MY FRIENDS THE ENEMY

About the Author

Nick van der Bijl BEM spent a total of 24 years in the Regular Army, mostly in the Intelligence Corps, but also three years in an armoured regiment. He saw active service in Northern Ireland and the Falkland conflict. On leaving the Regulars, he was commissioned into a Territorial Army infantry battalion. On leaving the Army, his second career was in NHS security management. He is the author of several books on post-1945 military history and was the Senior Producer and Writer for Brush Fire Films.

MY FRIENDS THE ENEMY

LIFE IN MILITARY INTELLIGENCE
DURING THE FALKLANDS WAR

NICK VAN DER BIJL

AMBERLEY

*I wish to dedicate this book to my colleagues in the
3 Commando Brigade Intelligence Section and those associated
with Intelligence assets within and to the Brigade.*

This edition published 2023

Amberley Publishing
The Hill, Stroud
Gloucestershire, GL5 4EP

www.amberley-books.com

Copyright © Nick van der Bijl, 2020, 2023

The right of Nick van der Bijl to be identified
as the Author of this work has been asserted in
accordance with the Copyrights, Designs and
Patents Act 1988.

ISBN 978 1 3981 1542 2 (paperback)
ISBN 978 1 4456 9419 1 (ebook)

British Library Cataloguing in Publication Data.
A catalogue record for this book is available
from the British Library.

Typesetting by Aura Technology and Software
Services, India. Printed in India.

CONTENTS

AUTHOR'S
ACKNOWLEDGEMENTS

Writing an account of one's personal experiences, particularly in war, is always somewhat daunting, for two reasons. First, suggestions that the author 'won the war'; second, interjecting your view into events in which presumptions have been set in concrete. Nevertheless, this is a personal account that I first drafted on the *Canberra* while returning to the United Kingdom from a diary that I kept throughout the Falklands War and from letters home. I also accessed documents collected during the war and since. It is in addition a personal story of my contribution to the Falklands War and was first submitted for publication to the Ministry of Defence in 1985.

There is no doubt when that the UK went to war against Argentina, the intelligence booklet on Argentinian Armed Forces was blank, apart from a couple of lines. This book sets out to tell the story of how the intelligence assets within the 3 Commando Brigade, which led the ground forces' contribution in the war, collected information and converted it into intelligence.

I must thank several people, in particular former Royal Marines Corporal Tom Priestley, who was part of the Brigade Intelligence Section and has been in frequent contact; Major-General

Julian Thompson, Brigade Commander, 3 Commando Brigade, who has kindly written the Foreword and has also supplied information; Colonels David Burrill, David Charters and John Hughes-Wilson, who all served HQ Land Forces Falklands Islands Intelligence; Colonel David Benest of 2 Para, and Señor Alejandro Amendelora, who supplied me with information from Argentina and answered my queries, and especially HQ Intelligence Corps, which has reviewed the content. There are others who shall remain nameless.

I am grateful to Connor Stait of Amberley Publishing who has given me another opportunity to contribute to the history of the Falklands War, to Cathy Stagg as a patient and supportive editor and to many other people who all contributed their part in getting this book into print. Thanks also to Richard Munro for the index.

Finally, I owe very special thanks to my wife, Penny, for her endurance in 1982 and while I wrote this account.

PROLOGUE

In 1904, Lieutenant-Colonel David Henderson (Argyle and Sutherland Highlanders) offered a definition in his *Field Intelligence: Its Principles and Practice* (HMSO):

> The successful intelligence officer must be cool, courageous and adroit, patient and imperceptible, discreet and trustworthy. They must understand the handling of troops and have knowledge of warfare. They must be able to win the confidence of their General, and to inspire confidence in their subordinates. They must have resolution to continue unceasingly their search for information, even in the most disheartening circumstances and after repeated failures. They must have the endurance to submit silently to criticism, much of which may be based on ignorance or jealousy – and they must be able to deal with people, to approach their source of information with tact and skill, whether such source be a patriot or an abandoned traitor.

Henderson wrote this assessment after his experience in the Field Intelligence Department during the Second Boer War and recommended that those engaged in intelligence in the field, except for Intelligence Staff Officers, should be formed into an 'Intelligence Corps'.

When the First World War broke out in 1914, his recommendation was adopted and the Intelligence Corps was formed as an all-ranks counter-intelligence protective security capability with responsibility to ensure that those serving with the Army, and the nationally sensitive information supplied to the Army, were safe from espionage, subversion, sabotage and, more recently, terrorism. Army units at all levels continued to form intelligence sections and to have knowledge of the military threat to British interests and enabled commanders to have sufficient credible intelligence to fight their battles. This was known as Operational Intelligence. In the early 1960s, the Intelligence Corps took responsibility for the provision of Operational Intelligence at the Ministry of Defence down the levels of command to brigades. Regiments continued to raise intelligence sections.

The word intelligence has its origins in the Latin verb *intelligere*, which is translated as 'to comprehend or perceive'. Using the 1982-era Intelligence Cycle, there were seven phases to convert information into an intelligence product:

(1) Identify the requirement

(2) Collect information from a range of agencies and sources

(3) Grade the information for quality and accuracy against other sources

(4) Assess by comparing new information with other information

(5) Disseminate to those who need the information in a suitable format in time to be of use

(6) Exploit the information

(7) Continually assess the quality and source of the information, ideally through feedback from users.

Sources include Human Intelligence, which is essentially extracting information from people; Signals Intelligence, which is achieved by exploiting the airwaves; Technical and Scientific Intelligence, the studying of weapons and equipment; and Documentary Intelligence, scrutinising of publications.

We all use intelligence to make decisions in the knowledge that some information is publicly available and some information is protected from prying eyes. The motto of the Intelligence Corps translates as 'Knowledge Gives Strength to the Arm'.

In spite of plenty of diplomatic and political signals of Argentinian intentions, notably the occupation of Southern Thule and the encroachment on South Georgia during the late 1970s and early 1980s, the failure of the Foreign and Commonwealth Office and the Ministry of Defence to predict Argentinian intentions against British interests in the South Atlantic was an intelligence failure. Also, the *Junta* in Buenos Aires believed that the United Kingdom – with its NATO, Northern Ireland and worldwide commitments and its apparent lack of interest in the South Atlantic – would not react to the Argentinian seizure of South Georgia; that was another intelligence failure.

FOREWORD BY MAJOR GENERAL JULIAN THOMPSON

I was privileged to know Nick van der Bijl when we served together before, during and after the Falklands War of 1982. Now, some thirty-eight years on, he is already an established author of military history books, and has co-authored one. He brings his skill as a writer and his experience as a soldier in many places round the globe to telling the story of the Intelligence Section in the headquarters of 3 Commando Brigade in the Falklands War. As he tells us in his Acknowledgement, this book *My Friends, The Enemy* is based on notes and papers collated during the voyage home from the Falklands in 1982. Nick brings to the task a deep knowledge of the events of the Falklands War grounded not only in research for three previous books on the subject, but also from having participated as a member of 3 Commando Brigade, which carried out the initial landings and fought in all but one of the major land battles. As the Staff Sergeant commanding the Intelligence Section and in addition as a trained and experienced interrogator, Nick's perspective encompassed both sides of the war – trying to fathom what the opposition was up to as well as being well briefed on our plans and intentions.

Without good intelligence a commander is virtually 'blind' and 'deaf' – cut off from reality. Good intelligence does not just consist of amassing facts, on the basis of the more the merrier. The skill of the successful intelligence operator is acquiring information and then assessing it. The evaluation of information is not merely a matter of judging whether it is accurate or not, but also includes the art of working out where it fits into the picture, and what it means. The aim, very rarely achieved outside works of fiction, is to present the commander with a complete forecast of what the enemy is planning and about to do. There were times when Nick and his team, with Captain Viv Rowe, my Intelligence Staff Officer, got near to achieving this – all credit to them.

When 'the whistle blew' in the early hours of Friday 2 April 1982, we were off to war with no notice at all. There was minimal intelligence on the Argentines – 'the enemy' was the Soviet Union and Warsaw Pact countries. That so much was garnered in so short a time and in such unpromising circumstances, is a credit to Nick and his Section. Starting with the battle to get a better space allocated for intelligence work in the headquarters ship, HMS *Fearless*, there were times when it was an uphill struggle – successfully overcome often by guile and cunning.

Just the story of how the enemy picture was built up is fascinating. For example, early on, much excellent information was garnered from intercepted telegrams sent between Argentine servicemen in the Falklands and their families in Argentina over the cable and wireless link between Stanley and Buenos Aires. In addition to giving name, rank and unit, there was a surprising amount of useful military information in many of them; far more than the equivalent of 'hello Mum, all well here'.

By interspersing personal detail with insights into what was going through his mind at various stages in the campaign and afterwards, Nick adds 'colour' to his narrative. It gives the reader some idea of the atmosphere of a brigade headquarters preparing for war, the planning involved, and daily life operating afloat and ashore in action. One of the most interesting aspects of Nick's story concerns interrogating Prisoners of War. He is a compassionate man, and operated strictly within the rules. I conjecture that his demeanour and attitude worked in his favour when establishing a rapport with those he interrogated. Although he speaks some Spanish, his task was made more difficult by the paucity of Spanish-speakers in the British Task Force. There were many more English speakers among the opposition than there were Spanish speakers on our side. Incidentally, this gave our adversaries a distinct advantage when it came to radio intercept of insecure tactical radio circuits once we were ashore.

Nick makes a key point when he says 'intelligence is essentially advisory, and commanders at all level take responsibility for accepting or rejecting it.' As a commander, indeed, until Major General Moore arrived on D plus 9, the senior land force commander, this rule applied to me: any misconceptions or misuse of intelligence was my responsibility and mine alone. In his prologue, Nick quotes from an intelligence pamphlet published at the beginning of the last century, which sets out the qualities of the successful intelligence officer and the relationship he must establish with the commander and how the former should work. I recommend that the reader look at this again after finishing the book and form an opinion on whether or not the Intelligence Section in the 3 Commando Brigade Royal Marines in 1982 came up to the mark. I will declare my hand and say, without equivocation, that they did. This is their story.

Julian Thompson
Commander 3 Commando Brigade Royal Marines
Falklands War 1982

I

PLYMOUTH

Friday 2 April 1982 dawned grey with a faint hint of sun. As usual after breakfast, I left my wife Penny and our six-month-old daughter Imogen in our married quarter on the Southway estate on the northern fringes of Plymouth and, on my trusty bicycle, hurtled 6 miles downhill to Stonehouse Barracks, entered through the impressive main gate, glided past HQ 3 Commando Brigade and skidded to a halt outside the Intelligence Section. The eighteenth-century barracks had been the base, and still is, of the Brigade since its return from Singapore in 1971. It also accommodates Commodore Amphibious Warfare, whose principal responsibility in 1982 was to assemble ships capable of transporting a Landing Force. My programme for the day was to join the Section for a short run, write the monthly Brigade Intelligence Summary of Soviet activities on the NATO Northern Flank and join the Brigade HQ and Signals Squadron scheduled for a fortnight's Easter leave. On the previous Monday, I had returned from two months of winter warfare training in northern Norway, first a month of Arctic Warfare Training with 42 Commando near Bardufoss, and then attached to the Allied Command Force Intelligence Section in southern Norway until we flew north for a NATO exercise. I knew virtually nothing about the media reports circulating that Argentina had escalated the South Atlantic crisis.

After showering, I was reading through the Northern Flank intelligence Summary when the telephone rang. It was Captain Viv Rowe, a Royal Marine who, using the new NATO terminology, was the Staff Officer, Grade 3, G2 (Intelligence) for HQ 3 Commando Brigade, asking me to join him at HQ Commando Forces at Hamoaze House, the Grade-2-listed house on Mount Wise that had been associated with the Royal Marines since 1934. Captain Rowe's title was usually shortened to 'G2'. Essentially, he was the Brigade Intelligence Officer and was responsible for advising the Brigade Commander on the intelligence picture. At his disposal, but not under his command, was the Brigade Intelligence Section. He had joined Brigade HQ from the School of Infantry at Warminster shortly before I deployed to Norway and was an experienced mountain leader and climber. I walked up the hill to Hamoaze House and was directed to an office on an upper floor by a member of the Women's Royal Naval Service where Captain Rowe told me, 'The Argentines have invaded the Falkland Islands and are thought to be preparing to seize South Georgia. A naval task force is being formed and 3 Commando Brigade is on 72-hours' notice to move as the Landing Force. The name of the operation is Operation *Corporate*. What do we know about Argentina?' On a wall, there was a map of South Georgia and a smaller one showing the Falklands. I advised him that we had very little information on Argentina because our focus was the Warsaw Pact and the Northern Group of Soviet Forces facing the NATO Northern Flank. I had previously been briefed that since the Brigade had an amphibious capability, it could also be deployed for 'out of area' operations.

I suggested that since Commander-in-Chief Fleet controlled the deployment of Naval Party 8901, which had been the Falkland Islands garrison since 1966, then it should know about the Argentinians. The Naval Party usually numbered about forty-five Royal Marines on a one-year rotation based at Moody Brook Barracks; the changeover date was usually 1st April. Its role was to provide the Falkland Islands garrison and train the Falkland Islands Defence Force and, in the event of an enemy landing in force, to deploy a 'trip wire' strategy of not defending and buy time for reinforcements. By any stretch of the imagination, it was a tall order.

Returning to the office, I briefed Colour-Sergeant Neil Smith on my conversation with Captain Rowe. Neil was the senior Royal Marine in the Intelligence Section. Nearing the end of his career, he had been a dog handler in the confrontation with Indonesia from 1963 to 1966, had served with the landing craft of the 4th Assault Squadron on HMS *Fearless* and had been a platoon weapons instructor at the Royal Marines Commando Training Centre. His intelligence experience was limited to Northern Ireland. A dedicated family man, he was regularly ribbed that his Skoda car usually belched out more clouds of exhaust than a Soviet T-55 tank. As the linchpin for the Section, he was to be my guide and mentor.

Although Argentina had posed a political and military threat to British interests in the South Atlantic for decades, someone seemed to have been remarkably slack about intelligence. It seemed that either the loss of the Falklands was an acceptable risk or, more likely, there was a Cold War mind-set that nothing will happen because nothing has happened and therefore intelligence assessments can mirror previous ones.

In contrast, the Army defence of Belize from Guatemalan aggression in Central America was built on a solid foundation of long-term and current intelligence, and an invasion would be met with aggression built on knowledge. More in hope than anything, I contacted the South America desk at the Defence Intelligence Staff at the Ministry of Defence, without any success. HQ United Kingdom Land Forces and the Foreign Armies Branch at the School of Service Intelligence could not help because the South Atlantic was a Navy problem. It was therefore clear that the Brigade had a clean intelligence sheet on which to start collecting, analysing and collating information on the Argentinians.

So, how did an Intelligence Corps staff-sergeant find himself searching for information on the Falklands and Argentina, about which he knew absolutely nothing?

My military experience began with the Aldenham School Combined Cadet Force in 1961. On leaving school in 1964, I enlisted as a potential officer badged in the 17/21st Lancers until the spring of 1965, when I failed the Regular Commissions Board. I was not entirely surprised because mathematics and science were a mystery to me. I took discharge and became a meat porter in Canterbury. After about a year, I joined the C (Canterbury) Squadron, Kent, and County of London Yeomanry (The Sharpshooters), a Territorial Army light reconnaissance unit based in the city, however, my ambition was strong and in January 1967, I enlisted into the Royal Dragoons (The Royals) and spent three very happy years on Centurion and then Chieftain tanks based in Detmold, West Germany. When the Royals merged with the Royal Horse Guards to form the Blues and Royals in 1969, I had sufficient education to transfer to the Intelligence Corps in July 1970 as an Operator, Intelligence and Security. This trade had two basic roles. Firstly, to provide commanders with sufficient intelligence in time to fight their battles; secondly, to conduct protective security and counter-intelligence to deter and prevent hostile intelligence services from conducting espionage, sabotage, subversion and terrorism against the Army and its associated civilian components. Secondary basic skills included Air Photographic Reading and Tactical Questioning.

For the next twelve years, I had a balanced career of both roles starting with protective security and counter-intelligence in West Germany. In 1971, I married Lance-Corporal Penny Weaver, who was a member of the Women's Royal Army Corps attached to the Intelligence Corps. From 1973, for two years, I was on Operation *Banner* with the 3rd Infantry Brigade Intelligence Section in Lurgan in Northern Ireland. This included ten days on the Ton-class minesweeper HMS *Lewiston* helping the Royal Navy to collect information by joining boarding parties. I also qualified as an assault boat coxswain. During two-and-a-half years in Hong Kong from 1976, I was the security point of contact during the construction of the high-rise Prince of Wales Building in the naval shore establishment HMS *Tamar* when HQ British Forces moved from Victoria Barracks. I attended a six-week Jungle Warfare Course in Brunei and on several exercises regularly paired up with Corporal Paul Sullivan of 2nd Battalion, The Parachute Regiment (2 Para), as my 'basha buddy'. Returning to the United Kingdom in 1979, I was posted to HQ 7th Field Force in Colchester, which included being detached to go on a six-month tour to southern Belize in Central America. I had attended the Long Interrogation Course in November 1981. So far, I had worn civilian clothes for about three quarters of my career.

When posted to the Commando Brigade in early 1981, I fulfilled a cherished ambition and began several weeks of training for the commando course, but the fallout of a diplomatic incident in Belize led me to withdrawing my application. However, the major commanding 8 Intelligence Company, which had responsibility for UK-based intelligence sections, persuaded me to change my mind and thus in June, with Penny expecting Imogen in October, we drove to Plymouth. The Commando Brigade was my fourth brigade posting. I had also served with ones in West Germany and in the UK. Apart from three Parachute Regiment brigade commanders, I was generally less than impressed with the interest shown in intelligence by the other brigade commanders and thus when I joined 3 Commando Brigade, I expected a similar culture. However, during my introductory interview with Brigadier Julian Thompson, he emphasised that he expected an effective Intelligence Section with good knowledge of the Soviet threat to the NATO Northern Flank. I was to continue drafting the monthly Intelligence Summary, enhance intelligence training and undertake specialist intelligence activities to enable him to fight his battle. I was impressed.

Until about 1960, headquarters in the Army and Royal Marines formed their intelligence sections from within. When the Intelligence Corps took over responsibility for operational intelligence, it supplied intelligence sections down to brigade level, including to 3 Commando Brigade, which was then based in Singapore and involved in the confrontation with Indonesia. After the Brigade returned to the UK in 1971, the Army in agreement with Director-General Royal Marines disbanded the Intelligence Corps section. Meanwhile, when Operation *Banner* commenced in Northern Ireland in 1969, the three brigade intelligence sections developed procedures and philosophies and gained considerable operational experience. All intelligence units were trained at the School of Service Intelligence in Ashford, Kent. When the Commando Brigade was assigned to provide an amphibious capability on the NATO Northern flank in 1972, the Brigade Major, Major Julian Thompson, reformed the Brigade HQ Intelligence Section from within the Royal Marines, but it was not trained at the School of Service Intelligence in Ashford, Kent. Instead, 81 Intelligence Section, which was part of 8 Intelligence Company at Bulford, provided training and support.

Brigade HQ was supported by the versatile 3 Commando Brigade and Signals Squadron. Elements included Defence Troop, Air Defence Troop equipped with portable Blowpipe surface-to-air missile firing posts, Communications Troop supporting the Brigade HQ with vehicle-mounted and portable radios and teleprinters, the Royal Marine Police Troop included a commando-trained Royal Military Police corporal as close protection to the Brigade Commander and an eight-strong Intelligence Section was formed from within the Brigade. By the late 1970s, the intelligence expertise gap was narrowed when an Intelligence Corps staff-sergeant was posted to the Section. When I joined, only two members had completed any formal intelligence training and I persuaded the predecessor to Captain Rowe that once the entire Section had passed the All Arms Intelligence course at the School of Service Intelligence, I would consider completing the commando course; in the meantime, I would do anything the Royal Marines set before me. While on winter warfare training in Norway, I had given several intelligence presentations on Soviet winter warfare tactics and amphibious capabilities.

Other members of the Section included Corporal Bob Birkett, a Yorkshireman, who was awaiting promotion to sergeant. Very fit, an expert skier, his specialist qualification was air defence. He had little experience in intelligence, except aircraft recognition. Corporal Colin 'Scotty' Scott was a sniper and although very fit, was niggled by a persistent knee injury that hindered his ambition to be a physical training instructor. In the mid-1980s, we again served together with the Joint Intelligence Staff, Cyprus, in an interesting period that included Westerners being taken hostage in Lebanon, aircraft hijacks to Cyprus, Palestinian 'freedom ships' limpet-mined in Limassol by Israeli frogmen and attacks on Libya by US F-111s. Lance-Corporal 'Taff' Evans was our strongman; he was powerfully built and due to begin a Royal Marines Police course on 5 April. When it was cancelled, he returned to be 'with the boyos'. He wrote regularly to his several girlfriends. I often felt the confines of our small unit restricted his unbounded energy and 'macho' lifestyle. His intelligence experience was limited. Marine 'Scouse' Atkinson came from Liverpool and was scheduled to be married on 10 April. After a very short period of soul searching, he decided that his destiny also lay 'with the lads'; Neil and I were not too happy about this but it was his decision. While he had no intelligence experience, we needed to understand the nature of the 'out of area operations' role of the Brigade and before deploying to Norway, I had tasked him to trawl for information on Argentina.

Marine Tom Priestley was the most experienced in intelligence. He had been drafted into the Intelligence Section when Major Thompson reformed it, had been trained by 81 Intelligence Section and remained involved, including at Royal Marines Poole and on two Operation *Banner* tours. In 1979, he took discharge from the Royal Marines intending to instruct at a sports centre, but he was plagued with injury and the great conversationalist that he was, he had talked his way back into the Royal Marines in 1980. While he was assisting in an Officers' Mess function in Stonehouse Barracks, an officer suggested that he was better employed in Brigade Intelligence and the next Monday he was drafted to the Section, where he remained until 1987. He had considered transferring to the Intelligence Corps. Tom was reliable and never afraid to be forthright. When manning the Command Post map, if he was asked to explain a particular map symbol, he would deliver a lengthy lesson on the art of map making.

Of our two illustrators, or draughtsmen, Corporal Brian Dodd was nearing the end of a varied career that included active service in Aden, the Far East and Northern Ireland. A qualified SCUBA diver and fit, we regularly had a lunchtime game of squash. Marine Ken Loftus had recently passed the Illustrator Course and drew excellent cartoons. While we were at Ascension Island, when his wife gave birth to their first child and there were some complications, Ken very nearly returned to UK. Both men frequently worked in ill-lit, cramped and dirty conditions; however, they always produced neat traces and charts.

Petty Officer Dick Birkett was the Brigade HQ photographer. He had very little experience in ground warfare and his webbing seemed to hang on him. Being festooned with camera equipment just added to his problems. An excellent scrounger, he was essential to our team. He was rather thin, and that he suffered from the cold weather was a source of concern.

In spite of its limited experience, I was impressed with the commitment of the Section, particularly because, unlike Army Brigade HQs that used intelligence sections to glue maps together and print table cards for Officers Mess functions, this one familiarised itself with the Intelligence Cycle, studied the Soviet threat to the NATO Northern Flank, helped arrange study days and, crucially, practised Intelligence on exercise. Over the next four months, it developed into a decent unit whose contribution has rarely been recognised.

On Fridays, 12.30pm was usually the 'end of play' for the week. The rumour that Argentina had invaded the Falklands in 1982 was regarded as an April Fool's joke, a day late, but by mid-morning, it was clear that a crisis had developed in the South Atlantic and that Argentina had launched Operation *Rosario* to recover *Las Malvinas* (The Falklands). With a little information arriving from the Ministry of Defence and media outlets, the Section plotted the events onto a map. Early reports suggested a three-pronged attack of marine infantry advancing into Port Stanley, commandos landing to the south of Mount Harriet forcing the surrender of Government House, and infantry capturing Stanley Airport. Naval Party 8901 and those members of the Falkland Islands Defence Force who mobilised did not stand a chance. Surrender was inevitable. Casualties on both sides were reported to be light.

As the British political response gathered pace and 3 Commando Brigade was brought on notice to move, Brigadier Thompson and key staff officers, including Captain Rowe, set up the 3 Commando Brigade Command Post alongside HQ Commando Forces at Hamoaze House on Mount Wise. In command of HQ Commando Forces and Royal Marines was Major-General Jeremy Moore, MC and Bar. The Brigade HQ Intelligence Section remained at Stonehouse Barracks. Since a 1:50,000 map of the Falklands was required for the Command Post, Scotty, who managed the Brigade HQ map requirement, found a few Falklands maps ordered by Major Ewen Southby-Tailyour for 1978 deployment in command of Naval Party 8901, which included circumnavigating the Islands in his yacht. When Scotty then telephoned an emergency order to 8 Map and Chart Depot RE at Guilford and was told it would take several days to assemble the order, he explained the urgency. When the Depot noticed that Falkland Islands maps lacked grid lines, its commanding officer, a Royal Engineer colonel, drove to Plymouth and briefed Captain Rowe and Captain Russ Tolley, a Royal Engineer and the Staff Officer responsible for mapping, that a Mercator's Projection adjustment within the Falkland Island made it difficult to create a common grid system across the twenty-nine sheets of the 1:50,000 series. A grid is a network of evenly spaced numbered horizontal and vertical lines used to fix locations on a map. The colonel said a solution had been found, but it was most unlikely that gridded maps could be drawn, printed and delivered quickly. In the meantime, we would have to use ungridded maps. He undertook to ensure that gridded maps were sent to Ascension. We also ordered other products, for example, large-scale maps of Port Stanley, 'going' terrain maps and coastal and airstrip data. The next day our driver Marine Sid Seaton drove Tom to Guildford but when they were told that the print run was not ready, they had lunch at the Women's Royal Army Corps Depot.

We later learnt Argentina had purchased several thousand maps of the Falklands in 1981 for a 'training paper exercise', but, it seemed, the intelligence clue of the country's intentions was missed. Then they reproduced them in their Military Institute of Geography, as stated on their maps.

Scotty also placed an order for maps with grid lines. In the meantime, we assembled the stationery used for NATO exercises and doubled the amount. Since we knew nothing about Argentina, the first principle of intelligence was applied to collect information from any source and convert it into formats suitable for a busy commander and his Staff Officers to understand. The priority was Argentina and its Armed Forces but time was very short. HQ Commando Forces and Brigade HQ did not have a decent library, as a victim of defence financial cuts, however, the Section had the *Military Balance 1978/79*, which provided a baseline. There were a few tattered, out-of-date copies of Jane's reference volumes on weapons, vehicles, aircraft and ships in the Intelligence Section. Captain Rowe therefore telephoned the head librarian at Plymouth City Library and reached agreement to sign out a complete set of Jane's (military-related publications named after John F. T. Jane, an Englishman who first published Jane's *All the World's Fighting Ships* in 1898) for 24 hours. Tom Priestley was duly despatched to the library to collect them and spent a couple of days photocopying information from these and other publications. He also supplemented the information from his collection of defence periodicals at home. Lance-Corporal 'Auzzie' Jones, of Air Defence Troop, supplied his collection of *International Defence Reviews* and *Recognition Journals*. Our usually unreliable photocopier worked overtime. When we departed, a Marine in the section who was left behind on draft had instructions to return the loans to Plymouth Library. The publications allowed us to make an initial assessment that the Argentinian Army was divided into five Corps with a total of 60,000 all ranks, of whom 40,000 were conscripts serving no more than one year. Brigades of three battalions and combat and service support were recruited regionally.

Media photographs are always good sources of intelligence. One interesting photograph showed a woman wearing a red anorak while carrying a bag and accompanied by a small girl as she passed a column of stationary Argentinian LVTP-7 (Landing Vehicle Tracked Personnel, Mark 7) amphibious tracked personnel carriers capable of carrying twenty-five, excluding the crew. Behind her on the pavement, there are groups of Falkland Islanders chatting. The photograph must have been taken on 2 April because the LTVPs had been used during the invasion and re-embarked during the day and returned to Argentina. A staged photograph showed LARC-5 (Lighter, Amphibious Resupply, Cargo, 5-ton) Number 15 passing captured Naval Party 8901 lying on Ross Road near the War Memorial. Other photographs that emerged over the next four days showed Amphibious Commandos, carrying FAL 7.62mm self-loading rifles, assembling prisoners on the lawn in front of Government House. Since the policy was that resistance to interrogation training was only given to Special Forces and aircrew, I wondered how the prisoners would deal with interrogation.

One question was why did Argentina take the massive political gamble to seize British dependencies in the South Atlantic? As the Spanish Empire in South America crumbled in the early 1800s, two British attempts in 1806 and 1807 to seize control of the Viceroyalty of the River Plate had been defeated in Buenos Aires and Montevideo respectively. José Francisco de San Martín, who was born in the Viceroyalty in 1778 and had gained military experience fighting the French during the Peninsula War, returned to South America in 1812 and, after defeating Spanish colonial forces in modern Argentina in 1814, had crossed the Andes with 5,000 men and helped the Chileans to eject the Spanish. He then went to Peru where Simon Bolivar completed the drive for independence. Civil wars in the first half of the nineteenth century by several provincial leaders opposing the centralist Buenos Aires eventually saw the formation of the Army. It became involved in several wars in South America during the 1860s and conquered the southern desert region of Patagonia. It largely remained outside politics and took the German Army as its cultural benchmark. Its Navy benchmarked the Royal Navy.

The British had played a significant role in the development of Argentina and had invested in railway and tramways construction, agriculture, whaling, the export of livestock and the financial and business sectors. Welsh-speaking immigrants first arrived in Patagonia in the mid-1860s in order to protect their culture and language. Harrods opened its only overseas store in Buenos Aires and taking afternoon tea became standard behaviour. The British introduced soccer and in 1910 Argentina played its first international rugby match against a touring British team. But a military coup in

1930 heralded a long period of political intervention by the Army, the most well-known leader being Colonel Juan Peron in 1943. But his left-wing ideology of rejecting capitalism and communism in favour of the State negotiating compromise between managers and workers led to him being ejected in 1955, and the Army concentrated on preventing his return to power. Two attempted coups in the mid-1960s and political faction-fighting affected military discipline and cohesion. By the early 1970s, insurgency groups, such as *Ejército Revolucionario del Pueblo* (ERP, People's Revolutionary Army), which followed the Marxist theories of Che Guevara, destabilised the north-west mountainous region of Tucuman Province. Then in 1976, a civilian/military dictatorship, usually known as a *Junta*, seized power in Operation *Condor* and installed *El Proceso de Reorganización Nacional* (The National Reorganisation Process). Backed by the USA and employing State terrorism, the Army and right-wing death squads hunted the ERP, Peronists and socialists in a brutal internal security regime of murder, kidnap and torture in a period known as the Dirty War. Between 9,000 and 30,000 people 'disappeared'. In December 1981, General Leopold Galtieri, an army engineer and enthusiastic supporter of the restorative National Reorganisation Process, was appointed President. Regarded by the USA as a bulwark against the spread of communism in Central and South America, he had permitted limited political reforms and expression of dissent, but this led to agitation for the return of democracy. As his *Junta* became increasingly unpopular, it badly needed a diversion and the long-running dispute with Great Britain over *Las Malvinas* (the Falklands) was chosen in the belief that London would not respond to the seizure of the islands; indeed, there was evidence to support this notion.

In 1976 when fifty people, some described as 'scientists' but most of whom were marine infantry, established a base on Southern Thule, this was interpreted in London as a preparatory deployment for an invasion of the Falklands and so Prime Minister James

Callaghan despatched a deterrent naval task force in Operation *Journeyman* that included a nuclear submarine. However, Argentina did not back down and the force withdrew. Three years later Mrs Margaret Thatcher led the Conservative Party to victory and she set about repairing the political, foreign affairs and financial damage caused by a disastrous Labour Government whose defence cuts had included reducing the Royal Navy presence in the South Atlantic by withdrawing the ice patrol ship HMS *Endurance*. Since Argentina also had strong anti-communist credentials and had supported the USA in its covert operations against the left-wing Sandinistas in Nicaragua, the *Junta* believed that US objections to existing European presence in the Americas would be to their advantage. The NATO commitments between the US and Britain excluded Britain's overseas interests.

Nicholas Ridley, the new Minister of State at the Foreign and Commonwealth Office, visited the Falklands in July 1979 and concluded that Great Britain could no longer support a military deterrence to Argentinian aggression.

In 1980 he secretly negotiated that after a fixed period, sovereignty would be transferred to Argentina. Not surprisingly, the proposal was rejected by the Falkland Islanders and by Parliament insisting that British people should not be transferred to a foreign power against their wishes and certainly not one with such a disreputable human rights record.

The cumulative effect of the stalled sovereignty negotiations, the implementation of the 1981 British Nationality Act that risked depriving the Falkland Islanders of their rights as full British citizens, the Defence White Paper advocating the withdrawal of HMS *Endurance* from the South Atlantic, the shelving of plans to rebuild the Moody Brook Barracks near Port Stanley as defence savings, and proposals to close the British Antarctic Survey base on South Georgia, all convinced Buenos Aires that Britain had little interest in the Falkland Islands.

Throughout the instability, the Argentinian Government had developed effective systems to monitor subversion within civilian populations. Some of these systems were discreetly transferred to offices of the *Lineas Aéreas del Estado* (LADE, State Air Lines) in Port Stanley; it had been managing regular flights between Comodoro Rivadavia and Port Stanley since the early 1970s. The Citizen's Band radio network was monitored. Two powerful radios lodged in the attic monitored communications between the Foreign and Commonwealth Office in London and Government House. The activities, mobilisation exercises and annual rotation of Naval Party 8901 and the combat efficiencies of the Falkland Islands Defence Force and Settlement Volunteers in the settlements outside Port Stanley were evaluated. For instance, as tension increased in 1982, Captain Adolfo Gaffoglio, the Argentinian representative in Port Stanley, reported the departure of HMS *Endurance* for South Georgia on 21 March with a Naval Party 8901 detachment on board. Intelligence sources included the resident Argentinian population of about fifteen people. Argentina probably knew more about the Falklands than the Foreign and Commonwealth Office.

After the Argentinian occupation on 2 April 1982, the *Junta* assured the Falkland Islanders that their customs and way of life would be respected. However, early intelligence indicated changes included the continental system of driving on the right being introduced and reinforced with 'keep right' signs painted on the road. The new instruction made driving easier for the military, particularly the conscript drivers, but was ignored by some Falkland Islanders when there were no Argentinians evident. The Falkland Islanders were less than impressed when Port Stanley was renamed Puerto Malvinas, then renamed Puerto Argentino on 21 April. (The name Malvinas derives from the French Îles Malouines, the name given to the islands by the French explorer Louis-Antoine de Bougainville in 1764 who landed on East Falkland.) Spanish was to be taught in schools and the currency would be changed to pesos. A curfew was imposed; when someone needed to break it, they were – in a clever piece of psychological warfare – instructed to hang a white cloth outside their house. There was virtually no information of what had happened in South Georgia.

We listened to the historic Saturday 3 April morning emergency House of Commons debate on the crisis to glean any intelligence but none emerged, except confirmation that Southern Thule and the Falkland Islands had been seized by Argentina and that Prime Minister Margaret Thatcher was upset. The Argentines annexed South Georgia during the day and captured the twenty-two Royal Marines taken to the island. Like those captured on the Falklands, none had received any resistance to interrogation training. The Ministry of Defence seemed to be closed for business.

For the Intelligence Section, those three days melted into intense work analysing and collecting information emerging from the South Atlantic. We hardly saw our families, but when we did it was to sleep and pack kit into webbing, bergens and huge naval kitbags for a deployment few believed would happen. The Brigade HQ and Signals Squadron, which administered Brigade HQ, decided that its detachments would each take a Swedish Bandvagn 202Es (BV), skis and winter warfare equipment and long wheelbase Land Rovers and trailers. The BV was formed by two rubber-track units, the driving compartment for the driver and a commander, and a passenger trailer capable of carrying a maximum of ten passengers. A conventional steering wheel connected to a hydraulic ram steers the vehicle. Maximum speed is 35 km/h on land, and 7 km/h on water. White as well as green camouflage nets were to be taken. For the first time in my career, I was issued a bayonet; this was getting too serious. Neil reminded me to pack a pair of soft shoes for the ship.

The next morning, Sunday, the Intelligence Section set up a briefing room at HQ Commando Forces so that Brigadier Thompson could issue his first formal Orders at 10am. At the invitation of

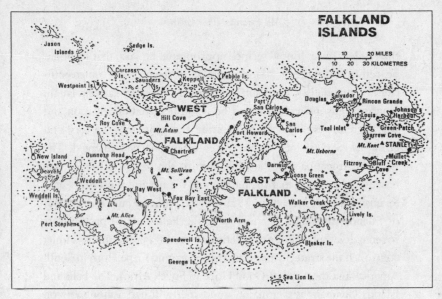

The first map produced by the Brigade Intelligence Section.

Major-General Moore, Neil laid out our intelligence handouts and a few maps for the delegates in his office. Pinned to the wall in the conference room opposite, between two screens, was a Union Flag with a hole in the centre. Several units had been added to the Brigade order of battle, including the 3rd Parachute Battalion, which had taken over Spearhead Battalion duties from 1st Welsh Guards on immediate notice to move. Major John Chester, the Chief-of-Staff, had recently joined Brigade HQ and was determined to begin the deployment as he intended to go on, with efficiency and effectiveness, but not even he could control the weather and several delegates were delayed by fog.

Brigadier Thompson welcomed the delegates and then handed over to Major Southby-Tailyour. An expert in amphibious warfare, he explained that the Union Jack was a trophy from the year when he had commanded Naval Party 8901. In a fit of schoolboy humour, he had relieved Government House of its flag and smuggled it back to England where it had lain forgotten in his attic as a morsel for the resident mice. It now seemed appropriate, he said, that it should be returned to the Falkland Islands. It seemed like nineteenth-century imperialistic jingoism, nevertheless, the story raised a laugh. Southby-Tailyour had written a book on his circumnavigation and was therefore well placed to describe the geography, history and economy. Several memorable pieces of intelligence emerged. The belief in Argentina was that the claim to the Falkland Islands was based on the notion that the nation was the natural successor to the Spanish Empire. Indeed, in 1820, the recently formed government of Buenos Aires had sent a ship to the Falklands to proclaim its sovereignty, but the British returned in 1833 and in so doing controlled the strategic maritime routes around Cape Horn in South America and the Cape of Good Hope in South Africa. The Falkland Islands Company was a major landowner and had a monopoly on all imports and exports as well as the control of shipping to and from the outlying settlements. Sheep are known as '365' because they are eaten throughout the year and wool was the principal export, he told us.

Oil, millions of barrels' worth, was thought to lie beneath the continental shelf. Peat was the main source of heating. A few tracks were suitable for vehicles. The average wind speed is 17 knots, as opposed to 4 knots in UK, and the weather can produce four seasons in one day. Winter was approaching. When Southby-Tailyour commented on the considerable influence of the Argentinian Consulate in the LADE offices, this set my counter-intelligence antenna bleeping and, suspecting that this was the centre of Argentine operations, I made a mental note that when, not if, we reached Port Stanley, the offices needed to be thoroughly searched.

Since we were expecting to recover South Georgia, Lieutenant Bob Veal RN, who had recently returned from a Joint Services expedition to the island, described it as crescent-shaped, 105 miles long and 18 miles at its widest point and as a mass of mountains, glaciers and icefields. The windward side is continuously battered by high seas. The permanent populations included seals, sea birds and masses of penguins. Several whaling stations, abandoned years ago, were rotting away. On the island were several scientists, based at Grytviken and on scientific field trips, and two women photographing birds. The chief scientist was the Magistrate and he was accountable to the Governor of the Falkland Islands.

Captain Rowe then gave an unavoidably short intelligence brief, largely because we had not received any intelligence from Ministry of Defence intelligence desks. The defence of the Falklands and South Georgia by the Royal Marines had been spirited but hopeless.

Argentinian dispositions were not known although television pictures indicated Port Stanley had been seized by a regimental marine landing team and was thought to be heavily militarised. Reinforcements could be summoned quickly. From our assessment of the landings, there was nothing unusual to report. Apart from in Port Stanley, there were no roads in the Falklands; there were a few tracks but apart from them, settlements were reliant upon coasters and light aircraft. Using slides provided by the former Royal Marines pilot appointed as the HQ Commando Forces Intelligence officer, I gave a brief on basic intelligence, such as uniforms, equipment and vehicles. Most of the slides were of American equipment that reflected our belief the Argentinian would follow US doctrines. Brigadier Thompson concluded by reminding everyone that the operation, Operation *Corporate,* was going to be difficult, ships would be overcrowded and the future was uncertain. 'Be flexible, keep smiling!' was to be our motto.

During the afternoon, Lance-Corporal Ivor Garcia, normally a driver at the Royal Marines Barracks, Deal, joined the Section. Having heard on the BBC that the Ministry of Defence was appealing for Spanish linguists, being a Gibraltarian, he telephoned Brigade HQ offering his services and was advised to make his way to Plymouth. He had served about seventeen years, his linguistic ability unexploited. His arrival was invaluable because we were very short of Spanish linguists. Before the posting to Belize, I had attended a three-week Spanish language course at the South Bank Polytechnic, Elephant and Castle, in London, followed by practice with a Spanish lady in Colchester. I had used the language in Belize and during two weeks of leave in Mexico, but I was, by no means, expert. I did, however, have a Spanish Language Guide TM30-600 booklet issued by the US War Department on 22 June 1943. I heard nothing from the Intelligence Corps.

That evening, as I drove home, I questioned the ridiculous notion that a Task Force being assembled to challenge Argentinian aggression would have to sail 8,000 miles through some of the world's worst seas in the South Atlantic winter, to go against an enemy about whom we knew very little but who had the ability to reinforce its occupation quickly and was thoroughly familiar with their newly acquired territory. Surely a rugby match at a neutral ground should solve the problem. To preserve operational security of our deployment, we were ordered to assemble at Stonehouse Barracks by midnight. With Imogen asleep in her cot in the back of the car, Penny drove through a drizzly Plymouth, which was quiet except for a 29 Commando Regiment RA convoy of 105mm Light Guns trundling through the shining streets to the Naval Dockyard from its barracks at The Citadel. I bade farewell to my beloved family and admit to having been rather unhappy at yet another long spell away from home. I had been on a seven-month unaccompanied tour in Belize for most of 1979, attended a three-week course in late 1980 and had returned from three months in Norway the previous weekend and now I was on my way somewhere else. I was very fortunate that Penny understood that long periods of separation was a fact of Service life, cushioned by the arrival of the postman delivering letters.

2

PORTSMOUTH TO ASCENSION ISLAND

In spite of the supposed secrecy about the mobilisation of Operation *Corporate*, the next morning, local journalists and photographers were swanning around Stonehouse Barracks seeking interviews and taking photographs, which I managed to avoid. I signed for my personal weapon, a 9mm Sterling submachine gun, four magazines, each capable of holding 25 rounds, and a cleaning box that contained a pull through to clean the barrel, a wire brush and a 4 inch by 2 inch cleaning cloth. The Sterling was light and its butt could be folded to the body, giving a length of about 19 inches. It was said to have a cyclic rate of 500 rounds per minute.

After a parade and kit check, as we boarded coaches supplied by Wallace Arnold Coaches I was passed a message for Scouse Atkinson that his fiancée was expecting a baby in November. The problem was he was in another bus and so Neil asked Brian Dodd to write the message on a large piece of paper. As the coaches left Stonehouse Barracks and were directed by the Royal Marines Police past crowds and relatives, some in tears and others wishing us the best of British, with a placard outside a hosiery factory reading 'Good Luck, Marines!' it was turning into an emotional moment but, luckily, comedy emerged. Instead of turning next right onto Millbay Road, as directed by the Sergeant-Major 'Buster' Brown of the Royal Marines Police at the Barrack Place junction, our driver drove down the hill to the next roundabout and turned right into Union Street. 'Buster' had recently rejoined the Brigade and his first major task was to ensure that everyone arrived at Portsmouth Naval Dockyard. As our coach blissfully passed him, there was a look of sheer horror on his face as the convoy split into two different directions. Passing through the centre of Plymouth, as our driver eventually caught up with the convoy on the A38, Neil persuaded him to overtake the coach carrying Scouse and held the note against the window, 'Girlfriend expecting baby in November. Wedding on return.'

About 3 hours later, we drew up alongside HMS *Fearless* in the Portsmouth Naval Dockyard. I knew her from an amphibious exercise in the autumn in which we embarked and disembarked by helicopter and landing craft, and 'stormed' a sandy beach near Poole shortly after midnight. The quay was crowded with lines of sailors, Royal Marines and civilians passing boxes and crates up gangways into the depths of the ship. Chacon containers (fire-fighting equipment storage units) were being lifted onto the Flight Deck by cranes. Moored on the other side of the quay was the forlorn hulk of the commando carrier HMS *Bulwark*, a veteran of other campaigns; also decommissioned and tied to a buoy was HMS *Intrepid*, sister to HMS *Fearless*, both victims of defence cuts. It was ironic to see two useless assault ships while merchant ships were being taken up from trade to join the Task Force. Filing on board through a control point in the Junior Rates' Galley that was allocating accommodation, Neil and I were directed to Number Two Chief Petty Officers Mess. For some reason, we assumed this to mean that the Chief Petty Officers' Lounge was being used for accommodation and so we lugged our kit up several decks and along narrow passages to find its bar propped up by three Chief Petty Officers. When they took exception to our Sterlings, Neil suggested the only reason we were on the ship was because there was a state of hostilities between UK and Argentina, and then accepted a beer from them. The lounge overlooked the Flight Deck and had several ale taps marked 'Harp' and 'Double Diamond'; in fact, the only brew was the strong 'Civil Service Brew' or 'CSB'.

We eventually found our Mess, which was one deck down, and I claimed a bunk above some lockers. This was to be the refuge for me and my sleeping bag for the next seven weeks. The Mess was a forty-bunk space divided into three sleeping areas and a recreational area that doubled as a sleeping area. When we arrived on board, a naval Westland Wasp helicopter was parked over the escape hatch to the Flight Deck until someone was invited to move it. Air-conditioning kept the Mess at a reasonable temperature. Lights burned all the time, either white bulbs or, after 'lights out', an orange glow. Neil and I shared a locker to store our weapons, bergens and webbing. The Mess was managed on normal Service Mess lines by the president and had its own galley and 'heads' (ablutions) of four showers, ten sinks and three cubicles, which were cleaned nightly by the Duty Watch, known as the 'Nighthawks'.

Unfortunately, I could not contact Penny because our married quarter had no telephone so before turning in that night, I telephoned my mother and asked her to buy Penny a birthday present and added I would probably be back home by the middle of the month – but just in case. At breakfast the next day, I was relieved to see a RAF Flight-Sergeant, who had been an instructor on the long interrogation course I had attended in the autumn. Not only did he have an understanding of intelligence, he had grown up in Central America, because of his father's career, and was bi-lingual. He proved to be an excellent asset and was patient, willing and shrewd but, I think, was slightly shocked to find himself on *Fearless* possibly going to war. Nevertheless, his presence meant that we had two decent Spanish speakers and one not so decent – me. The heavy boxes of the ungridded maps, which had taken up valuable space in our Land Rover and its trailer, now on the

Tank Deck, were manhandled to the office of Ship Sergeant Major 'Bogey' Knight near the Tank Deck where Scotty and Scouse made up unit orders by counting maps and boxing and addressing them ready for distribution, which they were still doing as we left Portsmouth the next day. As an experiment, the Illustrators tried calculating and inserting grid lines, but it was long and laborious.

The next day's weather was dull. During mid-morning, the warship let go and amid farewells from people ashore and salutes from other ships, she entered Portsmouth Harbour. Determined not to miss new experiences, I took my place on the Flight Deck with the Embarked Force and was brought to attention by orders given over the tannoy as we passed warships and shore establishments and then Standing at Ease until the next order. Once in the Solent, the dock at the stern was flooded and our four Landing Craft Utility (LCUs), which had been following like ducks, entered. The four smaller Landing Craft Vehicle Personnel (LCVPs) were already secured to their davits. The Executive Officer, Commander John Kelly, then briefed the Embarked Force on safety and announced that there were insufficient lifejackets for us, and that in an emergency survival suits would be issued. He did not make clear who would issue them or the location of the lockers. This seemed somewhat unsatisfactory, especially if locker keys could not be found and therefore in the spirit of self-survival, a mental note was made of where the survival gear was kept. During the early afternoon, the ship headed on a westerly course; when she was off Plymouth, Brigadier Thompson and his Tactical HQ were flown on board by helicopter. The ship then headed south in a freshening wind, grey skies and deepening swells.

HMS *Fearless* was not sleek. Broad across the beam, dominated by the Flight Deck, she was a tough lady classed as a Landing Platform Dock and had sufficient accommodation for a battalion of soldiers or a squadron of tanks. Laid down at Harland and Wolff, Belfast, in 1962 and commissioned three years later, she had an unladen displacement of 11,000 tons. Her main armament was four quadruple mounted SEACAT surface-to-air missiles. The 4th Assault Squadron operated her landing craft and beach assault equipment, including the Centurion Beach Armoured Recovery Vehicle, a tank, and lorried trackway. The LCUs were crewed by seven Royal Marines skippered by a colour-sergeant or sergeant, who was commander, regardless of the ranks of passengers. The LCVPs were skippered by a corporal supported by two Royal Marines. All had been trained at Royal Marines Poole. While the ship did not have a permanent flight of helicopters, it had the control and engineering facilities to support assault and light helicopters. Below the Flight Deck was the cavernous Tank Deck, divided into two levels that were connected by a steep ribbed hinged ramp. The ship could support the headquarters of a regimental battle group operating from the Amphibious Operations Room, which was on the same deck as the Bridge. The Room was essentially the operational headquarters of the Embarked Force of Army or Royal Marines.

A small annex was the Intelligence Section, however, it was too small to accommodate a Brigade Intelligence Section. Since the ship was not yet proposing to use its Electronic Warfare Room next to Operations Room, Major Chester secured it for us – as a temporary measure. While there was no space for maps, at least we could display our collated enemy Orders of Battle.

Watertight doors divided the ship into a maze of compartments connected by narrow passageways and stairs lined with pipes, electrical conduits and doors giving access to Mess decks, stores and work areas and the Sick Bay. The ship made her own fresh water and could resupply the Landing Ships Logistic and merchantmen, which did not have this ability. Her engineers and mechanics could manufacture and forge almost any item from a tiny screw to a shaft. There was also an operating theatre and a dentist, a small shop operated by the Navy, Army and Air Force

Institute (NAAFI) and a laundry manned by Hong Kong Chinese. Boxes of tinned food and other supplies were stored in gangways, which therefore reduced the space in them. The Junior Ranks lived in large Messes of three tiers of bunks, the lower two of which could be converted into 'settees'. Space underneath the 'settees' was used to store fighting orders and a suitcase. Each person had a lockable personal locker. Weapons were lodged in racks. Messes were equipped with a television mounted on a shelf. Some of the Petty Officers and Sergeants lived in a cabin-space near the Wardroom. *Fearless* TV broadcast a range of channels, which included national and local television. This proved useful when within range.

Officers in cabins on the upper decks had a degree of individual space that included a writing table. Since there was not enough room for all the officers on board, some junior officers shared cabins. The Wardroom itself was large and had comfortable armchairs. On the same deck as the Bridge was the cabin of the Commanding Officer, Captain Jeremy Larkin, a tall submariner. Naval tradition was that the Captain was not a member of the Wardroom and could only enter by invitation. All his domestic needs, including his meals, were managed by his steward. One intelligence source was his television and therefore we ensured that whenever the news was being broadcast, a member of the Intelligence Section loitered outside his cabin in order to identify equipment, personalities and places.

By 6 April, the ship had reached the Bay of Biscay and was pitching and rolling through the rough seas usually associated with the area by diving unpredictably toward Davy Jones's locker and then hauling herself toward the heavens. I was normally a decent sailor but the issued seasick pills seemed ineffective. When at about mid-morning Neil was asked to provide someone from the Intelligence Section to attend a Brigade HQ and Signals Squadron meeting to develop a training programme, this presented us with an opportunity to give regular updates on the South Atlantic crisis. Although somewhat queasy and reluctant to attend, I left the claustrophobic and windowless Electronic Warfare Room and made my way to the venue in Gun Room. This was usually the Junior Officers' Mess. It was opposite the Wardroom Galley, spewing out its unwelcome odours and my stomach churned. Lieutenant Pritchard, normally a Forward Air Controller, had been detailed as the Training Officer. I selected a comfortable armchair near a rectangular porthole, through which I could see white-tipped rollers marching towards the ship, lift her over the crest and dump her on the other side. Fighting the desire to vomit, I took notes as Lieutenant Pritchard opened the meeting by suggesting that while our eventual deployment was unclear, it was vital that preparations for hostilities must take precedence. Weapon training was a priority and therefore dry drills would commence immediately. The zeroing of sights would take place on the Flight Deck once the weather improved. Keeping weapons serviceable was essential and therefore they must be protected from the corrosion of seawater. The BVs would be fitted with their General Purpose Machine-Gun (GPMG) mountings. Revision of signal procedures was vital and all ranks were to master the newly issued *Clansman* range of VHF radios. Brigadier Thompson had ordered that all Embarked Force were to do 30 minutes' physical training daily. The conference over, I hoisted myself out of the armchair and staggered to the door feeling decidedly unwell. After some slices of veal at lunch and plenty of water to prevent dehydration, I returned to the EW Office, but nausea assaulted me and I staggered to the 'heads' across the deck and found an unoccupied cubicle. Agony over, while washing my hands, I was relieved that the retching I had heard next door was a naval officer. On returning to the Amphibious Operations Room, Neil, as annoyingly perky and fresh, said 'See you at supper!' I did and ate a good meal, as I always did in the Chief's Mess.

The Intelligence Section settled into a routine of assembling and collating intelligence for the daily Joint Briefing held by Brigadier Thompson and his key Brigade officers and Commodore Michael Clapp and his Amphibious Warfare Staff. Captain Rowe usually gave the intelligence brief. That both HQs were co-located in Stonehouse Barracks meant most officers knew each other, however, I found it interesting that Amphibious Warfare was not supported by an Intelligence Section.

Initially, we relied on the BBC World Service for reports. I had very little exposure to amphibious operations and did not know what to expect, however, that we were not receiving intelligence reports seemed odd. A couple of days after leaving Portsmouth, Brigadier Thompson mentioned something about the Argentinians to Captain Rowe, which he thought Rowe knew about. But Rowe had no idea what the Brigadier was telling him until it emerged he had been receiving highly classified signals from Commander-in-Chief Fleet. It appeared that differing Service cultures were having an impact. While the Royal Navy delivers signals to senior officers, the Army and Royal Marines practised a wider distribution. The Ministry of Defence appeared to be applying peacetime security constraints, however, a fundamental maxim of protective security is that 'Security Must Make Sense'. Remedial action was agreed that Brigade Intelligence must have access to Signals Intelligence. Unfortunately, the SAS on board did not offer its satellite communications.

Crucial to collation is the plotting of enemy positions. The Section maintained its won copy of the Operations Map in the Amphibious Operations Room, both on a scale of 1:50,000 – that is 1 centimetre on the map equates to 500 metres on the ground. Both maps were covered by clear plastic sheets so they could be marked, usually with a chinagraph (a grease pencil made of hardened coloured wax, useful for marking on hard, glossy non-porous surfaces). Blue was used for friendly forces' activities, red for the enemy and green for obstacles, such as minefields. We also maintained several maps of differing scales. Accuracy and speed of keeping them up to date and neat was crucial so they could be interpreted at formal and informal briefings.

Helpfully, NATO had produced a wide range of map marking symbols to depict organisations, sizes and activities. The basic symbol is a common-sized rectangle into which the type of unit is inserted, for instance, two diagonals lines corner to corner for infantry, a parachute for airborne and a small solid circle depicting a gun barrel for artillery. Symbols placed on top of the rectangle indicated type of units, for instance three dots representing a platoon, a single vertical line for a company and 'X' for a brigade. Identified units had name or numerical number entered alongside the rectangle. Fortunately, we had a template made from orange plastic containing a range of map marking symbols to ease map marking and drawing sketches.

Before leaving Plymouth, Brigadier Thompson and several of his staff had conducted a map study of the Falklands and had concluded that while Port Stanley was most likely to be the final objective, it was guarded by high ground covering approaches from the west, including Mount Kent, and sea to the north, east and south. Since the junior rank-and-file of the Argentinian Armed Forces were conscripts, operational weaknesses probably included inexperienced night-fighting capabilities, simple tactics and limited endurance. Early conclusions were that since the defence would probably hinge on occupying Port Stanley and waiting to be attacked, they had plenty of time to create a formidable barrier.

As the flow of intelligence increased, an Air Intelligence Cell was formed from a couple of RAF officers and the Flight-Sergeant to analyse the air threat. I was a little surprised that given their Special Forces role that neither the SBS nor the Mountain and Arctic Warfare Cadre had intelligence support, as did the SAS. Nevertheless, I had a long session with a SBS captain identifying possible beaches that would need to be recced. I found his willingness to share his views to be refreshing. We used the large Commodore's Dining Room, which was then occupied by two junior naval officers representing *Fearless* Intelligence. Afterwards, when I suggested that a joint intelligence section be formed, this was met with noisy support from Air Intelligence detachment but thundering silence from the Royal Navy. This was disappointing because if we landed, those delivering troops to beaches needed to know the enemy threat, but I was not too surprised. My experience on the minesweeper patrolling the Irish Sea from Belfast suggested the Royal Navy preferred to operate in a single service bubble.

One method to assess the combat efficiency of the Argentinians was to dissect the seizure of the Falkland Islands. During the early hours of 2 April, two Amphibious Commando Company detachments had landed about 800 metres east of Mullet Creek on the south coast and, heading north, they slipped past the single Royal Marine manning the Naval Party 8901 observation post on Sapper Hill. Then they had simultaneously attacked Moody Brook Barracks and Government House. Meanwhile, the 2nd Marine Infantry Battalion in LVTP-7s and LARC-5s amphibious tracked vehicles of the 1st Amphibious Vehicle Company landed in Yorke Bay and advanced against limited opposition into Stanley. At the same time, a platoon from C Company, 25th Infantry Regiment, had also landed at Yorke Bay and captured the airport. Naval Party 8901 and a small Royal Navy survey team from HMS *Endurance* were captured. The invasion force had then handed responsibility for the defence of the new territory of Las Malvinas to the 10th Mechanised Infantry Brigade commanded by Brigadier-General Oscar Luis Jofre. It had assembled as Army Group Port Stanley. A day later, the 22-strong HMS *Endurance* Royal Marines detachment, which had landed at Grytviken on South Georgia several days earlier, was overwhelmed in a short but fierce battle with a 1st Marine Infantry Battalion platoon and tactical divers known as *Buzo Tácticos*. The Royal Marines badly damaged a corvette, which came within range of an 84mm Carl Gustav anti-tank weapon. Factors were good intelligence and two well-executed operations.

Two days after leaving England, Brigadier Thompson had come into the Intelligence Section, as he frequently did, to discuss his ideas to capture Stanley and then said, 'Let me have your ideas within 24 hours.' Captain Rowe, Neil Smith and I had a discussion, then presented our own thoughts. The occupation of the Falklands seemed to be dividing into three tactical areas of operation. On East Falkland, Port Stanley was the seat of the occupation and therefore was psychologically and politically the prime objective, the most important bargaining tool. The town had a good airstrip, a sheltered anchorage for large ships and was the centre of communication with the outside world through the cable and wireless station. The defence would centre on the high ground to the east of the town – Mount Kent, Mount London, Two Sisters and Mount Harriet, facing west and covering south-western approaches from Fitzroy. The second sector was in the 'camp' and focused on C Company, 25th Infantry Regiment at Goose Green. The third sector appeared to be West Falkland, which was being occupied by an infantry regiment with companies and heavy weapons at Fox Bay and Port Howard and a 'rover' company periodically visiting settlements. UK television images had shown Italian OTO-Melara 105mm Pack Howitzers, a useful air portable gun with a maximum range of 10,400 metres and formerly used by 29th Commando Regiment RA.

Unfortunately, Brigade Intelligence and 29 Commando Regiment Artillery Intelligence Section were on different ships and without regular communication we were reliant upon the Regiment's Tactical HQ, which was on *Fearless*, and *Jane's Artillery of the World* for information. One main problem was that we initially did not know where the artillery fitted into the enemy order of battle. It did seem that brigades had an Artillery Group and therefore the assumption was the guns would be controlled by an artillery commander. It then emerged brigades were equipped with a field artillery group that had the same designation as its parent formation. *Jane's* told us that the Argentinians had a variety of towed 155mm guns that included the old US 'Long Tom' and the Argentinian CITEFA F3 Howitzer. The latter could be converted into self-propelled but there were no indications that any had been landed. Air defence included the useful West German twin-barrelled 20mm Rheinmetall 202 (Rh-202) and a variety of single-barrel Oerlikon, ranging from 30mm to 40mm. These calibres also served a useful ground support role. Several settlements in the 'camp' had decent airstrips capable of handling Pucará counter-insurgency aircraft, including at Goose Green. Mainland airfields provided bombers, fast attack aircraft, transport and air photographic reconnaissance. We viewed the enemy attitude toward general warfare to be one of seeing it as an almost gallant or chivalrous affair – capture the capital equals capture the nation.

When a general identified as Brigadier-General Menendez was appointed governor, we assumed this to be General Luciano Benjamin Menendez who had achieved something of a hard reputation during anti-guerrilla operations in Tucuman province. Among newspapers used in our collation was a report and a photograph of the general and we gave it to Brigadier Thompson to remind him of his opponent. Unfortunately, we were mistaken. General de Brigade Mario Benjamin Menendez, a fifty-two-year-old career cavalryman with a reputation as a conciliator, had been nominated as the governor of Las Malvinas.

As *Fearless* headed south past the Straits of Gibraltar into calm seas and sunny days, we were joined by a convoy of transports and auxiliaries escorted by warships from Gibraltar. Otherwise, few ships were sighted. The one moment of excitement was a Polish Auxiliary Gatherer of Intelligence sprouting aerials loitering in the path of the convoy. An RAF Nimrod dropped some packages, which were recovered by a ship's boat, and the Type-22 destroyer HMS *Broadsword* drew close enough for a jackstay to be rigged between the two ships allowing more packages to be transferred. As the warships parted, the officers saluted, waved their caps and the bosuns blew their shrill whistles – in the best of Royal Navy traditions. Off Madeira, the Type-21 frigate HMS *Antelope* came alongside *Fearless* on her starboard side and transferred more packages by jackstay. Further south off the coast of West Africa, the increasingly hot days were cooled by a breeze generated by the speed of the ship. I regularly took fresh air on one of the Bridge wings and watched the blue seas being disturbed by flying fish leaping from the bows and porpoises surfing through the waves. One afternoon, I was invited by the Gunnery Officer to join him in the Gun Direction Platform as he exercised the Bridge port and starboard 40mm Bofors in live firing. I gathered from his language and impatient demeanour that both crews needed practice. Each night as darkness spread from the west, orders were given over the tannoy 'Do you hear there! Darken ship! Darken ship! Darken ship!'

HMS *Fearless* left the convoy on the 14th and continued at full speed for a strategic conference scheduled at Ascension Island on the 17th. Two days later, as we approached the equator, during the regular Squadron Meeting Sergeant-Major 'Dutch' Holland handed me a summons to appear before the Court of King Neptune to answer charges that 'Representing the Embarked Force, did attempt to sail across the Royal Equator, in a uniform not readily known in these parts, namely that of a pongo (soldier), thereby attempting to avoid payment and is therefore due initiation'. 'Dutch' and I had been on the same Arctic Warfare Training course in Norway and had shared the same room. During the weekly Saturday morning 10-mile cross-country ski circuit, we had our private race. In an attempt to deflect my appointment with Neptune, I protested and mitigated that I had crossed the equator twice before as a child, once sailing from the UK to East Africa and then from East Africa around the Cape of Good Hope and back to the UK, but my appeal fell on deaf ears as I could not produce any evidence. I therefore had no choice but accept my fate as a repeat offender. Dressed in Arctic waterproofs, an Intelligence Corps stable belt and a winter hat with the earflaps turned down, in front of the baying masses, I was given a last request of a fat, horrible and sloppy kiss from the moustachioed Queen of The Ocean. I was pulled to a stool over a canvas pool of filthy water and, after being insulted and abused of being a 'pongo', I was doused in a foul, brown liquid, forced to swallow a disgusting concoction of a sausage covered in flour and curry powder. King Neptune then poked me with his trident and I was then tipped in the pool where I was mercilessly attacked by 'polar bears' and 'penguins'. Great fun and one up to 'Dutch'!

Meanwhile in the UK, as the crisis had escalated, Commodore Clapp, Commander Amphibious Warfare, was appointed to lead Task Group 317 and to command amphibious operations and then on 12 April, Major-General Moore was appointed Commander Land Forces Falkland Islands as Commander of Task Unit 317.0. Under his command, he had the equivalent of a division consisting of Task Unit 317.1.1 (3 Commando Brigade) and Task Unit 317.1.2 (5 Infantry Brigade), which had been mobilised on 9 April, Good Friday. There was undoubted relief among Royal Marines that a respected officer with a distinguished record and experience in amphibious operations had been selected as Commander Land Forces.

Although 5 Brigade lost its two parachute battalions transferred to the Commando Brigade, they were replaced by 2nd Scots Guards and 1st Welsh Guards. When Brigade HQ wrote *An Account of the Activities of 5 Infantry Brigade in the Falklands Islands Campaign 1982*, its order of battle failed to include its integral 81 Intelligence Section of lieutenant, an experienced staff-sergeant, a sergeant and a couple of corporals and lance-corporals, all Intelligence

Corps. The report made no mentions of its activities and no recommendations were made about intelligence and security.

Although the Intelligence Corps was comparatively small in 1982 with about 2,400 all ranks, about two-thirds were available for operations. It had significant commitments on Operation *Banner* in Northern Ireland, to NATO in West German, in Belize, Cyprus, Hong Kong and a long string of small worldwide deployments; nevertheless, it provided intelligence staff and an intelligence section to HQ Commander-in-Chief Fleet at Northwood. Major David Burrill was instructing at the Foreign Armed Forces Branch at the School of Service Intelligence when he was appointed SO2 G2 (Intelligence and Security) with responsibility to provide intelligence on the Armed Forces of a country that was outside the Army remit. He was supported by a small Intelligence Corps section that consisted of a commando-trained warrant officer currently posted to HQ SAS and a corporal from a UK-based security section. When he arrived at Northwood on 9 April, the sum total of the intelligence was listed on five sheets of paper, of which two were classified. When Major-General Moore moved his HQ to Northwood from Plymouth, Captain David Charters, then serving with Intelligence and Security Group (Germany), was appointed SO3 G2 (Intelligence and Security) and the Intelligence Section was reinforced by two UK-based staff-sergeants and a sergeant, all of whom I knew. The detachment was operational by 9 April. The expertise that the Intelligence Corps brought to Northwood was welcomed, even if some education on naval and military vocabulary and terminology was required by both sides. The intelligence picture was quickly created from official sources, as well as open-source material from newspapers, magazines and periodicals. Since Northwood was the hub of Operation *Corporate*, VIP visits were common. Major Burrill witnessed the firm grasp that Prime Minister Mrs Margaret Thatcher had on military considerations and her determination to succeed.

3

ASCENSION ISLAND

Penny's birthday, 17 April, dawned tropically bright. As *Fearless* gently dipped and rose through the long Atlantic swell, I strolled around the Flight Deck and wished her Happy Birthday. In the clear serenity of the early morning sun, a large white cloud capped the volcanic Ascension Island and soon after breakfast, the anchor splashed into the sea off Georgetown and the ship swung at the mercy of the current. Her fuel stocks were very low. Around us were anchored the two aircraft-carriers and warships that had arrived during the previous days. Two frigates patrolled the horizon and Sea Harriers and helicopters flew in the clear blue skies. I had distinct recollections of the island from going ashore in about November 1954 en route from Mombasa with my mother and brother to go to boarding school in Seaford.

Ascension lies just south of the equator and west of the central African coast and measures about 34 square miles, dominated by Green Mountain. Georgetown, the capital on the western coast, was a collection of single-storey and white-painted colonial buildings. To the south is Wideawake Airfield, so named from a noisy colony of sooty terns. Built with the agreement of the British Government in 1942 by US engineers as a transatlantic staging post during the Second World War, it had been abandoned until 1956 when the Americans returned during the Cold War and expanded it during the mid-1960s to accommodate large aircraft. The US National Aeronautics and Space Administration (NASA) used the island as an emergency base for the space shuttle programme and as a tracking station. The British Government Communications Headquarters and the US National Security Agency (NSA) had established signals intercept stations on the islands during the Cold War. From 1966, the BBC Atlantic Relay Station broadcast short-wave programmes to Africa and South America. In 1982, its airstrip and anchorage became an important asset during Operation *Corporate*.

At about midnight on 16 April, Admiral Fieldhouse and his Northwood planning team had left RAF Brize Norton in a RAF VC-10 and landed at Wideawake at about the same time as *Fearless* dropped anchor at breakfast time the next day. The 3 Commando Brigade planning team was flown by helicopter to HMS *Hermes* to meet the planners. The aircraft-carrier was anchored on our port side and was smaller than I expected. Our expectation of masses of intelligence was high.

Two factors forced another move for the Intelligence Section. First, the ship was reactivating the Electronic Warfare Office and, secondly, our section had become too small and we moved to a new space, this time to a long, narrow compartment alongside Commodore Clapp and his Amphibious Warfare staff in the Chapel two decks below the Amphibious Warfare Room. The move made sense because he needed access to intelligence to plan the landings. Colour-Sergeant Mick Marshalsay, the Brigade HQ Chief Clerk, and his Royal Marines writers, who had been in the Chapel, moved to the annex adjacent to the Amphibious Operations Room. Although a shipwright built a space for Mick, it did not exactly amount to decent working conditions but apparently was all that could be spared. While Commodore Clapp and his staff made us welcome, Neil and I were determined that we needed to be nearer to Brigade HQ in the Amphibious Operations Room, otherwise the Intelligence

Section would be in danger of being out of sight, out of mind. After completing the move, the Intelligence Section stood down for some rest and recuperation after a fortnight of hard work.

Among the consignments flown on board was a pallet of maps addressed to the Intelligence Section. True to his word, the colonel at the Map Depot had ensured they were gridded and again Scotty and Scouse Atkinson set about distributing them within the Brigade.

I was the Embarked Force Senior Non-Commissioned Officer for the day. It was not particularly onerous and involved such routines as visiting the Tank Deck Guard. When I was told that naval officers were tasking the Guard for other duties, I countermanded the order and expected a backlash. Nothing happened. In the evening, I did Rounds with Flight-Lieutenant Marshall-Hasdell, who was in our Air Intelligence Section, and between us it was a case of the blind leading the blind. We were fortunate that Embarked Forces spaces were clean, if overcrowded and poorly ventilated.

In the afternoon, word reached us that the Brigade planning team was returning and we looked forward to the good things the Ministry of Defence and Northwood had produced. Captain Rowe said the conference had gone well, although there had been differences of opinion about the mission and our objectives. There had been some discussion that there was a greater threat to the landing force once it landed than there was to the ships. My view was the best way to isolate a landing force was to sink their ships. It was agreed that the air space must be won to pave the way for ground operations. But we were disappointed by the quality of the information sent from Northwood. We had been isolated at sea for two weeks and yet basic orders of battle had not been supplied, instead US systems and doctrines were sent, which bore little relation to the conscript nature of a South American army. We needed basic intelligence, such as compositions of formations and units, command and control structures, tactics and uniforms and ranks. Very useful, however, was a Technical Intelligence booklet entitled *Argentine Army Equipment Technical Data Sheets* that included photographs and Technical Intelligence data of equipment, vehicles and weapon systems. Several debriefing reports of Falkland Islanders repatriated to UK within days of the Argentinian invasion and several annotated photographs showing positions, equipment and activities taken surreptitiously were invaluable. These included:

Two 'Tigercat' positions defending a probable 105mm artillery position on Stanley Common and a probable command vehicle or trailer fitted with a whip antenna.
Comment. The presence of 'Tigercat' suggested marines. The artillery was probably a 105mm Pack Howitzer.

A Skyguard fire-control radar annotated 'either 3 or 6 AAA guns.'
Comment. Skyguard was used to control the Swiss Oerlikon twin 35mm GDF anti-aircraft guns. (AAA = anti-aircraft artillery.)

On the summit of a low hill was a possible 'howitzer type' gun.
Comment. Probably a 105mm Pack Howitzer.

A field kitchen believed to be in the area of Sapper Hill.
Comment. The kitchen appears to be a sanger constructed of corrugated iron; the chimney is on the left of the construction. Note the two bivouac tents on the right. The Land Rover has probably been captured from Naval Party 8901.
(A sanger or sangar is a temporary fortified position with breastwork originally constructed of stones, now built of sandbags, gabions or similar materials. They are normally built where digging trenches would not be practicable. The word derives from the Persian word *sang*, meaning stone.)

Possible optical/radar guidance equipment, a box-bodied vehicle and two tents near a water tank.
Comment. Our 1:25,000 map showed the water tank supplying Port Stanley was in the West Ward on the south-western outskirts near the reservoir.

Argentinian activity around the Meteorological Station in the East Ward of Port Stanley.

Comment. Note the Argentinian flag. Identified was a Mercedes truck with a canvas behind a well-constructed bunker. Behind the truck, several soldiers were erecting an antennae. A soldier is on the watchtower.

Another photograph showed several people carrying shopping and chatting on Ross Road lined with stationary LVTP-7s. In the foreground of one photograph was a lady wearing a red jacket, with two children, and carrying shopping. The photograph must have been taken on 2 April because the LVTPs were still ashore.

Other photos came from several media outlets, including from a Brazilian periodical, showed:

A military ambulance passing a LVTP-7.

Troops disembarking from the LSL *Cabo San Antonio*.

Troops and AML-90 armoured cars waiting at Comodoro Rivadavia.

Two infantry conscripts eating a meal by a sign that reads 'NP 8901 OC, Port Stanley, Falkland Islands'. The photograph is titled *Argentine soldiers eat field rations at the docks after takeover of the Islands*. In fact, the photograph was taken at Moody Brook Barracks.

Soldiers digging in on Victory Green, Ross Road.

Soldiers carrying large kitbags disembarking from C-130.

Several Amphibious Commandos after the capture of Government House. One is armed with a 9mm Sterling, apparently fitted with a silencer.

Disappointingly, there were no debrief reports of the members of Naval Party 8901 although there were debriefs of the Royal Marines captured at South Georgia and several repatriated civilians debriefed at RAF Brize Norton by an intelligence team. The Intelligence Corps lieutenant-colonel leading the team had been ordered to deliver the information to a Cabinet meeting at 10 Downing Street, timed for 5pm. But, as so often happens, the debriefings took longer than expected and when he was then held up in the Friday rush hour, the lieutenant-colonel instructed his Army driver to 'attract the attention' of the police. When the lieutenant-colonel explained to the police officer who he was and that he had urgent information for Prime Minister Thatcher, the officer led the driver on a high-speed drive through London that included traffic lights switched to green. The lieutenant-colonel arrived with a couple of minutes to spare. It later emerged that the unit commanded by the lieutenant-colonel had not been tasked to debrief Naval Party 8901 and thus a golden opportunity for very recent intelligence disappeared. Our next problem was to disseminate the intelligence throughout the Amphibious Task Force.

When the Combined Task Group 317.8 (Carrier Battle Group), commanded by Rear-Admiral John Woodward, left for the South Atlantic on 18 April, it was almost on the horizon when there was a sudden burst of activity from the two aircraft-carriers, HMS *Hermes* and HMS *Invincible*. Sea Harriers and helicopters could be seen buzzing around and then the two ships scurried back to their anchorages. It later emerged that a sonar contact had indicated a possible submarine. Nothing was found; it was probably a whale. The Argentinian Navy had four submarines, two of which were US Second World War-vintage *Guppy* class and two German Type 209 imports.

Two days after arriving at Ascension, Neil gave the Royal Marines in the Intelligence Section a day of rest and recuperation on the understanding there was always one on duty. The Flight-Sergeant and I took a day off to rediscover our landlubber legs by hitching a lift ashore by helicopter. How the ground swayed once I stepped onto *terra firma*! Wideawake was already becoming the busiest airport in the world, its runway a hive of buzzing helicopters, noisy Vulcan bombers and Victor tankers on test and screaming VC-10s arriving and departing. Such had been the urgency of leaving the UK that contingency loading plans had been replaced by simply loading vehicles, stores and equipment into the ships in any order and then letting go the ropes. Dispersal areas were thus the organised chaos of supply dumps as the Commando Logistic Regiment worked hard to ensure the right equipment was in the right place. 5 Infantry Brigade following behind had no such opportunity. Help was welcomed. A friend, Warrant Officer Jim Taylor REME, serving with the Commando Logistic Regiment on board an LSL, had hooked an underslung net containing stores to a 3 Commando Brigade Air Squadron Scout, but as the helicopter lifted to take the strain, his fingers were trapped as the net tightened. The pilot ignored frantic signals to land and set off for Wideawake with Air Operations struggling to inform him by radio that a stowaway was precariously clinging to the net. When Jim and the net were unceremoniously unhooked on the apron and a crowd asked him what on earth he was up to, it took him some time to explain that his flight was involuntary, showing his skinned fingers, and saying that he had no intention of dropping into the sea, which was reputed to be patrolled by hammerhead sharks. Although Hammerheads do not actively seek out human prey, they will attack if provoked.

We set off for Georgetown and had hardly gone 50 yards before a motorist picked us up and invited us to the Colony Club overlooking a dusty cricket pitch and a hotel. The nearby St Mary's Church was delightful and contained several plaques, including one to a ship's captain who had fallen off his bridge and died. Purple bougainvillea bushes and green palm trees were a picturesque backdrop to the white bungalows and harsh red and black volcanic stones and rocks. The main shop was managed by the Navy, Army and Air Force Institute (NAAFI) but it soon ran short of provisions to the extent that Task Force customers were banned the next day. My only souvenir from Ascension Island was an inscribed T-shirt. We then decided to go to Two Boats Village, a settlement in the centre of the island and were driven there by a BBC engineer who first took us to the One Boat Golf Club about halfway between Georgetown and Two Boats village where, over a delicious cold beer, he mentioned his side-line of photographing young ladies from cruise ships on secluded sandy beaches and then selling the photographs to magazines. Apparently it was all very easy. He then drove us to Two Boats, where he lived, and dropped us at the Club, but the swimming pool was crowded with airmen from the RAF Tactical Communications Wing, which was usually based at RAF Brize Norton, lounging on sunbeds, as if they owned the place, muttering 'Not more Marines!'

'Actually no,' I replied 'but not far off!' We lazed beside the pool, swam a few lengths, had a few beers, fell asleep in the sun and fed the tan. We were given a lift back to Wideawake by a man scheduled to leave Ascension next day and after a huge meal in a United States Air Force canteen, then hitched a helicopter to *Fearless,* thoroughly refreshed after our run ashore.

On *Fearless,* there was a continuous rumble of activity as watches came on and went off duty and pipes broadcast announcements throughout the ship, such as 'Stand by FOXTROT 4!' as the LCU returned to the ship or 'Do you hear there! Do you hear there! Flying Stations!' for helicopter operations. The pipes originated from the bosun's mate console on the bridge. One was a Yorkshireman who had a broad accent and I have no doubt that members of the Embarked Force have lasting memories of him piping 'The AOO is to go to the AOR (Amphibious Operations Officer is to go to the Amphibious Operations Room)' in his rich accent. When it became evident he was being contacted to announce some spurious message request just to listen to his broad accent, this led to his removal from the microphone. However, by popular request he returned, and a cheer reverberated around the ship as he piped, 'The AOO is to go to the AOR'.

A couple of days after arriving, the Ministry of Defence announced that we were to receive Local Overseas Allowance for Ascension Island, the announcement was a welcome addition to the 'hard living' allowance we received for 'suffering' the rigours of shipboard life. However, it was something of a surprise. It was also amazing that stores and equipment, which normally took years to be issued, suddenly become available. For instance, the Intelligence Section received a complete set of the latest Jane's defence volumes within about a week of ordering them. On the other hand, Ordnance Squadron of the Commando Logistic Regiment had a difficult time sourcing spares for our Mark XI Land Rover; their list was for Mark IIIs.

For the six-and-a-half weeks I was on *Fearless* I kept to a routine because I felt it important to have a regulated life on board. 'Reveille' at 6.30am was an insistent whistle piped throughout the ship and I re-joined the hustle and bustle of the ship after a shave, shower and preferred breakfast of scrambled egg, fried bread and tomatoes or baked beans followed by grapefruit or cereal and two mugs of tea. The usual rig (dress) was lightweight trousers, shirt and soft-soled desert boots. It was important that either Neil or I or both attended the daily 8.15am Brigade HQ and Signals Squadron parade on the upper deck amidships in which working parties were detailed and the training programme announced. The Intelligence Section was on permanent call to support Brigade HQ and was therefore excused most duties, such as guards and fatigue parties and the junior ranks were supplied with watchkeeper chits to prevent them queuing for meals.

One controversial matter that became a focus of tension was the Navy apparently regarding the Embarked Force as a valuable source of labour and expecting them to provide parties to chip paint, scrub floors and clean compartments. Indeed, I often heard it said that whenever the Embarked Force was on board, the two LPDs were the cleanest ships in the Fleet. However, on this deployment, the Royal Marines and Army needed to prepare for war with weapon training, radio procedures, first aid, tactics and helicopter drills. The Navy also practised their drills, such as Damage Control exercise for Nuclear, Biological, Chemical and Defence (NBCD) piped by 'Exercise! Exercise! Exercise! All hands to Action Stations. NBCD State Yellow. Assume Condition Yankee!' The announcement was followed by an organised rush to Action Stations, each man wearing a white anti-flash hood and long white gauntlets and carrying his respirator. The incident was usually in some inaccessible part of the ship. While this was happening, the Embarked Force were closed up in their messes or work areas. Interestingly, I do not recall any 'Abandon Ship' exercises.

The Intelligence Section spent the mornings interpreting the latest intelligence reports, which, frustratingly, still tended to be raw information, highly classified and usually still without comment. The two Illustrators then compiled diagrams of orders of battle collated by the rest of us.

Northwood had yet to supply a threat assessment of the Argentine air capability and thus when one report identified MB-339 Aermacchi aircraft at Air Force Base Stanley, our conclusion was that they and the FMA IA 58 Pucarás gave the Argentinians a decent ground attack fighter capability, particularly as both could operate from settlement grass strips. Another report suggesting a probable Army Commando Company base and headquarters at Stanley Junior School led to requests for more information about Argentinian commando units because they had gained something of an unenviable reputation during the Dirty War. Neil and I usually attended mid-morning Stand Easy (coffee break) at 10.30am in the Chief's Mess during which we would brief the Chiefs and military SNCOs from a map pinned on a wall. Chief Petty Officer 'Bungy' Williams seemed exceptionally well briefed on 'need to know' information, possibly originating from Wardroom stewards reporting conversations.

Major Richard Dixon, who commanded the Brigade HQ and Signals Squadron and also the Embarked Force, held a daily conference at 11am at which either Neil or I usually gave a formal update. Subjects included extra cigarettes to be issued prior to the landings, that twenty-seven new arrivals would have to sleep on the Tank Deck and that all Embarked Force not on duty would be required to assist in refuelling-at-sea and the stowage of transferred stores. Whistling was not allowed, which intrigued me. Apparently, it brought the ship bad luck and only chefs were allowed to whistle because it meant they were not eating rations. It is said that Christian Fletcher had initiated the mutiny on HMS *Bounty* by whistling.

Lunch, usually a light meal and snacks, was at 12.30pm. For some reason, which no one explained to me, hot drinks were not served. At 1pm, I briefed Mess 2MI (Junior Ranks Starboard Aft). I had management responsibility for this mess because it consisted mainly of Army from 29th Commando Regiment gunners, 59 Commando Independent Squadron sappers and the commando-trained Corporal 'Dixie' Dean of the Royal Military Police and Brigadier Thompson's close protection. For instance, there was a complaint that some Chief Petty Officers had used the aft 'heads' just before an inspection. Lance-Bombardier Stone had a defective rifle; it was repaired by a ship's armourer. Next came a most difficult decision, siesta or return to the Intelligence Section, as one's conscience demanded. I also contributed to other briefings by giving presentations on conduct after capture and Prisoner of War handling, usually to a large audience of Royal Navy and Embarked Force Other Ranks.

Far more difficult was preparing and being the voice on three video presentations produced by *Fearless* TV describing enemy equipment that were circulated around the Amphibious Task Group as a briefing mechanism. Captain David Nicholls, who had the unenviable appointment of being the Commando Brigade

Public Relations Officer, was a great help during the editing stage. The first video was made on the way to Ascension Island and was an introduction to enemy equipment. Since I did not feel competent enough to talk about the maritime threat, this was delegated to the ship's Intelligence Section of two junior officers. The other two were part of a larger programme and made after we had departed from Ascension Island. One used photographs to describe more enemy equipment and the other showed photographs from intelligence sources, emphasising that with the probability of hostilities and that with the approach of winter, life for the Argentinians would be hostile, primitive and uncertain. When there was a suggestion the Intelligence Section prepare a daily briefing for circulation throughout the Amphibious Task Group, a belief emerged that the Embarked Force wanted to take over the studio and our suggestion was blocked. One criticism after the war was the lack of information.

I usually attended the second Embarked Force physical training session of 30 minutes circuit training at 5.30pm for Brigade HQ officers, senior non-commissioned officers and anyone from the ship's company. If I missed circuit training, I would pound up and down the Tank Deck ramp for about 30 minutes doing exercises at each turn. When the Docking Bay at Ascension was dry, I sprinted from the stern to the ramp and jogged back, repeating the course at least fifty times. I would then wreck all the good work by buying an ice-cream, and then shower. There was always much banter in the washrooms as the off-duty watch mingled with the sweaty Embarked Force in a small space in which the floor was awash with soapy water that swished to and fro as the ship lurched in the swell. I usually rinsed my feet under the salt-water tap to prevent foot infections and harden my soles.

Supper, the last meal of the day, was always appetising with roasts, pies and curry followed by a sweet. Indeed, the menus produced by the Navy chefs were first class. Afterwards, it was relaxation in the Chief's Lounge or in the Mess watching *Fearless* TV showing videos, my favourite being a Mike Oldfield concert featuring the albums 'Hergest Ridge' and 'Tubular Bells'. At 8pm, the evening programme was fronted by a Leading Seaman, whose hair parting regularly changed positions, reading the news, previewing programmes and listing the `stitch-ups' – everyone's favourite. A `stitch-up' is public teasing about an individual or a group's habits, tastes or activities. The Wardroom stewards came in for much teasing. Commander Kelly, the Executive Officer, then usually appeared to announce changes to the daily routine or to dish out some reprimand; how we yearned for him to congratulate someone. He or Captain Larken then commented upon the political situation by reading extracts from the newspapers received by the 30th Signals Regiment Rear Link Detachment on board. Unfortunately, the extracts were once intercepted and Commander Kelly was fed false information, to the amusement of almost everyone because Messes had received the correct version earlier in the evening. Then followed a short programme, such as *Top of the Pops* or *The Benny Hill Show* and finally a feature film ranging in type from *A Bridge Too Far* to *Grease*. Not one 'blue' film was shown. Afterwards, I usually returned to the Intelligence Section to read and analyse the latest intelligence reports, review our collation in case we had missed something and, usually, write a letter. Before turning in, I generally made a mug of cocoa and climbed a ladder to the upper deck and spent a few minutes of contemplation savouring the tranquillity of the night as the gently swaying Gun Direction Platform and superstructure briefly blocked out the myriad constellations and galaxies. I always posted a message to Penny and Imogen relayed through the moon and stars spread across the curtain of the tropical night. With the gentle rocking of the ship, sleep came easy.

The Intelligence Section was strengthened with the welcome return of Sergeant Roy Packer, the 59 Independent Commando

Squadron RE Intelligence sergeant who had normally worked with us in Plymouth. The Air Intelligence detachment had increased and now consisted of Lieutenant-Commander Callaghan, the Brigade Air Liaison Officer, Flight-Lieutenant Dennis Marshall-Hasdell, a commando-trained Forward Air Controller, our RAF Flight-Sergeant, and Flight-Lieutenant Tony White, loaned from Commodore Amphibious Warfare. He was a Buccaneer navigator, usually based at RAF Lossiemouth, and he tried to extract some sympathy by claiming he had been given just a few hours' notice before deployment. It was a mystery why he, front-line aircrew, had been appointed as an intelligence officer, nevertheless, he was typical aircrew – hardworking and fun – and he wore his flying suit. Lieutenant-Commander Dobinson, a photographic interpreter from RAF Brampton, joined the HMS *Fearless* Intelligence Cell that consisted of three junior officers and a carpenter. For the first time the land, air and naval intelligence functions on board were working as a joint organisation but were not centralised.

About a fortnight after arriving at Ascension, Brigadier Thompson arrived in the Intelligence Section with a signal from HQ Intelligence Corps stating that I had been promoted to Warrant Officer Class Two and that I had been posted to Northern Ireland forthwith. I advised the Brigadier that the Intelligence Corps establishment for the Section was a staff sergeant and unless my Corps was prepared to change that establishment, then I would rather remain with 3 Commando Brigade.

Our frustrations at not being able to circulate intelligence sent by Commander-in-Chief Fleet was temporarily resolved one evening when Neil and I were having a CSB pint with a Chief Petty Officer in the Chief's lounge, who had recently arrived from UK and was managing the Ship's Electronic Warfare capability. The previous night, his team had been twiddling the knobs of their equipment when they had intercepted the Cable and Wireless telephone and telegram link between Stanley and Buenos Aires and stumbled on the welfare telegram link between Argentinian servicemen on the Falklands and their families. We frankly did not believe him until the next morning when he arrived at the Intelligence Section clutching a wad of telegrams and suggested there was not much of interest. How wrong he was! Each telegram included rank, name and unit details of the sender and names and addresses of the recipient. The content often included descriptions of military activity and also personal information that might be useful in interrogations. The telegrams were often more informative than the bland Commander-in-Chief Fleet signals. We were astonished at the breach of security and when Northwood was advised, they considered the link was most likely an Argentinian disinformation operation and that we should ignore it. While that was a fair comment, we were not convinced and the next day we tested the authenticity of the telegrams by comparing them with information received from Northwood. An analysis showed the sources of information complemented each other and so the Chief undertook to pass on any intercepted welfare telegrams – on a strict 'need to know' basis.

Five days after arriving at Ascension, Rigid Raiders of 1st Raiding Squadron Royal Marines ferried several of the Brigade Intelligence Section to *Canberra* to attend the only Intelligence Officers conference of the campaign. *Fearless* was swaying in the swell and some questioned the wisdom of descending a rope dangling from the stern into a small craft bobbing in seas that had fast currents and fish that bite. The Rigid Raiders skipped at speed to the leeward side of the liner where the next obstacle was that the landing pontoon was higher than the gunwales of the Raiders. Watching the arrivals was an audience of paras and commandos who were taking bets on who would mistime the step onto the pontoon; the trick was to step with total, but casual, confidence onto the platform at the crest of a wave. After coming from the dour gangways of a warship, I marvelled at the spacious corridors, large recreation areas, lounges, shops and waiter service in the restaurants. Apparently, canny Embarked Force from other ships were using the liner as an informal rest and recreation centre as a change from the lifestyle of the Grey Funnel Line.

After the unit Intelligence Sections had gathered in a room near the Photographic Shop, Captain Rowe opened the conference by briefing that the Argentinians had established an Air Bridge from the mainland to consolidate their hold and reinforce their troops. Our previous assessment that Port Stanley, Goose Green, Fox Bay and Port Howard were strongholds had not changed. Television images confirmed that Argentinian troops were having an uncomfortable time surviving the early South Atlantic autumn weather. After Lieutenant-Commander Callaghan briefed us on the air threat, I gave a short brief on equipment recognition and refreshed on the importance of effective prisoner handling, the basics of the Third Geneva Convention and the need for operational security. It was critical to remind troops of the value of intelligence and that the two-way passage of information developed in Northern Ireland was the benchmark. Without intelligence, commanders at all levels are 'blind and deaf'.

Two members of Naval Party 8901 captured in Stanley and now serving with J Company, 42 Commando, told their story, the good news being that the Argentinians generally complied with the Geneva Conventions. We reported that in the event of having to fight in the built-up area of Port Stanley, the Intelligence Section was using a 1966 1:2,500 Ordnance Survey map to plot brick buildings that could be converted into strongholds. Examples were Government House, the Secretariat, Police Station, Falkland Islands Company offices and several houses near the public jetty. The main discussion point was illustrated by justifiable comments about the lack of intelligence. Captain Rowe explained that the combination of high classifications and privacy gradings imposed by Commander-in-Chief Fleet meant that distribution was strictly on a 'need to know' basis and that Brigadier Thompson had ordered that sensitive intelligence was not to be shared. He assured the conference that it was not our policy to withhold information that could be released and we undertook to continue writing daily Intelligence Summaries from open and non-sensitive sources that could be communicated throughout the Landing Force without breaching operational security.

Indeed, that evening, Captain Larken announced on *Fearless* TV that as a consequence of a breach of operational security concerning several dates that Brigadier Thompson had said could only be verbally shared being published on an Embarked Force written daily orders, with immediate effect, private mail would be censored. There was the justifiable fear that written orders could be heaved over the side of ships as 'gash' (rubbish), float ashore and end up in Buenos Aires. Instructions issued throughout the Brigade included that letters were not to identify where we were, even though the US broadcasting station on Ascension had been beaming details of our presence to the world's media. A saving grace was that the censors were the padres and chaplains. While the measure lasted three days, it was a salutary lesson that not sharing information with the enemy was crucial. I was not too surprised by the breach. The two Security Companies of the Intelligence Corps with the British Army of the Rhine in West Germany had checked the locations of major HQs on exercises, collected rubbish left behind and they often gave presentations to senior commanders on the sort of information that could end up in Soviet hands.

On 24 April, the Argentinian merchantman *Río de la Plata* was sighted lingering some 5 miles offshore and when a helicopter was scrambled to shadow her, air photographs sent to Brigade Intelligence appeared to show, at the stern, canoes beneath tarpaulins. The combination of reports that the Argentinian Navy had mini-submarines, the merchantman had recently been in Lisbon and had embarked Argentinian Special Forces, and that a patrolling destroyer had picked up unidentified sonar contact, led to Action Stations throughout the anchorage. Within half-an-hour, the ships scattered to the four points of the compass. The next day, the threat panic escalated when a foreign yellow lifejacket found floating offshore was assumed to be Argentinian. 40 Commando therefore conducted a cordon-and-search operation across the island concentrating on the woods and fields and Green Mountain. Nothing was found, nevertheless, the threat was considered to be sufficiently serious that it prompted the Navy to order Operation *Awkward* to defend anchored ships against divers and mini-submarines. Henceforth, the perimeter of the anchorage was guarded by destroyers and frigates and within it, ships were encouraged to keep moving along a racetrack from English Bay to the beaches off Wideawake that became known as 'Georgetown Races' or 'The Wacky Races'. In common with other ships that were stationary, *Fearless* launched a whaler manned by two seamen who chugged around the ship dropping small depth charges into the sea at irregular intervals in order to deter divers. A demand that armed Embarked Force patrol the decks was resisted on the grounds that the defence of the ship was the responsibility of the ship. When divers regularly inspected the hull, Dick Birkett, who reputedly could hardly swim a stroke but nevertheless was a qualified naval diver, helped. As evening approached, ships left the anchorage and returned the following morning.

In addition to cross-decking of personnel and stores to ensure everything was in the right place, the two Troops of B Squadron, The Blues and Royals, were ferried on board *Fearless* by LCU. Each Troop consisted of two Scimitars equipped with 30mm Rarden gun and two Scorpions fitted with a 76mm gun. They were supported by a Royal and Electrical Engineer-manned Samson armoured recovery vehicle. Unfortunately there were no bunks and the troopers set up a laager on the Tank Deck. Having served with the Regiment for three years, I met a couple of former colleagues. The Squadron zeroed their guns and experimented by firing their guns over the lowered ramps of the LCUs, not exactly a stable platform but a practical solution for delivering close fire support for a beach assault.

Throughout the stopover at Ascension Island, drills and exercises familiarised troops with helicopter assaults, landing craft drills by day and night, and combined helicopter and landing craft landings controlled by headquarters, live firing on temporary ranges and command post exercises to test procedures. The feasibility of using helicopters to drop patrols was tested one afternoon when Flight-Sergeant Roberts, who was a Parachute Jump Instructor in my Mess, with three officers and a para, jumped by static line from a Sea King, watched by audiences as they drifted down into the sea. Apparently, there was one instance of ill-discipline when three gunners on a LSL defied anyone to remove them from the foc'sle. No one was persuaded and the trio had seats booked on the next VC-10 home. 3 Para on *Canberra* were said to be restless and one presumed that, sooner or later, they would attempt to throw anyone wearing a Commando Green Beret over the side, followed presumably by anyone wearing a Red Beret. Gifts arriving from the public were humbling but most welcome. I was desperately short of decent books. The people of Southampton collected 9,000 books and the 'dockies' at Portsmouth had a whip-round to buy videos. Prized was one of 3,000 copies of the December issue of *Men Only* donated by W. H. Smith. In relation to entertainment, the Commando Forces Band, which on operations supplied logistic and casualty support to the Brigade, gave a very pleasant performance on *Fearless* on 25 April during a tropical evening fed by a warm breeze whispering across the decks. The traditional fishing competition saw lines of sailors with fishing rods and Royal Marines and soldiers with a variety of lines endeavouring to catch a shark, or more likely any fish. The several comedians included a Royal Marine with a length of thin rope and something that represented a hook, on which dangled some meat, nonchalantly heaving his 'rod' over the side four times – and catching four tuna.

British resolve was demonstrated on 25 April when M Company, 42 Commando, led the recapture of South Georgia. SAS secrecy and their unwillingness to acknowledge expert regional opinion had led to the loss of two valuable helicopters and winter warfare equipment, quite apart from risking the operational security of the operation. Several days later, when the RFA *Tidespring* arrived from South Georgia with 156 Prisoners of War and several civilians, the two-man interrogation team on board sent us a red-covered book entitled *Reglamento del Grupo de Infanteria de Marina en el Combate* (Marine Infantry Group in Battle). For the first time, we had a detailed reference to Argentinian tactics and a benchmark for the Argentinian Army. The pair had been flown to *Tidespring* by a CH-47 Chinook and the prisoners were interrogated en route. Their results were our first glimpse of the Argentinians.

4

THE DEFENCE OF LAS MALVINAS

By the time that HMS *Fearless* was preparing to depart for the South Atlantic after three weeks at Ascension Island, Brigade Intelligence Section had developed an order of battle of the Argentinian forces on the Falkland Islands that we believed to be accurate. The interception of the welfare telegrams had proved crucial. Admittedly, the assessment had been benchmarked against the Guatemalan Army, which the British had been facing in Belize for several years. I had seen it from close quarters. There were no available alternatives.

The *Ejército Argentina* (Argentinian Army) had modern equipment, principally from Western origins. Deeply involved in politics, as were all three Services, it had gained international notoriety from its excesses in the Dirty War, otherwise it was inexperienced. Organised into five Corps, 2 Corps defended the border with Uruguay and Paraguay; defending the northen border with Bolivia was 3 Corps; 1 Corps was based in mid-Argentina; 4 Corps was based in the vicinity of Buenos Aires and 5 Corps defended the south including the border with Chile and the Atlantic coast.

Since the word 'division' rarely appeared in intelligence assessments, there was some uncertainty over whether the Army had a divisional structure. The order of battle seemed to be organised around eight

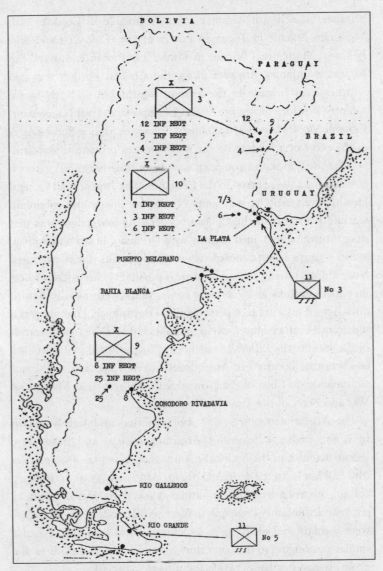

Contemporary map produced by the Commando Brigade Intelligence Section showing the mainland bases of the three brigades and their infantry regiments that deployed to the Falklands.

brigades, namely 4th Airborne Infantry Brigade in Córdoba; 5th Mountain Brigade in Tucumán Province; 9th (*Colonel Luis Jorge Fontana*) Mechanised Brigade in Santa Cruz Province; 6th and 8th Mountain Infantry Brigades along the Chilean border; the cold weather 11th Brigade in the extreme south; 3rd and 7th Jungle Infantry Brigades facing Brazil and Uruguay and 10th (*Lieutenant-General Nicolás Levalle*) Mechanised Brigade defending Buenos Aires in the event of a landing on the north-eastern provincial seaboard. 'Mechanised' indicates equipped with armoured personnel carriers, however, none were taken to the Falklands. The Argentinian General Headquarters sent its best units of marine, jungle and mountain warfare regiments to the Chilean border. The assessment was that since Argentina remained friendly with Uruguay, Brazil and Bolivia, 1 and 5 Corps seemed most likely to provide units. Light armoured recce units on roads and tracks were a possibility. In order to foster unit identification and *esprit de corps*, units were usually named after Argentinian military personalities. For instance, Fontana was a nineteenth-century officer, explorer, politician and the first governor of Chubut Province. Levalle was born in Italy, fought in most of the conflicts that occurred in Argentina between 1852 and 1893, was Commander-in-Chief of the General Staff and served as Minister of War and Navy of the Argentine Republic.

The Argentinian officer was well educated and largely drawn from the higher echelons of Argentine society and most were indoctrinated into the national mantra that *Malvinas es Argentina* (the Falklands are part of Argentina). After two years in military college, officers served for a minimum of two years. First-lieutenants commanded infantry companies. Warrant officers and senior NCOs were regulars and likely to be experienced and hard. Most had a similar upbringing to the conscripts, were professional soldiers and probably had combat experience during the Dirty War.

The Argentine conscript was an unknown quantity but was likely to be similar to other worldwide conscripts who regarded military national service as a tiresome chore. However, armies can produce good conscript soldiers, provided they are well trained, as was the case with the British Army throughout the Second World War and in its post-war campaigns until the late 1950. Therefore there was no reason to underestimate these conscripts. From 1976, all males aged 18 years were inducted into military service, although some received exemptions for a variety of reasons including being unable to reach the required physical standards. After induction, the training cycle lasted from March to October, after which the conscripts were released in stages until the next induction. While some brigades and regiments organised platoon-sized commando and heli-borne detachments from the best recruits after basic training, conscripts were used on fatigues and were often referred to as *Las Colimba*s from their perceived daily routine of Correr (Run!), *im*par (Clean!), and *ba*rrer (Sweep!). Discipline was harsh, field punishment not uncommon and religion a way of life. Marine conscription was for three years and their training produced generally well-prepared and motivated units.

In 1982, the annual Army conscription of *Soldados Clase 63* of men born in 1963 had started in February and thus some of those sent to the Falklands were inexperienced and inadequately trained. When the Task Force set sail in early April, the Army recalled *Soldados Clase 62*, who had been discharged in December 1981. Most supported the seizure of the Falklands and were keen to do their bit to ensure that '*Las Malvinas es Argentina*'. While middle to senior leadership lacked the appropriate skills, there is substantial evidence that junior leaders were effective.

The *Armada Argentina* (Argentinian Navy) was a threat to the naval element of the Task Force. Brigade Intelligence was concerned for several reasons. The British-built aircraft carrier *Veinticinco de Mayo*, formerly HMS *Venerable* launched in 1945, could provide close air support and light bombing missions. The Second World War US cruiser *General Belgrano*, two British-built Type 42 destroyers and several German frigates and corvettes could provide naval gunfire support. The four submarines, two of Second World War US vintage and two German boats with a long endurance, had the capability to intercept Task Force convoys and also land agents and raiding parties. Amphibious support was assessed to be durable with a variety of ships suitable for the inhospitable South Atlantic and Antarctic Oceans. Much depended on the ability and skill of the officers and NCOs to train the conscript sailors. The *Prefectura Naval Argentina* (PNA – Argentine Coastguard) had a useful sea and air capability but little was known about its paramilitary capability. Since the Falklands was within the contested zone, PNA cutters and helicopters were likely to be encountered. The Argentinian Marine Corps was something of an elite that could trace its origins to the colonial Spanish naval infantry. It had fought the British in 1806 and 1807. Naval Air Command had a mix of interceptors, fighter ground attack, training, helicopters, fighters and transport aircraft. McDonnell Douglas A-4Q Skyhawks and Dassault-Breguet Super Étendards, which were carrier-borne, had the ability to launch.

Since Northwood had yet to produce an authoritative view of the *Fuerza Aérea Argentina* (Argentine Air Force) threat, Flight-Lieutenant White produced an assessment but then experienced some difficulty in persuading the Royal Navy and Amphibious Warfare that the air threat was a considerable one and that his lone voice should not be treated as an unintelligible whisper. His research suggested that the Air Force had a wide range of aircraft. Interceptors and fighters included the US-built Skyhawks, Delta-winged French Dassault Mirage IIIs, the Israeli variant being known as the Dagger, and the Super Étendards. Most of the Argentinian pilots were believed to be American- or Israeli-trained and therefore tactics would reflect their instructors; in fighter ground attack for example, the tactic was likely to be line astern and not the 'finger four' formation favoured by the RAF. This meant attacks were likely to be narrow and sustained. White believed the Exocet surface-to-surface missile was a major threat to ships and used graphs and charts to predict the height at which a missile would strike the side of the ship and called it 'The Exocet Line'. Two Air Force reconnaissance Boeing 707s, nicknamed the `Shads' (the Shadows), were already roaming the Atlantic. The British Canberra was a useful high-level bomber and the Learjet had a decent air photography capability. The FMA 1A 58 Pucará ground attack aircraft was regarded as a significant threat because it could lay down extensive firepower over a small area. There was no intelligence suggesting that strike aircraft were based at Air Force Base Stanley and therefore air raids would be launched from the eastern seaboard airfields, such as Comodoro Rivadavia, and would probably be supported by KC-130H refuelling tankers. This would offer pilots reasonable linger time.

As with most air forces, the Argentinian Air Force could muster civil transport to move troops and equipment, but much would depend on the serviceability of the runway at Stanley Airport. From monitoring UK television pictures before we left Portsmouth, we had identified Fokker F-27 Friendships and F-28 Fellowships. Helicopters were an important resource on both sides. *Military Balance* listed Argentina as having CH-47 Chinooks, Bell-212s, Huey UH-1H Iroquois of Vietnam fame, Pumas and French Alouettes, indicating a reasonable troop lift capability, gunship escort and fire suppression.

At Port Stanley, Government House housed the Joint HQ under the overall control of Brigadier-General Menendez. HQ Army Group Falklands was thought to be in the Secretariat. Initially, the defence appeared to be static and by the end of April, the Stanley defence appeared to be organised into three tactical areas of responsibility of Army Groups at Port Stanley, Goose Green and Port Howard/Fox Bay.

Army Group Port Stanley consisted of an estimated 8,400 all ranks under the command of Brigadier-General Oscar Jofre, the commander of the 10th Mechanised Infantry Brigade. Brigade HQ was thought to be at the Falkland Islands Defence Force Drill Hall. Defending the Outer Defence Zone on the high ground to the west was the 4th Infantry Regiment in the area of Mount Wall, Two Sisters and Mount Harriet; on its right on Mount Longdon and Wireless Ridge was 7th Infantry Regiment, which was usually based in the city of Buenos Aires. Defending the southern gateway to Stanley at Pony Pass and in depth to the Outer Defence Zone was the Marine Infantry Combat Landing Group built around the 5th Marine Infantry Battalion with its HQ on Mount Tumbledown. It was supported by a .50-inch Browning machine-gun company and an amphibious engineer company. Defending Air Force Base Stanley was A Company, 25th Special Infantry Regiment, from 9th Infantry Brigade, supported by an amphibious engineer company. The Regiment was commanded by the hard-line Argentine/Lebanese Lieutenant-Colonel Mohamed Alí Seineldín. His wife had designed the shoulder flash of a soldier on the Falkland Islands.

Supported by a highly motivated training team, he brought out the best in his men in a tough but short commando course. When 9th Brigade was warned for deployment, Seineldín renamed his regiment the 25th Special Infantry Regiment and enlarged it to five companies of about 100 men. A substantial number of the regiment had been either commandos or paratroopers. Argentine journalists nicknamed the unit the *Seineldín Commando Regiment*.

In general support were the 10th and 181st Armoured Car Squadrons, both thought to be equipped with twelve Panhard AML-90 armoured cars. Other Brigade assets included 10th Engineer Company, 10th Communication Company and 10th Logistic Company. 3rd Artillery Group from 3rd Infantry Brigade and the 4th Parachute Artillery Group formed the field artillery assets. Batteries usually consisted of six 105mm Pack Howitzers. B Battery, Marine Field Artillery also had six Pack Howitzers. British gunners were familiar with the Pack Howitzer.

Air defence of Port Stanley was strong. The 601 Air Defence Artillery Group defended the ground forces with a Westinghouse TPS-43/44 long-range radar supporting a Roland and four Tigercat surface-to-air missile systems and six Skyguard fire control radars supporting two Oerlikon 35mm GDF-002 twin cannons and three Oerlikon 20mm single barrel anti-aircraft cannons. B Battery, 101st Anti-Aircraft Group was equipped with eight Hispano-Suiza 30mm guns and ten 12.7mm machine guns. Some Infantry units were equipped with Blowpipe. The 1st Marine Air Defence Battery on Stanley Common deployed three Tigercat surface-to-air missiles, which was the ground version of the naval Seacat system, and twelve Hispano HS-831 30mm anti-aircraft guns to support the defence of Mount Tumbledown.

The Air Force defended Air Force Base Stanley with three Oerlikon GDF-002s south-west of the airport supported by a Super Fledermaus fire control radar. Nine Rheinmetall Rh-202 twin 20 mm anti-aircraft guns (Rh202) were close to the runway.

Army Chief of Staff Troops supplied units prefixed with the number 601, such as 601 Electronic Warfare Company and 601 Engineer Battalion. It was assessed that since helicopters had been used in Tucuman Province and the Dirty War, the 601 Combat Aviation Battalion would be effective and had sufficient helicopters for a single battalion lift covered by suppressive fire from gunships. To prevent the resource being destroyed by naval gunfire or an air attack, the helicopters were mostly located in a base on Mount Kent. 1st Corps provided units prefixed with the number 181, such as 181 Intelligence Company, a counter-intelligence unit believed to be at 18 Ross Road, and 181 Military Police Company at the Junior School.

The Argentinian Army did not have Special Forces until the early 1970s when commandos were raised in response to internal security unrest, however, the fear of such highly trained groups being used in a *coup d'état* saw them shelved. In 1975, they were reformed for the Dirty War but were again disbanded after the 1978 Football World Cup. Thereafter commando companies were raised when required. Two Special Forces units had been identified as part of Army Group Falklands, namely 601 Commando Company and the border guards of 601 National Gendarmerie Squadron. A gendarmerie unit is a military organisation with jurisdiction in civil law enforcement.

Initially, 9th Infantry Brigade under command of Brigadier-General Americo Daher defended East Falkland with its C Company, 25th Infantry Regiment, based at Goose Green. Also at the settlement was Military Air Base *Condor* with a flight of Pucarás. It was defended by six Air Force Rh-202s supported by an ELTA short range radar. An air photograph later showed two CH-47 Chinooks parked near the settlement. At Fox Bay was 8th Infantry Regiment, commanded by Lieutenant-Colonel Ernesto Repossi, and 9th Engineer Company. Reports suggested that a battery of 105mm Pack Howitzers from the 4th Parachute Artillery Group varied between Port Howard and Stanley. In mid-May, reports emerged that the health of the troops was poor and at least two civilian doctors had been transferred from Port Stanley to deal with malnutrition, influenza, exposure and gunshot wounds.

3rd Mechanised Infantry Brigade was based in the north-east coastal province of Mesopotamia (named this by the first Spanish settlers because it resembled the lush ground between the Euphrates and Tigris rivers in modern Iraq) which is in Northern Argentina. Its districts include Corrientes and Misiones.

When the hostilities escalated in April, Brigadier-General Omar Parada was warned to reinforce Argentina's defence against Chile. When he recalled reservists demobilised in December, the response was good with men catching the troop train as it travelled south to defend the Atlantic coast against British incursions. It was then deployed by rail to deter an opportunist Chilean incursion, but shortly after crossing the Colorado River in mid-Argentina, Parada was ordered to replace 9th Infantry Brigade in the southern province of Santa Cruz, which had deployed to the Falklands. The regiment was then diverted to Bahia Blanco to embark on the Amphibious Support transport *Ciudad de Cordoba* bound for Port Stanley. But the ship hit rocks soon after sailing and returned to port for repairs. She was prevented from sailing to the Falklands by imposition of the Total Exclusion Zone; nevertheless, the brigade eventually landed in Port Stanley on 24 April. The remainder first deployed to Mount Wall as part of the Outer Defence Zone, but of its ten 81mm mortars, eight were damaged. Piaggi was also missing most of his radios, the company field kitchens and fourteen MAG machine guns with B Company.

On landing, Parada lost 4th Regiment to 10th Brigade defending Port Stanley and 5th Regiment to 9th Brigade at Port Howard on West Falklands. 5th Regiment was commanded by Colonel Juan Mabragaña; it was traditionally commanded by a full colonel. The regiment was titled Task Force Reconquest. A and C Companies, 12th Regiment, C Company, 25th Infantry Regiment and two Army 35mm Oerlikons reformed into the about 500-strong Task Force Mercedes. About 50 per cent of the soldiers of the 12th *General Arenales* Infantry Regiment were new conscripts with less than six months' service. Many of the remainder were recalled reservists with between twelve and fourteen months' service.

When Brigadier-General Parada was prevented from deploying with his Brigade HQ, a disagreement typical of the rivalry that plagued the entire Argentinian Armed Forces broke out when Lieutenant-Colonel Ítalo Piaggi, who commanded 12th Infantry Regiment, was appointed to command the Task Force, but the Air Force commander of Military Air Base Goose Green, Vice-Commodore Wilson Pedrozo, objected saying he should command. Not even talks between Parada and Brigadier-General Luis Castellanos, the senior Air Force commander, could resolve the issue, nevertheless they instructed both officers to co-ordinate their activities. The concept 'Joint' between the Armed Forces did not exist. For several days, we lost sight of the 12th Infantry Regiment third company until it emerged that B Company Combat Team *Solari*, as part of the Strategic Reserve, was defending the helicopter base on Mount Kent.

The Strategic Reserve, also referred to as Z Reserve, haunted us for weeks, however, the intelligence billed it as a composite infantry regiment, possibly with supporting artillery, communications, engineers and logistics supported by the helicopters of 601 Combat Aviation Battalion. It was thought to be based near Fitzroy.

As Brigade Intelligence analysed the structure of Army Group Falklands in April, military logic suggested the three brigades would defend the three strongholds of Port Stanley, Goose Green and West Falkland, but by the about the third week, intelligence from Northwood was suggesting that only the headquarters of 3rd and 10th Brigade had landed. A report then indicated that Army Group Falklands had reformed into two areas of operational command and that Brigadier-General Daher, the commander of 9th Brigade, had been appointed to Chief-of-Staff. The two formations were Army Group defending the Port Stanley sector and Army Group Littoral under command of Brigadier-General Parada entrusted to defend the rest of the Falklands. He wanted to command from Goose Green, but when an initial survey revealed weaknesses in communications, Brigadier-General Menéndez instructed him to remain in Stanley and manage the transfer of heavy equipment expected by Army Group Falklands because as a brigadier-general, he had more influence that a logistics major. Nevertheless, Parada tried to move to Goose Green. When the *Bahía Paraíso* arrived to collect casualties from Stanley and the field hospital at Port Howard, he tried to persuade the captain to take him and the small headquarters to the settlement. When the captain refused on the grounds of using a hospital ship for military purposes contravened the Geneva Conventions, Parada offered to dress as a doctor for the crossing – without success.

Meanwhile, on 17 April, Colonel Francisco Cervo, the Head of intelligence, Army Group Falklands, had written a threat assessment for Brigadier-General Menendez in which he considered the factors of a British landing. He used as its basis knowledge of British doctrines largely assembled from manuals, rather than estimating the probable composition of the Landing Force. For instance, he did not know if the 'Landing Force', that is 3 Commando Brigade, was part of the 'English Naval Task Force heading toward the South Atlantic'. He believed the aim of the British would be either to destroy Argentinian forces or to capture all or part of the Falklands to achieve an advantageous negotiation position. He believed the British had two options:

Option 1

Amphibious assault on 18 April against Army Group Stanley defending the Freslnet Peninsula east of the Murrell River and north of Blanco Bay, north of Port Stanley. The overall aim was to establish a sufficient presence on the peninsula to gain an advantageous presence for negotiations. The proposed method of operation would be:

Phase one. SAS and SBS reconnoitre Argentinian positions, act as guides for landing craft and helicopters during the landings and raid command posts and important military installations.

Phase Two. A helicopter assault of 500 to seize either a west to east line, Mount Estancia or Mount Kent to Mount Longdon, or north to south Strike Off Point north of Mount Round to Mount Longdon to seize new ground or disrupt the defence.

Phase Three. Landings by two Royal Marines Commandos to consolidate gains.

Support

Reinforcements delivered by landing craft and 'air transport'.
Naval gunfire support.
Artillery fire thought to be an artillery group.
Electronic warfare.
Engineers.
Six groups of irregular forces, each of eight to ten men.

Advantages

Would fulfil the strategic objective to recover Stanley, the capital.

Eliminate or cause serious damage to Army Group Stanley and the Argentine claim to the Falklands.

The decreasing seasonal window of autumn to winter would minimises diplomatic intervention.

Disadvantages

Because the majority of the Argentinian troops were based in Stanley, a landing could result in heavy British casualties, which would be politically unacceptable.

Argentinian air defence was effective.

Complete or partial damage to Stanley and substantial civilian casualties could lead to accusation that liberating the Falklands was 'false'. The defence would be robust with the political risk of intervention by the USA or the Soviet Union.

Option 2

Amphibious landing north-east of Soledad Island on 25 April.

Phase one. SAS and SBS reconnoitre Argentinian positions, act as guides for landing craft and helicopters during the landings and create alarm by raiding command posts and important military installations. An additional factor was unconventional operations conducted by hostile civilians before or during landings.

Phase Two. Establish beachheads in weakly held or undefended sectors:

Zone 1. Black Rocks (Fox Point). North-east limit – Fitzroy.

Zone 2. St Louis Peninsula.

Zone 3. North-west limit – Northern mouth of Falkland Sound.

North-east limit – Northern mouth of Port Salvador.

In all instances, troops to be landed by helicopters from ships loitering twenty kilometres from the selected landing zone.

Phase Three. Helicopter assault by a Royal Marines Commando of 500 men in a single lift to seize and consolidate a beachhead. Reinforcements. Royal Marines Commando landed from six tank landing craft, a parachute battalion, an infantry battalion, an armoured battalion, one to two Rapier air defence batteries, engineer squadron, signals squadron and logistic support. Within twenty-four hours, twenty VTOL fighters-bombers (Harriers) transported in containers and set up on unprepared ground.

Advantages

The assault would not be against the Army Group Stanley. Landing would be with minimum casualties. Would give the British a useful political foothold from which to negotiate at little military cost. The locations of the Zones made a land counterattack difficult and therefore control of the sea was essential.

Disadvantages

Take longer to capture Stanley before diplomatic intervention. Lack of roads meant heavy reliance on helicopters to move troops, equipment and supplies. The third conclusion is that 'whatever happens they will have to attack Puerto Malvinas as the only way of obtaining the objectives of the expedition, with the already-mentioned risks to the civilian population and the high political implication that this implies.'

Reviewing the conclusions to the analysis, the document suggests that Option 1 of a landing on the Fresinet Peninsula would probably result in high British casualties and damage to civilian property in Stanley, neither of which would result with rapid success. Option 2 would allow a methodical advance to Stanley, but the risk would be a ceasefire before Stanley was recaptured. Overall, the calculations were that Argentina had numerical superiority in naval gunfire, air support, artillery of forty-eight 105mm guns to twenty-two British guns and longer ranges of

17 kilometres to 10.6 kilometres. The range could be extended to 20 kilometres from naval gunfire 114mm (4.5-inch) guns. In relation to air, it was concluded that British aircraft would be vulnerable to antiaircraft batteries during the day, but not at night. Consequently, night operations would give the British the best chance of success.

Likely execution of a British operation would be:

Amphibious reconnaissance by SBS from one or more submarines.

Selection of the assault beach and its isolation by air superiority.

Clearing minefields.

Final reconnaissance by the SBS and, eventually, the SAS, especially the night before amphibious landings.

Helicopter assault to seize a beach perimeter.

Conventional landings.

Land Rapier air defence.

Unloading of Harriers from the container ship and build aircraft apron.

Attack Argentine positions with 'powerful' air and naval support.

In both options, the British would be heavily reliant on helicopters and therefore the more the Argentinians could shoot down or immobilise, the greater delay to the landings.

The assessment has several weaknesses. Option 1 had been used during the Argentine invasion, which had been well planned and was compiled from basic intelligence. An accurate assessment of British intentions was available from international radio and television beaming reports and images as the Task Force assembled. In respect of artillery, both sides used 105mm guns, although the range of the British Light Gun was greater than the Pack Howitzer. Both navies had ships equipped with 4.5-inch main armament. The Task Force did not have sufficient helicopters to deliver 500 men in one lift.

5

DOWN SOUTH

During the morning of 30 April, Brigadier Thompson came into
the Chapel, as was his daily custom, to see Commodore Clapp,
closely followed by Major Chester, the Brigade Major, which
was not usually a good sign, and mentioned that Commander
Kelly had been asked for more accommodation as Commodore
Amphibious Warfare needed the Chapel in order to plan an
amphibious assault. Some acting was required to make out our
situation was worse than it already was and so Neil despatched
Scotty and Taff to work on the floor in the corridor. Commander
Kelly duly arrived, however, his inquiries, to our initial horror,
were interrupted by Lieutenant-Colonel Holroyd-Smith, who
commanded 29th Commando Regiment RA, asking for the order
of battle of an enemy battery. As we made heavy weather of
searching our files piled on the floor, he complained that it was
utterly pointless having information if there was nowhere to
display it. Within a couple of hours, a shipwright told us that we
were being moved to the Gun Room. The Gun Room is an annex
to the Wardroom on large ships so that junior naval officers can
relax out of sight of senior officers. He divided the space in two,
less than half for the officers and the remainder, which included
a large table, for us. At last and for the first time since leaving

Portsmouth, we could display a 1:50,000 map of the Falklands on the dividing wall with known and probable Argentinian positions. The Commando Brigade Intelligence Section now consisted of:

One Royal Marines colour-sergeant,
One Intelligence Corps staff-sergeant,
Two Royal Marines corporals, each commanding a section,
One Royal Marines lance-corporal,
Two Royal Marines,
Royal Marines corporal and a Marine illustrator,
Royal Marines translator/interpreter of Gibraltarian extraction,
Royal Navy petty officer photographer,
Air Intelligence cell of two RAF officers,
Specialist Interrogation team of the Intelligence Corps staff-
     sergeant and the RAF Flight Sergeant.

In addition was Captain Rowe, the Brigade Staff intelligence officer.

Meanwhile, the British Government escalated the South Atlantic crisis by issuing a warning that it intended to widen the 200-mile Maritime Exclusion Zone it had established around the Falklands on 12 April to a Total Exclusion Zone on the 30th and that ships or aircraft operating in this zone were liable to be challenged. If identified to be Argentinian, hostile action was a possibility. On the same day, Major-General Moore visited Brigadier Thompson on *Fearless* and gave a short address over the public address system, however, I was doing my daily exercises, and so I have no idea what he said.

The Task Force, at last, took the offensive on 1 May when two 50 Squadron Vulcan bombers roared over the anchorage and, supported by Victor air tankers, headed south on Operation *Black Buck 1*, the first of seven, to bomb Air Force Base Stanley. In a robust interview on *Panorama* the next day when Prime

Minister Thatcher again insisted that there would be no talks until Argentina withdrew from the Falklands, I rather felt that our bluff would be called. The following day, Sea Harriers sank a fast patrol boat and damaged a Falkland Islands Company coaster that was being used as an auxiliary off Port Stanley.

Hostilities escalated when the submarine HMS *Conqueror* sank the elderly Argentinian battleship the *General Belgrano* the next day. This first blow against the Argentinian Navy was of some significance and effectively removed the threat of naval gunfire support. Questions about the morality of the sinking and the subsequent protestations of some politicians and civil servants were irrelevant. The following day, Vulcans again bombed Air Force Base Stanley but it remained operational. During a three-aircraft strike against Military Air Base *Condor* at Goose Green, Lieutenant Nick Taylor RN, of 800 Naval Air Squadron, failed to return. Originally, it was believed he had been caught in his leader's bomb blast until other evidence suggested his height was low. It is a matter of conjecture if the Argentinian air defence had taken note of Mr Hanrahan's observation. HMS *Sheffield* was so severely damaged by an air-launched Exocet that she eventually sank under tow. Her loss seemed to have a profound effect on the Royal Navy; it was, after all, the first warship loss in action since 1945, excluding two destroyers mined off Albania in 1946.

Air photographs delivered to Brigade Intelligence about two days after the bombing of Air Force Base showed one bomb of the twenty-two dropped had hit the western edge of the runway, nevertheless the psychological value of the attack was priceless. While the principal purposes of naval aviation are to protect ships from air attack and submarines, conduct search and rescue and support amphibious landings, the purposes of air forces include domination of the skies and support of military operations. Common to both is reconnaissance, but beating up targets at sea and on the ground is more exciting than precise flying at high level taking photographs. No. 1 (Fighter) Squadron on *Hermes* was experienced in air photographic recces, but since air operations on both carriers were controlled by the Navy, it meant, with some justification, that the defence of the ships against Exocets, which certainly focused naval minds, was top priority. Additional factors were poor weather preventing flying and the distance between the carriers and the ground forces. The combination of these factors meant that the air photographic recce in support of ground operations was sometimes lacking and that annotated air photographs lost their intelligence value. Air photographic interpretation was another core Intelligence Corps skill. On board HMS *Hermes*, Sergeant Chris Bowman of the Intelligence Corps was the only Army Photographic Interpreter in the Reconnaissance Intelligence Cell. Squadron Leader Pook MBE DFC wrote in his book *RAF Harrier Ground Attack, Falklands* (2011):

> This splendid character worked tirelessly for us, trying to get the maximum amount of intelligence from every film received. Despite his commitment to the Captain, he still managed to find time to get up to No 2 Pilots' Briefing Room to brief us personally on anything he thought important – it usually was.

The appearance of the air photographs allowed us to persuade those unfamiliar with annotated air photography of its utility by inviting, actually insisting that, anyone who visited the Intelligence Section take the 'Blind as a Bat' test based on three air photographs of Military Air Base *Condor*:

1. *How many Chinooks are there in Goose Green?* Three parked near the houses of the settlement. They had probably delivered troops, stores and equipment

2. *How many Pucarás are on the settlement airstrip?* Seven. Six are dispersed widely and the seventh appears to be on its nose.
3. *Where did the Sea Harrier crash?* A dark scar at the north-eastern corner of the airfield perimeter.

Apart from the entertainment and educational value, the photographs confirmed, as we suspected, that the grass strip near Goose Green was operational and posed a considerable risk.

Aircraft from HMS *Invincible* and *Hermes* also began competing with Argentinian air defence and raided Stanley Common and Darwin Peninsula. But the hacks of 1982 lacked the same sense of military security as those in 1945 and when the BBC journalist Brian Hanrahan breached operational security by broadcasting 'I'm not allowed to say how many planes joined the raid, but I counted them all out, and I counted them all back', it was the first of several thoughtless breaches of operational security by the BBC. Hanrahan essentially advised Argentinian air defence that there was room for improvement. It is interesting that the breaches appeared not to be as serious as breaches that had resulted in the censorship at Ascension. Indeed, it was disturbing to watch on *Fearless* TV current affairs programmes in which venerable generals, admirals, air marshals and historians did the job of Argentinian intelligence by speculating on Task Force possible courses of action.

Meanwhile, as the SBS landed patrols to reconnoitre coastal settlements and potential sites and the SAS conducted inland surveys, Brigade Intelligence analysed enemy threats against nineteen beaches thought to be suitable for landings.

On East Falkland, in the Stanley area, the Argentinians had landed on the sandy beaches of Yorke Bay against weak opposition. A direct assault in the Stanley area was risky because the town was defended by Army Group Port Stanley, an infantry brigade and a

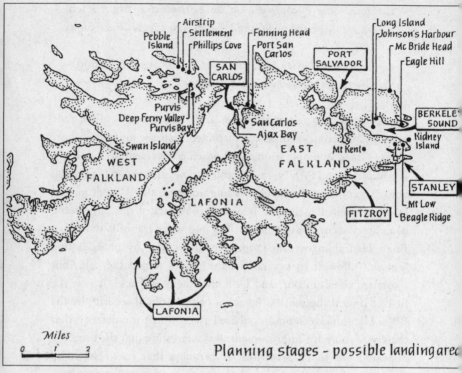

Analysis of possible landing sites.

marine infantry battle group supported by field artillery and air defence artillery. Fighting in the built area of Stanley would soak up troops. The approaches were probably mined. Berkeley Sound to the north housed Port Louis, the original capital of the Falkland Islands. Green Patch had reasonable breakout facilities but was sufficiently close to Stanley for a counterattack. There were no known defences.

Port Salvador Waters on the northern coast had suitable beaches at Douglas, Port Salvador and Teal, and was also attractive because it was close to Stanley. But the approaches could be mined or blockaded.

San Carlos Water, a sheltered two-fingered stretch of water spilling into Falkland Sound, had good access to the settlements at Port San Carlos and San Carlos and the abandoned mutton refrigeration plant at Ajax Bay. The inlet was surrounded by hills that could provide a degree of protection for the anchorage and beachheads. But across Falkland Sound was a brigade-sized Task Force 'Reconquest' spread between Port Howard and Fox Bay and to the south was Task Force Mercedes at Goose Green. The settlement had been designated as the Forward Army Base and provided a useful platform for a counterattack and possessed the operational Military Air Base *Condor*. There was no artillery. From debriefs of several 'Kelpers' (Falkland Islanders are nicknamed Kelpers), repatriated to the UK, we had good intelligence on Port San Carlos; in particular Mrs Carole Miller, the settlement manager, had provided a good map and useful information. We also had a sketch of the San Carlos beaches. Stanley was about 100 miles to the east across poor terrain.

Brenton Loch to the north of Goose Green provided similar advantages to San Carlos Water but about 6 miles of flat and open country to the south was Task Force Mercedes at Goose Green. The isthmus of Lafonia to the south of Goose Green had three large exposed inlets along its eastern coast, but the boggy terrain was devoid of cover and therefore unsuitable for breakout operations. To the north was the threat from Goose Green.

The south coast from Darwin to Fitzroy was overlooked by the Wickham Heights. An advantage was the motorable track, on the map, that led from Darwin through Pony Pass to Stanley that could be used by armoured fighting vehicles. The beaches to the east included Port Pleasant, Fitzroy and Bluff Cove. Important objectives would be to seize the footbridge between Fitzroy and Bluff Cove before the enemy blew it up and to capture Pony Pass to prevent enemy exploitation from Port Stanley.

On West Falkland, Port Howard and Fox Bay had good anchorages and jetty facilities for large ships and were close enough to jump across Falkland Sound to East Falkland, but the Argentinian regiments at both settlements would have to be neutralised. Another possibility was to land at Chartres or Hill Cove, establish a secure beachhead and create an airstrip.

As part of our preparations, on 5 May, the Brigade HQ and Signals Squadron landed at English Bay for range work and training. After we formed up on the road, 'Dutch' Holland, who knew of my aversion to drill, grinned, 'Staff, march the Squadron to the range.' I played the game with a deft point to the right, 'Turn that way, please, gentlemen' and managed to reach the ranges without losing anyone. Afterwards, Roy Packer and I climbed Green Mountain. Alternating running and fast walking, we crossed the desolate lowland volcanic landscape to an abandoned coastal artillery emplacement and then headed up a road through bush and eucalyptus, damp glades of banana and papaya trees to peaceful English market gardens, with lettuce, tomatoes and cucumbers, nestling among cottages. After refilling our water bottles at a building that a gentleman said was the former hospital, we climbed up the rolling downs, complete with cattle and long wavy grass, to a ridge with water catchment ramps near the former Royal Marines barracks. The windward side of the island was lush from moisture blown from Africa. At the summit we followed a short, muddy track through bamboo and emerged into a cool clearing with a pond of cool, clear water. After stamping our passports in a small birdhouse, we took off our boots and allowed our feet to be nibbled by small fish. After the frenetic energy of *Fearless*, it was a serene place that brought memories of the jungle in Brunei and Belize, and after a tranquil doze we ran down through the extraordinary changes in the landscape to the beach at English Bay to find our colleagues swimming and lazing around on the beach. The steep shelf and fierce current had caught one or two out of their depth. My brother and I had swum off the beach in 1954. In the late afternoon, a LCVP nosed through the swimmers and dropped its ramps onto the beach and returned us to *Fearless*.

3 Commando Brigade was fortunate that in its order of battle was Y (Electronic Warfare) Troop, which was part of the Brigade Headquarters and Signals Squadron. Electronic Warfare sets out to attack enemy transmissions without being discovered. Signals Intelligence gathers intelligence, primarily by interception. For Operation *Corporate,* the Troop was commanded by a Royal Signals captain and consisted of several Royal Marines signallers and Royal Signals from 13th and 14th Signals Regiment on short-term emergency postings from West Germany. They had left the UK on the RFA *Sir Geraint* on 7 April. Signals Intelligence was an intelligence source to be exploited, alongside Prisoners of War and captured documents.

On 7 May, a small convoy of ships, including HMS *Intrepid* and the P&O Roll On/Roll Off ferry MV *Norland* carrying 2 Para, arrived at Ascension, having left the UK on 26 April. Tom Priestley was on duty in the Gun Room when two visitors entered and one of them, an Intelligence Corps major, admonished him for not handling some classified signals correctly. Fortunately, the Brigade Signals Officer was in the Gun Room and hosted the officer. It emerged that one visitor was Major David Thorp, who commanded the air-portable Special Task Detachment and had arrived on HMS *Intrepid*. He wrote an account of his war in his *Silent Listener* (History Press, 2011). The Detachment was a Ministry of Defence Electronic Warfare asset and consisted of seven Intelligence Corps, most, if not all, Spanish speakers. When the Detachment was warned for deployment in the third week of April, initially without its vehicles, due to the lack of space, Major Thorp advised the Ministry of Defence that his unit could not therefore deploy. Space was found. When Thorp attended a briefing at Northwood, he expected his unit to be independent but when he was told that it would be subordinate to Y Troop, he was displeased because he believed its operators were not trained in Signals Intelligence, had limited linguistic capability and he would be reporting to a captain. The decision made sense because Y Troop was part of the Commando Brigade order of battle and was familiar with amphibious operations. When the Detachment boarded *Intrepid*, it set up in the Electronic Warfare Room. While its arrival was a welcome reinforcement to the intelligence community, its value was undermined when it became clear that the Detachment would apply the 'No Clearance, No Briefing' principle. Indeed, its deployment as part of the Amphibious Task Group appeared to be so secret that not even Commodore Clapp knew it was part of his organisation until near the end of the war.

As a strong breeze cooled a warm day, the Amphibious Task Group slipped from the shelter of Ascension and headed south, hoping to disappear from prying eyes into the vast watery wastes of the South Atlantic. A few hours later *Fearless* followed and adopted Defence Stations with the crew split into 4-hours-on, 4-hours-off watches. Having represented the Army in the Fastnet Race in 1981, I knew just how tiring this can be until one becomes accustomed to the routine. The ship began exercising Action Stations and Damage Control. The Embarked Force were not involved, although several SNCOs having breakfast on one exercise were admonished by a naval officer for not participating in the spirit of the exercise. Our time would come ashore. Orange-coloured Immersion Suits and life-jackets were issued, which in addition to the white anti-flash hoods and a pair of gauntlets issued in the UK, brought home the reality of the situation.

By next morning, there was no sign of Ascension or its white top hat, instead the southern hemisphere autumn was approaching and the clouds in the grey sky were a touch menacing. Around us, other ships of the Task Group ploughed through the dark with endless white-capped rollers being thrown aside in white swathes. Included in the convoy was the *Atlantic Conveyor*, which had successfully experimented with launching Harriers from her decks at Ascension.

Escorts scouted ahead and protected the flanks and rear. Every so often, bright lights would twinkle from bridges as messages were passed by signal lamp. During the afternoon, I briefed the Blues and Royals on the situation and about the enemy.

We had lost our information flow from Electronic Warfare and were now reliant on the Signal Intelligence product from Commander-in-Chief Fleet, which meant we were again prevented from sharing intelligence. Most of the information was still arriving without the vital 'comment' to set the content into some context. So far, no intelligence had reached the Intelligence Section from the SAS and SBS patrols that had landed. Either there was nothing to report, which is as important as a report, or the Intelligence Section was not in the intelligence loop. My suspicions of the latter seemed to be confirmed when, one evening, a Special Forces officer and a Brigade Staff officer came into the Gun Room, went to the Intelligence map and whispered to each other. When I edged a little closer, it was frustrating to overhear a discussion about Argentinian activities. In order for intelligence sections, of any size, to function at their optimum ability, they must have all the available information so that the enemy situation can be plotted and analysed before commanders commit troops to battle. Unfortunately the 'need to know' principle was being applied a little too rigorously by a couple of units.

Letters had been an important part of my life since going to boarding school and I welcomed the opportunity to write letters, not only to share personal thoughts but also record events. Receiving letters and parcels was always a significant morale booster and thus I was impressed with the high category that mail was given in the logistic chain. On the voyage from Portsmouth, I knew that at Ascension Island there were likely to be letters from home, but as we headed toward the Roaring Forties, and whatever hand fate dealt us, I thought this would cease. Sending mail became opportunistic. On 8 May, I had written to Penny:

> By the time you receive this letter it will have been transferred from HMS *Fearless* onto a frigate, taken to Ascension Island and then flown to you in UK. I thought the letter I wrote last night might be the last for some time but this opportunity arose. This may be the last but I will continue writing, trusting my letters will eventually reach you.

With the South Atlantic crisis no nearer to a political solution, the nearer we closed to the Falklands, the greater was the risk of some sort of confrontation. Army Group Stanley experienced naval gunfire and then hostilities were ramped up on 9 May when Argentina was warned that any Argentinian vessel within 150 miles of the centre of the Total Exclusion Zone would be attacked. The capture of the trawler *Narwal* generated further excitement. She had been detected collecting Electronic Intelligence shielded by the Argentinian mercantile marine ensign since 30 April, including by the destroyer HMS *Yarmouth* towing the crippled HMS *Sheffield*. The SBS boarded the trawler and among the twenty-eight crew was a naval communications expert. Some Technical and Documentary Intelligence was seized. She sank next day while under tow.

11 May was a day of distractions which began with a practice Action Stations in the early hours, much to everyone's annoyance. Then in the morning, a C-130 Hercules flying from Ascension made twelve passes and parachuted pallets into the sea, which were

recovered by landing craft and by sea boats that were bouncing around the uneven sea and avoiding a whale nudging a pallet. To our delight some packages contained mail. Several years later I met the loadmaster and gave him some photos of the drop. Included in the mail was a detailed debriefing report from a Falklands Public Works Department official who had been repatriated in late April. The report gave such details as:

Government House was occupied by Brigadier-General Menendez and telephone cables had been laid from the Army, Navy and Air Force headquarters on the islands.
Army HQ is in the Town Hall.
The Navy HQ in St John St not heavily guarded.
Air Force HQ is at Stanley House.

The report also listed several positions of weapons, including surface-to-air missile location screened by canvas, and troop concentrations.

About mid-afternoon, Action Stations was sounded when two Soviet Long Range Air Force Tupolev TU-95 *Bear* maritime reconnaissance aircraft, ostensibly en route from Cuba to Angola, circled the convoy, one low about 1 mile off and the other flying top cover. Their long, thin bodies and high, thick tails were distinctive against grey, mottled clouds split by shafts of sunlight arrowing into the sea. Their appearance was unwelcome because efforts to lose the ships in the vast southern ocean had probably been compromised. They may have been operating with a submarine, but in any event, our position, details of ships and heading would find its way to Buenos Aires. Soon after the aircraft disappeared heading toward Africa, Action Stations was again sounded when Sonar identified a contact and a look-out spotted a periscope. The convoy initiated violent manoeuvres, but suddenly there were more contacts and then more and then even more, far too many to represent the three submarines the Argentinian Navy had. We had apparently run into a large school of whales, which confused the sonar; and their waterspouts resembled periscopes.

As our information accumulated and a greater range was arriving on board, whenever Neil and I entered the Mess or the Chief's Lounge, we usually faced a barrage of questions. While always prepared to answer, sometimes it took some persuading to convince our messmates that ours was accurate, even if the sources of 'Bungy' Williams were still picking up snippets.

In spite of the long period that the Embarked Force were confined to the ship, my experience was that disagreements were soon resolved. As was expected of soldiers, I professed ignorance of matters naval and instead of declaring 'I am going below to the Tank Deck and will be starboard for'ad', I would say 'I am going downstairs to the car park and will be on the right hand side at the front'. Even though the ship was wobbling all over the place, fitness was still important. However, more people had boarded at Ascension and to make room, I cut my exercise period to about 15 minutes daily. When someone suggested that to help the Embarked Force acclimatise to the cold of a Falklands winter, it would be a jolly good idea if the heating was turned off, temperatures fell alarmingly. Soldiers and marines are good at acclimatisation and most thought the measure to be farcical, as did most sailors. As the ship began to chill, rivulets of water appeared on the bulkheads and deck, furniture became damp and lights bulbs started exploding, common sense prevailed and the heating returned, much to our relief. During the day, the frigate HMS *Alacrity* passing through Falkland Sound south to north checking for sea mines sank the coaster *Isla de los Esatdos* near Fox Bay, which was carrying several thousand litres of aviation fuel and blew up.

For most of the morning the next day, *Fearless* replenished. At one stage, a RFA tanker was on one side and on the other was

RFA *Stromness*. This time, I was standing next to a sailor who explained what was happening and mentioned that the Royal Navy was one of the few navies that replenished side by side. It was certainly impressive to watch two ships steaming alongside each other, about 200 to 300 yards apart, the sea in between boiling, angry, unable to escape and always threatening to draw the two ships together. I was astonished to learn that steering the ship was relayed from the bridge to the coxswain about two decks below. A thick pipe jerked with fuel and a jackstay transferred stores and equipment. Soon after the ships drew apart, a large school of porpoises passed by, playing and leaping, often in unison. It was a beautiful sight, these dark-backed mammals completely free and at home. The RFA was replaced by a frigate, which creamed in from astern to pass some packages. At about midday, the SAS detachment sent a catch-all invitation to watch them test their new weapon, an American 60mm light mortar. Invited again to the Gun Direction Platform by the naval lieutenant, we watched as the two-man mortar crew stabilised the baseplate with sandbags and then pop the first bomb into the tube. There was a mild thud and the projectile shot out in a high arc and as it splashed into the sea, there was a loud cheer – direct hit! The team fired several practice rounds, which drew a cheer each time. At last, someone on *Fearless* had hit something, even if it was the sea.

During the day, Major-General Moore had signalled Brigadier Thompson his orders:

> You are to secure a bridgehead on East Falkland, into which reinforcements can be landed, in which an airstrip can be established and from which operations to repossess the Falkland Islands can be achieved.
>
> You are to push forward from the bridgehead area so far as the maintenance of its security allows, to gain information, to

establish moral and physical domination over the enemy and to forward the ultimate objectives of repossession.

You will retain operational control of all forces in the Falklands until I establish my Headquarters in the area. It is my intention to do this, aboard HMS *Fearless*, as early as practicable after the landing. I expect this to be approximately on D+7.

It is then my intention to land 5 Infantry Brigade into the beachhead and develop operations for the complete repossession of the Falklands.

The Intelligence Section had known for a couple of days that San Carlos Water was to be the Amphibious Operations Area and had been focusing on collecting information on the general area of Falkland Sound, in particular Task Force Mercedes at Goose Green and West Falkland. Brigade Intelligence now had a decent appreciation of the enemy. So far, Army Group Falklands had remained static in its three bunkers at Stanley, Goose Green and Fox Bay/Port Howard. Its amphibious capability had been withdrawn in early April and there was no intelligence suggesting exercises to counter landings. A significant threat remained the air assault and gunship helicopters of 601 Combat Aviation Battalion and fighter ground attack provided by Air Force Pucarás and Naval Air Command MB-339s, and T-34 Mentors operating from grass airstrips were evident with Army Group Falklands.

In late April, intelligence had emerged about *Estación Aeronaval Calderón,* which translates as Naval Air Base Cauldron, but the location was missing except that it might be on an island as a base for light aircraft, or a diversionary airfield for turboprop aircraft en route from Argentina to Stanley, or a possible search-and-rescue helicopter base. Land Forces Falkland Islands (LFFI) Intelligence, the senior Intelligence organisation supporting the headquarters of General Moore, took on the task and, by a process of elimination, focused on

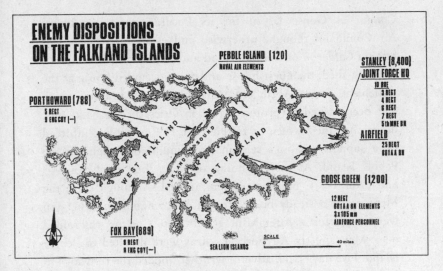

Deployment of Army Group Falklands dated 15 May 1982.

four locations. When D Squadron SAS was tasked to find the base by 15 May or never, during the night of 11/12th May, a Boat Troop patrol paddled to Pebble Island and reported an operational airstrip with Naval and Air Force aircraft. A Royal Engineers Briefing Map dated April 1982 shows one settlement on Pebble Island. The two principal features are the 237-foot-high Marble Mountain Peak at the eastern tip of the island and First Mountain at 227 foot overlooking the settlement, otherwise the terrain is low, particularly to the east where there are several lakes and large ponds. A jetty on the sheltered south shore could handle coasters. The 650-foot grass runway A15(a) lay to the east of the settlement and Airstrip A14(b) was on the sheltered southern beaches of Elephant Bay and was described to be 1,000 feet of firm beach and below the high water mark. Inter-service rivalry and complaints at the poor state of the grass runway led to the Argentinian Air Force declining to operate with the Navy in favour of using Military Air Base

Condor at Goose Green for its Pucará operations. Naval Air Command thought otherwise and established Naval Air Station *Calderon* on Pebble Island and requisitioned the sheep-shearing shed, the guest house and an unoccupied house at the settlement. On 26 April, 3rd Marine Infantry Battalion, which had been tasked to protect naval facilities on the Falklands, despatched the 74 men of 1st Platoon, H Company, reinforced by a support weapons section and amphibious engineers, to Pebble Island. At the beginning of May, four 1st Naval Air Squadron T-34C Mentor trainers arrived. Although slow, the Mentor was a steady bomb, rocket and 7.62mm machine-gun weapon platform. After Military Air Base *Condor* was raided on 1 May, the six Air Force Pucarás were diverted to Pebble Island. Five days later, adverse weather flooded the runway and it was declared unfit for fixed-wing operations.

There was a colder, greyer dawn on 13 May. At about breakfast time, when the tannoy reported an 846 Naval Air Squadron Sea King on an early morning courier run had lost power and was preparing to ditch, there was a general rush on deck to witness the disaster. The stricken helicopter made one pass alongside *Fearless*, thick black smoke streaming from an engine but when it then failed to land on the Flight Deck, the ship made an emergency turn into the wind, heeling over at an alarming angle, and slowed down as the helicopter approached from astern at an agonisingly slow rate, hover shakily and then smacked rather heavily onto the Flight Deck. As emergency crews dashed forward with extinguishers and axes, the side door flew open and out tumbled a stream of white-faced passengers to a round of applause from the 'stadium'. The pilot was generally awarded ten points for style.

During the lunchbreak, the Intelligence Section arranged conference facilities in the Wardroom so that Brigadier Thompson could issue Orders for Operation *Sutton*, the code name given to the landings. As approximately forty delegates arrived, the Section checked them against an attendance list and then I directed major unit commanding officers to armchairs at the front, officers commanding smaller units in the rows behind and the remainder filling up at the back. I perched on a Wardroom table at the back, barely conscious of the pitching ship but aware of the anticipation.

At 2pm, Brigadier Thompson strode up the dais. 'Good afternoon, gentlemen. Mission. To land at Port San Carlos, San Carlos and Ajax Bay and to establish a beachhead for mounting offensive operations leading to the recapture of the Falkland Islands.' He repeated the mission and continued 'Design for battle. A silent night attack by landing craft with the object of securing all high ground by first light'. It was perhaps typical of the Commando Brigade that it was going to land in the middle of the enemy position.

Major Southby-Tailyour then have gave one of his information terrain briefings. He was followed by Captain Rowe using slides prepared by the Illustrators to give the Intelligence summary. The 3,000 men of Commando Brigade would be facing 11,000 Argentinians deployed into three strongholds at Port Stanley and Goose Green on East Falkland and Port Howard/ Fox Bay on West Falkland. The enemy had superiority in artillery. The weakest factor was the Argentinian Navy, which would be pressed to achieve superiority. Since Northwood had yet to provide an air assessment, Flight-Lieutenant White had drafted the Air Intelligence picture. Stanley Airport was thought to be non-operational for fast aircraft and therefore in-flight refuelling flying to and from the mainland was a necessity and also a hindrance. The Army had a decent helicopter capability and the Air Force and Naval Air Command both had aircraft suited to ground attack and low level bombing.

Brigadier Thompson then addressed the major unit commanding officer by first name and prefaced his orders by the phase, 'I want you to...' As befitted their role, the three-phase assault would be led by the Royal Marines:

First wave

40 Commando. Land on *Blue Beach* at San Carlos. Supported by a Blues and Royals troop.

45 Commando. Land on *Red Beach* at Ajax Bay, clear the refrigeration plant and secure Sussex Mountain.

Second wave

2 Para. Pass through 45 Commando and consolidate on Sussex Mountain.

3 Para. Land at *Green Beach* and secure Port San Carlos. Supported by a Blues and Royals troop.

Floating Reserve

42 Commando. On *Canberra*.

Artillery

29th Commando Regiment Group and T (Shah Shujahs) Battery of Rapiers to be flown ashore at the highest priority.

Naval gunfire support provided by 148 Commando Battery.

Logistics

Commando Logistic Regiment to establish ammunition dump, stores and hospital at *Red Beach*.

Diversions

D Squadron SAS to convince Task Force Mercedes that a regiment was attacking – 'noise, firepower but no close engagement'.

HMS *Glamorgan* to be active in Berkeley Sound and keep Army Group Stanley occupied.

3 Commando Brigade was to wait for 5 Infantry Brigade but if an opportunity arose to advance toward Stanley, it would be exploited. Brigadier Thompson mentioned several key issues. In the event of an opposed landing, impetus was essential and

therefore the wounded were to be left where they fell. Every unit was to appoint a Brigade HQ liaison officer who, before entering the Command Post, was to be debriefed by the Intelligence Section. On departure, they were to collect the contents of their distribution tray near the entrance and visit the Section for an update and collect Essential Elements of Intelligence required by Brigade HQ.

The Chief-of-Staff, Major Chester, then issued co-ordinating instructions and emphasised that date and time of D-Day would be circulated by Commodore Clapp in a signal identified as OPGEN Mike once the political decision had been made. He reminded the Orders Group that in British amphibious operations, H-hour was the time when the first landing craft beached and L-hour was the touchdown time for the first wave of a helicopter assault. Easy to remember, he said, because, illogically, H-Hour was for landing craft and L-Hour for helicopters. He covered several points, including marked maps, personal letters and personal documents not to be taken ashore, nobody to take photographs and since Special Forces patrols would be ashore, be aware of recognition signals.

Major Gerry Wells-Cole, the Deputy Assistant Adjutant and Quarter Master General (DAA&QMG), then explained the logistic plan that included handling and administration of Prisoners of War. The derelict refrigeration plant at Ajax Bay had been identified as the probable field hospital and prison camp. Prisoner management had been side-stepped for decades and it followed that a considerable amount of learning on the job was going to be required, particularly by the Commando Logistic Regiment, which had the problem of administering prisoners and ensuring that Intelligence had access to them.

Two Amphibious Warfare officers using complicated vufoils described the landing and naval gunfire support. One officer near me commented, 'Although I am sure they understood it, I had the general impression no one had a clue what they were talking about.'

In the time honoured way at the end of Orders Groups, Brigadier Thompson asked, 'Questions?' There were none, which, in my view, reflected on the quality of the Orders. Dismissing the conference, he concluded, 'May I remind you that this will be no picnic. Good luck and stay flexible.' He later wrote a book about 3 Commando Brigade in the Falklands entitled *No Picnic*. The conference, which had lasted about 2 hours, broke up in a hubbub of anticipation. As unit commanders left, the Intelligence Section supplied them with a package that included maps, photos and local information about their objectives. Very few knew when the landings were to take place. The first opportunity was between 16 and 25 May.

The Intelligence Section was immediately briefed by Captain Rowe, in particular discussing indicators that the enemy had either identified or were threatening the assault beaches, such as increased enemy activity in and around San Carlos Water, the mobilisation of 601 Combat Aviation Battalion, the deployment of the Strategic Reserve and evidence that Task Forces Mercedes and Reconquest were preparing to counterattack San Carlos Water.

Later in the day, intelligence emerged of an Argentinian presence in San Carlos Water of 601 Combat Aviation Battalion helicopters landing a 601 Commando Company patrol at Port San Carlos, which had then secured San Carlos and occupied Fanning Head. This was a real worry and concerns were raised that Operation *Sutton* had been compromised. A watching brief was therefore put in place.

During the evening, Captain Larken and Commander Kelly used *Fearless* TV to brief the ship on Operation *Sutton*, however when the Commander started reading the Articles of War, the anticipation fell away. The Articles were a set of regulations governing the conduct of the Armed Forces in battle but had fallen out of use in the Army when they were omitted from the 1955 Army Act. They had been retained by the Royal Navy. The Geneva Conventions were covered in training.

Early on 14 May, D Squadron, supported by naval gunfire support, raided the Pebble Island airstrip and damaged aircraft and vandalised equipment. However, air photographs delivered the next day indicated the grass airstrip was still serviceable, weather permitting. Nevertheless, while the raid removed a significant threat, a naval bombardment would have probably achieved a better result. About midday, for the third time since we left Ascension, a C-130 Hercules dropped more packages, but this time the sea boats and landing craft had difficulty recovering them because of the rough seas. As *Fearless* entered the Roaring Forties, an albatross invariably rode the wind astern as the ship lurched through steepening waves. With no sign of a ceasefire, the more surreal the confrontation had become. Initially, there had been a rush of nationalism and jingoism with the whole country appearing to support the Government, but I wondered how the loss of HMS *Sheffield* had affected public opinion. It was probably best to treat our deployment as a peacetime exercise – at least for the moment.

At his daily conference next day, Major Dixon issued his Operation *Sutton* Orders to the Brigade HQ and Signals Squadron representatives that included Air Defence Troop, Communications Troop, Defence Troop, Quartermaster Troop, Royal Marines Police Troop, Y (Electronic Warfare) Troop, the Blues and Royals and Forward Air Controllers. A key issue was the continuity required to support the Command Post by always having a foot on the ground. It had been practised many times. The 'D' Group (Command Post) would command the landings from the *Fearless* Amphibious Operations Room until ordered to land. HQ 'B' (BVs) would land on *Blue Beach* and be ready to receive the Command Post. Rear HQ would remain on *Fearless* until ordered ashore and would provide casualty replacements. HQ 'A' (Land Rovers) would land on *Red Beach* as a reserve in case HQ 'B' was put out of action.

To ensure that the Command Post was always supported, the Intelligence Section split into two sections. 'A' Section would support 'D' Group and 'B' Section remain on *Fearless* to support Rear HQ and also maintain the information flow from Commander-in-Chief Fleet until called forward. 'A' Section consisted of Corporal Bob Birkett with his detachment of Taff Evans, Tom Priestley, the illustrator Ken Loftus and Roy Packer of Engineer Intelligence. 'B' Section commanded by Corporal Colin Scott was supported by Scouse Atkinson, Brian Dodd, the senior illustrator and the naval photographer Dick Birkett. Brigadier Thompson formed a Tactical HQ of an engineer, a gunner, a logistician and intelligence, namely myself, to go ashore by helicopter behind 40 Commando landing on *Blue Beach*. All the Tactical HQ requirements, including radios and spare batteries to be man-packed in addition to our personal equipment, which inevitably meant heavy bergens.

Major Dixon listed several tactical priorities that included good camouflage, trenches, Command Post protection, respirators and Nuclear, Biological and Chemical overboots to be carried in bergens and no marked maps or Operations and Logistic Orders to be taken ashore. Assault lifejackets were to be worn in helicopters, but not in landing craft. First line ammunition was to be issued forthwith; I received 250 rounds of 9mm for my Sterling. Vehicles were to be fully fuelled and to carry at least one spare full jerrycan. As usual, the tannoy would announce arrivals and departures of landing craft and helicopters. 'Stick leaders' were to familiarise themselves with their teams and ensure that their 'stick' was in the right place at the right time. Spare kit and equipment were to be stored in kitbags on the Tank Deck. The medics would be giving tetanus injections, and morphine phials were to be worn as necklaces. Blankets and sheets were returned to Supplies and, henceforth, our sleeping bags became our refuges (mine had been since I left Portsmouth).

At midday, as I was giving an Intelligence brief to the Squadron Orders Group in the Wardroom when halfway through stewards began to lay up the tables for lunch and then naval officers threaded their way through the seated delegates to the bar while others ordered their meals, talking noisily and with little regard, although some tuned into the briefing.

Major Dixon had warned me that I was to deal with the interrogation of prisoners and that the Royal Marines Police Troop could guard and administer them until passed to the Commando Logistic Regiment, which had responsibility for prisoner administration. This was excellent news. Sadly, interrogation and its value as an intelligence tool was, and remains, widely misunderstood and consequently the Ministry of Defence was more than defensive about its use. And training in the handling of mass prisoners, let alone a single prisoner, was rare. Members of the Intelligence Corps were trained in counter-intelligence interviewing as part of basic training. The purpose of interrogation is simple – the systematic extraction of information from a selected willing or unwilling person in time for it to be of use. Not every prisoner is interrogated. The primary aim is to develop a dialogue. However, interrogation exercises were generally unrealistic and designed to give 'prone to capture' personnel, in particular aircrew and Special Forces, some experience in resisting interrogation, except for providing Service number, rank, full name and date of birth, as required by the Geneva Convention. The Ministry of Defence 'prone to capture' policy had been rather undermined in April when Naval Party 8901 and the Royal Marines from HMS *Endurance* were captured. None were Special Forces. In planning the interrogation, I adopted the standard system:

Tactical questioning at unit level by unit intelligence officers.

Interrogation at Brigade HQ by a Joint Forward Interrogation Team for battlefield and medium term information.

Detailed Interrogation by an interrogation unit. I had noted the derelict refrigeration plant at *Red Beach*.

But we were short of Spanish interpreters and always hovering in the background would be delegates from the International Committee of the Red Cross monitoring prisoner welfare.

Meanwhile another mystery was being addressed by Brigade Intelligence. During the morning of the 14th, intelligence reports indicated that an 8th Infantry Regiment platoon of thirty-seven men had been transferred from Fox Bay to Task Force Mercedes at Goose Green. This was assumed to be a reinforcement. That evening, a report indicated that a unit known as EC *Guemes* had delivered a platoon to Port San Carlos and a platoon to Fanning Head. A glance at the map showed it to be a feature that overlooks Falkland Sound and the entrance to San Carlos Water. 'EC' meant nothing until I mentioned it to Captain Rod Bell, the Adjutant of the Brigade HQ and Signals Squadron. He was the son of a British UN official in Costa Rica, who had joined the Royal Marines apparently speaking better Spanish then English. 'That's easy, "EC" stands for *Equipo Combate* which means combat team. *Guemes* means "eagle".' The transfer of the 8th Infantry platoon seemed to compensate for the deployment of Combat Team *Guemes* to Port San Carlos and Fanning Head. But why Fanning Head? Had the landings been compromised?

From a document later captured by 3 Para at Port San Carlos, on 13 May Lieutenant-Colonel Piaggi, the 12th Infantry Regiment Commanding Officer, instructed First-Lieutenant Carlos Esteban, from C Company, 25th Infantry Regiment, to command EC *Guemes* and 'to block and control the entrance to San Carlos Water and to observe for enemy naval activity and possible landings at

Port Howard, Fox Bay and Darwin'. He was to place an 88mm Instalaza anti-tank gun on Fanning Head. Esteban was given a company that consisted of a rifle platoon each from 12th Infantry Regiment and C Company, 25th Infantry Regiment and a support weapon and supply section.

When EC *Guemes* arrived the next day at Port San Carlos, 601 Commando Company were sheltering from poor weather in the Community Centre. Esteban established his Command Post, logistic support and reserve section in the Centre and deployed a strong rifle section and the Instalaza to Fanning Head. Unknown to the Argentinians, the previous evening, a SBS patrol operating in the Port San Carlos area had been alerted by the helicopter activity and started sending reports direct to its headquarters on *Fearless*. The Intelligence Section nicknamed the Argentinians the 'Fanning Hill Mob'. As soon as Brigadier Thompson was advised about the deployment and an intelligence report that the Strategic Reserve had been operating north of Darwin, he adjusted his landing plan to ensure that *Blue* and *Red Beaches* were seized simultaneously. The seizure of Sussex Mountain to block Task Forces Mercedes was crucial.

First wave
2 Para. Land on *Blue Beach One* at San Carlos and block any enemy units advancing from Goose Green by occupying Sussex Mountains.

40 Commando. Land on *Blue Beach One.*

Second wave
45 Commando. Land on the *Red Beach* at Ajax Bay.

3 Para. Land at *Green Beach* and secure Port San Carlos.

Floating Reserve
42 Commando. On *Canberra.*

Fanning Head
3 SBS. Neutralise the 'Fanning Head Mob.'

Diversions
D Squadron to convince Task Force Mercedes that a regiment was attacking Goose Green. D Squadron was to simulate an attack with 'noise, firepower but no close engagement'.

HMS *Glamorgan* to be active in Berkeley Sound and keep Army Group Stanley occupied.

Some Royal Marines were less than impressed that their traditional first ashore role had been usurped by the Parachute Regiment, in particular the 2nd Battalion, which had only recently joined the Amphibious Task Group.

The Intelligence Section believed it had developed an accurate order of battle and deployment of the Argentinian forces of the Falkland Islands; however there were significant gaps, in particular strategy and tactics, endurance and Argentinian commitment to the defence of the Falklands.

Unknown to and not reported to 3 Commando Brigade Intelligence by the Special Task Detachment was that it had identified that the 2nd Airborne Infantry Regiment and 602 Commando Company were part of Task Force Mercedes at Goose Green, bringing the total number of troops to an estimated 1,500 men. When a report received by the Intelligence Section suggested the 12th Infantry Regiment consisted of 382 all ranks, this confirmed that the third rifle, B Company, was missing. It had previously been identified as Combat Team *Solari* with the Strategic Reserve. Another report suggested that the operational capability of the 8th Infantry Regiment at Fox Bay was weak with 285 men listed as casualties, comprising 125 with influenza symptoms, 96 with gastro-enteritis, 43 with homesickness, 3 killed in action, 10 with limb dislocations,

8 wounded, including four with burns. With the combination of having had a platoon transferred to Goose Green and its long casualty list, the combat effectiveness of the regiment was about 50 per cent and in no state to counterattack.

The next day, the Amphibious Task Group, some twenty-one ships ranging from the elegant *Canberra* to the workmanlike LSLs, were loitering just inside the 700-mile fighter range of Argentinian aircraft, outside the Total Exclusion Zone and about 300 miles from Port Stanley. Harriers were ready to 'Hack the Shad' said to be in the area. The 'Shad' was a Boeing 707 adapted for long-range maritime reconnaissance. Several Action Stations against unidentified aircraft heightened the tension, particularly as the tannoy was not broadcasting situation reports. As escorts ranged to and fro, naval signallers clacked their messages with signal lights.

It had been nearly seven weeks since we left Plymouth and although the crucial sense of humour was alive and well, there was tension about the possibility of an opposed landing. Certainly, reasonable precautions had been taken to reduce casualties, and while any war induces grief and while I still hoped for a political solution, protection of sovereignty is essential.

5 Infantry Brigade was apparently some five days behind us, which was good news, for it meant that the 3,500 men of the Commando Brigade would not be facing 13,000 enemy for too long. Underestimating the enemy would be fatal. During the day, an order from Northwood instructed that no two major infantry units were to be on the same ship. Quite why such an order had not been issued at Ascension undermined confidence in Northwood because it meant a considerable re-organisation in the South Atlantic and not far from enemy territory. Nevertheless, 40 Commando were transferred by landing craft from the comfort of *Canberra* to HMS *Fearless*. With 1,400 troops on board, life promised to be more uncomfortable. The ditching of a Sea King

carrying SAS with the loss of 21 servicemen induced sadness. There was a suggestion that a bird had been sucked into the engine cowling.

During the day, Composite Rations, always known as 'Compo', were issued. First developed during the Second World War as a method to feed troops after a landing until field kitchens arrived, the individual variant was known as '24-hour Ration Pack, General Service' or 'rat pack'. Packed in a cardboard box and designed to provide sufficient calories for a 24-hour period, the 'rat packs' had four menus of a tinned breakfast, such as bacon grill, and a main meal, such as steak and kidney pudding and ginger pudding, all airtight in 5-ounce tins. One menu had an ounce of dried apple flakes in a foil container, two packets of biscuits AB, a packet of Garibaldi biscuits and packets of enough coffee, tea bags and powdered milk for drinks in a large mug, and two Oxo cubes. A small plastic packet contained matches, toilet paper and tin opener. Other items included an oatmeal biscuit, a chocolate bar, boiled sweets and Dextrose orange or lemon energy tablets. The theory was that different 'rat packs' would be issued to vary main meals, but that was usually difficult to achieve and therefore it was always 'take it or leave it' and eat when you can. Cooking varied and ranged from smokeless hexamine blocks and a simple stove or individual gas cookers.

I filled my four Sterling magazines each with twenty-five rounds, put twenty-five in my jacket, fifty rounds in my webbing and twenty-five rounds in my bergen. I packed my mobile Intelligence Office in a Royal Hong Kong Regiment (Volunteers) jungle pack with maps, stationery, interrogation documentation and a spare 'rat pack'. In my bergen, as part of my share of carrying Brigade HQ needs, I also packed a spare Clansman radio battery and carried a belt of 150 rounds of linked machine-gun ammunition. Total weight was about 100 lbs. The purpose of the 'Intelligence Office' was to be self-sufficient once I left Brigade HQ. I waxed my boots, again, oiled the blade of a butcher's knife I carried and placed my unwanted baggage in my seaman's kitbag onto the HQ and Signals Squadron pile on the Tank Deck. All in order and ready to go.

As the Task Force awaited political approval to enter the Total Exclusion Zone, all seemed quiet on the intelligence front. There were no reports of enemy activity in the San Carlos Water sector. Tension increased at 10.14pm when Captain Larken ordered Action Stations and the extinguishing of 'galley fires', just as they had been in Nelson's time. Meals would henceforth be Action Messing. Our Mess was taken over as a First Aid Post commanded by the Ship's Paymaster.

D-1 (20 May) broke with grey skies and the wind whistling through the rigging and stanchions. At 8am, the Amphibious Task Group crossed into the Total Exclusion Zone and headed towards Stanley, about 200 miles to the south-west, in an air defence formation. Breakfast was meat, beans and a roll placed into my mug, and while uninviting, it was essential not to go hungry. As *Fearless* ploughed through the white-tipped, grey-green waves, swathes of briny broke against the foc'sle and scurried into the scuppers. Oerlikon gunners and watchkeepers in foul-weather gear scanned the horizon. Signal lamps flashed. It could have been a scene from the Second World War film *The Cruel Sea*. All enemy submarines had been accounted for except one, which was said to be inside the Exclusion Zone. Would we get away with it?

Lunch was another meal of bread and soup. I was looking forward to unwrapping a 'rat pack' once ashore. As the night began sweeping across the horizon, the convoy shook into an anti-submarine formation and altered course to the north-west, which took the ships past Stanley on our port beam and we headed to the north coast of the Falklands. Neil Smith told me to rest, which I did by watching *Saturday Night Fever*, *The Taking of Pelham 1-2-3* and *Benny Hill* on *Fearless* TV, which raised spirits. The gale blew itself out. Air Raid *Red* was sounded and then reduced to Air Raid *White* – no aircraft observed but Action Stations to be maintained. At about 11pm, the convoy changed course to the south-west and headed for Falkland Sound. Still no reaction from the defenders.

6

SAN CARLOS WATER

D-Day, 21 May. Waking up at about 3.30am and conscious that the motion of the ship was gentle, I went to the Gun Room where Neil told me the latest intelligence was that there was no significant activity from the three Argentinian Army Groups. From the port quarterdeck, I saw that *Fearless* was loitering south of Fanning Head and the only interruption to the silence of the night was the gentle rumbling of her engines. Just south of the entrance into San Carlos Water, small blue lights bobbed on the dark, gentle sea indicating that landing craft carrying the first assault wave were lined up on the Line of Departure. The silence was then shattered by HMS *Antrim* opening fire on the 'Fanning Head Mob' position and as the landing craft accelerated, there were momentary flashes of fluorescent white water and then the file of blue slowly disappeared into San Carlos Water. I returned to the Intelligence Section. The next hour was tense as we waited for news of the landing. Were the Argentinians waiting? Where? How many? How would they react? No news. As I sat in my chair, Neil told me, 'Go to bed. You will need your sleep.' And so I did. A couple of hours later, Neil briefed me that the SBS had neutralised the 'Fanning Head Mob' with both sides apparently expending a considerable quantity of ammunition but with few bodies and wounded to show for it.

Meanwhile *Fearless* had entered into San Carlos Water. I went aft on deck for my first glimpse of the Falkland Islands, a dramatic moment after all the days at sea. A weak autumn sun spilled across the tranquil, treeless, moorland hills. Only the grey hulls of the warships and black ones of the merchantmen betrayed our purpose. *Canberra* lent misplaced style. There was no evidence of an Argentinian counterattack from anywhere and then 'Air Raid Warning Red! Air Raid Warning Red!' was broadcast over the tannoy. I dashed into the shelter of the ship, slammed the door and flung the clips over to lock. Inside, there was no great commotion,

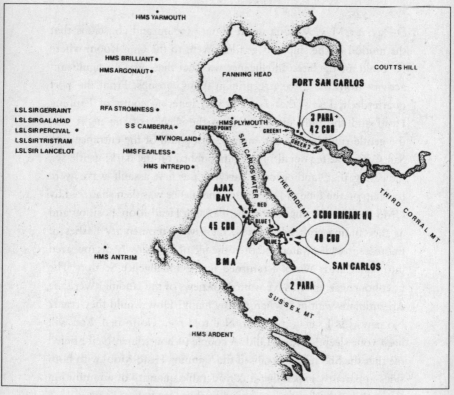

Operation Sutton landings.

so I reverted to cool, calm and collected. The ship was already at
Action Stations. Steadying myself and opening the door, I saw a small,
camouflaged aircraft flying along San Carlos Water under inaccurate
machine-gun fire, tracer and the steady thud of Bofors guns. It later
turned out that at the request of Combat Team *Guemes*, Naval Air
Command at Stanley had instructed the 1st Naval Attack Squadron
to investigate reports of enemy landings in Falkland Sound, San
Carlos Water and Grantham Sound. Lieutenants Guillermo Crippa
and Horacio Talaria, both flying MB-339s, took off from Air Force
Base Stanley at about 7am, however, Talaria's aircraft developed
a fault and he returned to base. Such was the strength of the
intelligence that Crippa was instructed to continue his task. Even
though mist and the sun was causing glare, at about 8.30am, he
approached San Carlos Water from the north and later recalled:

As I came over San Carlos itself, I came face to face with a Sea
Lynx helicopter. I was going to attack when I saw the ships in the
distance. I decided to forget about the helicopter and go for other
targets. I flew straight to the first ship, which was lying at anchor.
I don't know which of us was more surprised. I came under
attack and they started firing at me. I was taken aback by the
number of ships there were in the area and I thought to myself:
If I go back and tell them there are so many ships they'll never
believe me. I circled and came back trying to hug the terrain and
I drew a little map on my knee-pad before I returned to Puerto
Argentino. It was strange because it was a beautiful day, very
peaceful and the Islands looked lovely. It was incredible to think
there was a war going on. (*Speaking Out*)

Those who witnessed Crippa's gallant flight are unlikely to forget it.
His rocket and 30mm cannon attack on the frigate HMS *Argonaut*
damaged a Seacat position and wounded two sailors. And then
under fire from rail-mounted GPMGs and Blowpipe on *Canberra*, a

Seacat missile fired from HMS *Intrepid* and HMS *Plymouth*'s 4.5in main armament, he negotiated San Carlos Water and returned to Stanley reporting that the British had landed. He was awarded Argentina's highest award for gallantry. I later learnt from the Argentinian pilot shot down during the Battle of Goose Green that San Carlos Water was part of a regular early morning patrol and that Crippa was equally surprised to find the inlet jammed with enemy ships as were the British by his audacious flight.

When the tannoy announced that the Tactical HQ was to report to the Tank Deck, I was a little surprised because I had been briefed that Brigadier Thompson was going ashore by helicopter, nevertheless, I collected my webbing, hoisted my bergen and 'crash pack' onto one shoulder and clutching my SMG staggered out into the companionway and began the tortuous journey to the Tank Deck, negotiating narrow ladders and eventually arrived at the assembly station. I watched with 'professional interest' as the 4th Assault Squadron manoeuvred their Centurion Beach Armoured Recovery Vehicle and some lorried trackway onto a LCU. The disembarkation controller then told us that *Blue Beach One* was not yet suitable for vehicles and the landing schedule had slipped. Another Air Raid Warning *Red* was announced and fast aircraft screamed low overhead. It was about 9.30am. I returned to the Intelligence Section where Neil told me Daggers had badly damaged HMS *Ardent* on guard off Cat Island. Daggers were Israeli-built Mirage 5 ground attack aircraft equipped with two 30mm cannon and could deliver two 1,000 lb or four 500 lb bombs. The unexpected air raids had resulted in the landing plan being changed with 42 Commando being landed from the white-hulled *Canberra* as a priority. Tactical HQ had dropped down the priority ladder. I learnt in the Amphibious Operations Room that 3 Para landing on *Green Beach* had clashed with Combat Team *Guemes* near Port San Carlos and as the enemy ground fire shot down two Commando Brigade Air Squadron Gazelles east of the settlement and damaged a third, they were withdrawing. Three aircrew had been killed. An immediate operational investigation concluded that the helicopters had been working on the original timetable and were unaware that 3 Para had been held up by Combat Team *Guemes*. The D Squadron diversion north of Darwin had attracted no response from Task Force Mercedes.

Neil and I went aft for a break and watched landing craft packed with life-jacketed troops crowded into the well decks and Sea Kings flying the 29th Commando Regiment 105mm Light Guns and trailers, these swinging lazily on long cables. The Rapiers of T (Shah Sujah's Troop) Battery were landed into the proposed firing posts. Although there were reports that some had been damaged during stowage at Ascension and during the poor weather at sea, everyone was willing that these unassuming gunners could sort out their problems – because they were vital. A Rigid Raider then swung in below the stern and a crewman dressed in a green survival suit and combat lifejacket climbed up the rope ladder. 'Where is the Int Sect?'

'We're part of it. How can we help?' I replied and he handed me a crumpled document sent by Captain Orpen-Smellie, the 3 Para Intelligence Officer, showing the organisation of Combat Team *Guemes*. It was our first item of Documentary Intelligence direct from the enemy. The Royal Marine was shivering with cold so I offered a cup of coffee from my flask, 'How's it been?' When he said he had been sent to recover the body of one of the helicopter aircrew, I noticed slivers of blood intermingled with sea water swishing to and fro in his boat. Another air raid warning was followed by running boots, shouted orders, screaming aircraft, columns of sheer white marble, the clatter of machine-guns and then silence apart from the Bosun's Mate calmly giving information over the tannoy.

At midday, when Neil and I went for lunch and in conversation said we were landing, the Navy chefs produced a welcome meal

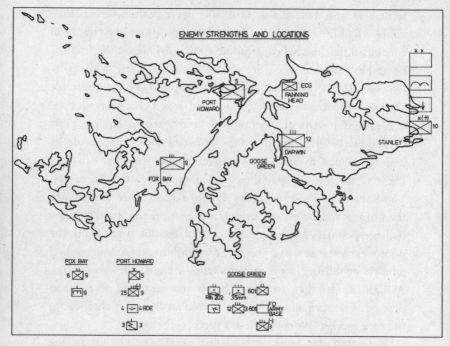

Operation Sutton. Estimated Army Group Littoral order of battle on 21 May.

of tinned sausages, baked beans, bread and fruit. As I returned to the Tank Deck for an update, there was yet another raid of sudden violence. Being in a ship under attack was most disconcerting. Returning to the Intelligence Section, reports from *Blue Beach One* indicated that the 4th Assault Squadron were using a lorry carrying metal trackway to lay a road over soft sand and mud on *Blue Beach*.

At some stage, when orders confirmed that Brigade HQ would land after dark, Neil and I agreed that I would go ashore with Bob Birkett and 'B' Intelligence Section and he and the rest of the Section would remain on *Fearless* supporting the Amphibious Operations Room until called forward. The afternoon passed with more air raids. In between visits to the Intelligence Section for updates, usually 'nothing to report', there was always something happening on the Tank Deck, landing craft arriving and departing, vehicles being prepared for landing and always someone with whom to pass the time of day. Still no reaction from Army Group Falklands.

As darkness fell after a hectic day, the Intelligence Section took stock. 3 Commando Brigade was ashore. 3 Para and 42 Commando had landed on the two *Green Beaches*. 40 Commando had cleared San Carlos and had raised the Union Flag. 2 Para had landed on *Blue Beach* and were dug in on Sussex Mountain ready to deal with a counterattack from Task Force Mercedes. 45 Commando had seized the refrigeration plant at *Red Beach* and were dug in on Sussex Mountain in depth to 2 Para. Combat Team *Guemes* in Port San Carlos and the 'Fanning Hill Mob' had been neutralised and there was no intelligence indicating an Argentinian counterattack from Goose Green and West Falkland. The destruction of two Puma and a Chinook helicopter in the 601 Combat Aviation hide on Mount Kent Harriers would reduce the capability of the Argentinians to move troops quickly. Fifteen enemy aircraft were claimed destroyed. But the cost had been high. HMS *Ardent* sunk with the loss of twenty-two killed and thirty-six wounded, HMS *Argonaut* was damaged by bombs although her weapon systems were still functioning and HMS *Brilliant* was hit by a bomb which failed to explode. HMS *Broadsword* had also been hit by a bomb which ripped into her Flight Deck but failed to explode and the aft deck of HMS *Antrim* had been penetrated by a bomb which ended up in the after 'heads' but failed to explode. There were unconfirmed reports of an Exocet being fired at *Canberra,* which seemed most unlikely. It was rumoured that the Combat Air Patrol had not provided overhead cover because the weather at sea had been poor. Some were suggesting the Task Force commander was nervous about exposing his ships – the Exocet Syndrome, again.

Flight-Lieutenant Glover of No. 1 (Fighter) Squadron, flying a RAF GR3 Harrier, had been shot down by ground fire off Port Howard and was missing. It was later learnt that he had been captured badly wounded and was flown to a military hospital in Argentina as a prisoner. As RAF aircrew were defined to be 'prone to capture', I hoped that he attended resistance to interrogation training. He was released in June.

In spite of the unexpected intensity and unfamiliar ferocity of the air raids, morale was high. About 11pm, the order came over the tannoy, 'Brigade HQ, stand by to embark!' At last! Shaking hands with Neil, I looked forward to seeing him ashore the following morning. Brigadier Thompson had been flown ashore shortly before dusk with his radio operator. I joined Defence Troop, which was commanded by Lieutenant Metcalfe, on the Tank Deck, which was dark except for a few shielded orange lights. When someone wanted a photograph of the Troop, I was reluctant in case I was captured but failed to conceal myself sufficiently! I usually rode with Sergeant Steve Pope commanding the 'stick' of five BV 202s of Tactical HQ and dumped my bergen in his BV and waited. On the instruction 'Embark,' the drivers reversed into the LCUs and left the engines gently ticking over to prevent a stalled vehicle blocking the ramp. The remainder of us then filed onto the landing craft, Tactical HQ aft while Defence Troop, tasked to secure our landing, assembled behind the ramp. The LCU engine burst into life and as the ramp slowly raised, we went astern into San Carlos Water, the scene of so much unexpected drama during the day, but now quiet and dark, and the coxswain took us from the comfort of our home at anchor. The landing craft picked up speed, her blunt bows gently dipping into the low swell and throwing up the occasional salt spume. It was just possible to see the dark mass of land. Above, stars glittered. As we passed blacked-out ships at anchor, silent and shadowy, we saw occasional glimmers of lights in San Carlos settlement. After about an hour the LCU slowed down and from the shore, a yellow flash briefly split the night. 'Standby' from the bridge. I adjusted my webbing, checked the magazine on my Sterling and watched as Defence Troop gathered in two files and the BV gunners manned the coaxial GPMGs. The LCU slowly edged forward and then almost imperceptibly grounded on *Blue Beach*. My watch showed midnight.

The ramp splashed into the water at an alarming angle. Someone was going to get wet and then at 'Troops Out', the traditional command to disembark, Defence Troop splashed into the water and waded ashore up to their knees. The rest of us clambered onto the BVs which jolted forward onto the ramp, slid into the sea and after a few metres trundled up the steel trackway. The dark beach was a hive of activity with one landing craft discharging its cargo of stores and another slowly backing off. The Beach Armoured Recovery Vehicle appeared to be bogged down and someone was hitting metal with metal. I jumped down and met some guides who indicated the exit track and reported, 'No mines and no enemy.' That was comforting. The BVs clambered up from the busy beach, motored up a steep muddy track and stopped on the outskirts of the sleeping settlement, silent except for an occasional barking dog. Drizzle began to fall, not entirely unexpected because it always rained on exercise, so why not on operations! Suddenly from the direction of Port San Carlos, the night was split by flashes and flares, followed by the crump of mortars and irregular chatter of small arms fire that fell away only to reach another crescendo. What was happening? Had 3 Para been attacked by the survivors from Fanning Head? Was it a counterattack? We simply did not know and I had no communications with the Intelligence Section on *Fearless*. The column drew up alongside a hedge of gorse bushes and, as engines were switched off, local defence sentries were posted and then someone uttered that dreaded phrase 'Dig in'.

Although digging-in was not my favourite military pastime, the noise and flashes of battle to the north made the normally onerous task more inspiring. Picks and shovels were unhooked and we took it in turns to chip at the soil. After about an hour, an engineer grader/digger motored up the track and was intercepted by Sergeant-Major Pete Ellis RE, who was with the 59 Independent Commando Engineer Field Squadron Command Post. When he asked the lance-corporal driver to help excavate our weapon pits, the driver agreed that although his vehicle was leaking oil and he was on his way to another task, he would help as long as practical. Within a short time, several weapon pits had been dug around the BVs. Steve Pope then told me to get my head down, not only because my time for long hours without sleep would come, but I was apparently lousy at digging. It was about 3.30am. There was still gunfire from Fanning Head.

The landing of Tactical HQ meant that we lost the intelligence from Commander-in-Chief Fleet and henceforth our Intelligence Cycle of collection, collation, conversion into intelligence, grading according to reliability of sources, and dissemination and exploitation was reliant on patrols and observation posts, captured documents, Prisoners of War and local knowledge and, with luck, the delivery of air photographic interpretation.

While interrogation and Documentary Intelligence usually produced substantial information on enemy organisation, morale and future operations, generally commanders were not familiar with assessing Essential Elements of Intelligence and therefore information collection tended to be of a general nature, as opposed to the acquisition of targeted intelligence.

I was not sure how Y Troop and the Special Task Detachment were going to support the Brigade, bearing in mind we were largely divorced from the sources available en route from UK. (*See* plate section for examples of Documentary Intelligence gathered during this operation.)

D+1 for me did not begin well. Shortly before dawn, Steve shook me, 'Stand to'. I rapidly unzipped my sleeping bag, grabbed my fighting order and Sterling and scrambled to our weapon pit already occupied by Steve and his driver. 'Where are they?' I asked.

'Nowhere, it's only stand-to,' Steve replied. I relaxed and waited for stand-down and then I saw that Regimental Sergeant Major Pete Ranft was checking the position. Unfortunately, I had forgotten my smock and wondered how I could retrieve it without him noticing. I could not and prepared myself to be humiliated, 'Where's your jacket, Nick?'

'In the tent, sir,' I replied, 'I forgot to put it on in my rush to defend the HQ.'

'Mmm', he murmured and walked on. Nothing more needed to be said – lesson relearnt! Dawn broke clear and bright. The battle had died down. I later learnt it was enemy ammunition and weapons found at Fanning Head being destroyed.

The Intelligence Corps has a long history in Counter Intelligence and Protective Security that began in 1914. Its involvement in battlefield Operational Intelligence emerged in the early 1960s. Indeed, about 60 per cent of my career, so far, had been with the former. In the absence of Director of Naval Security representation, which normally managed Royal Marines security, I commenced a discreet counter-intelligence operation to protect the Brigade rear areas by visiting settlement managers to identify anyone who might pose a subversive, sabotage and espionage threat. I suspected the threat would be greater in the urban area of Port Stanley than in the close-knit settlements. During the morning, I toured San Carlos with Lieutenant Gibson, the 40 Commando Intelligence Officer. It seemed the Argentinians had hardly visited the area until a small detachment dressed in camouflage uniforms had landed from a Chinook in mid-May. While most stayed in the sheep-shearing shed, one patrol was despatched to the hills overlooking San Carlos and had returned three days later with most of the soldiers suffering from exposure and sickness. Thereafter there was no further patrolling and the only fraternisation was for food. One person believed the troops to be Marines, however I believed they were 601 Commando Company sweeping the area prior to the insertion of Combat Team *Guemes*. The Chinook was undoubtedly from the 601 Combat Aviation Battalion. Mr Paddy Short, the San Carlos settlement manager, invited me into his well-appointed house and explained that he was essentially the foreman for the absentee manager, who was apparently related to a Conservative politician. The absentee manager had achieved some local notoriety when he seemed to criticise Naval Party 8901 and openly supported the Argentinian invasion. We gave him the benefit of the doubt, as misguided and ill-informed.

During the night, most of Brigade HQ Main had landed from Mexeflotes motorised rafts and was established along a gorse-lined track underneath some trees bordering a small market garden, near a quaint white house with a red roof and with two large whale bones above the garden gate. I was ashore with Intelligence Section 'B' of Bob Birkett with his detachment of Taff Evans, Tom Priestley, the illustrator Ken Loftus and Roy Packer of Engineer Intelligence quietly settling in and waiting for command to be passed from HMS *Fearless*. Our Flight-Sergeant representing the Joint Service Interrogation Unit on *Norland* was already dealing with nine prisoners captured at Fanning Head. Three wounded Argentinians had been transferred to *Canberra*. Ivor Garcia had landed with Y (Electronic Warfare) Troop as an interpreter. While Neil on HMS *Fearless* was our main source for Commander-in-Chief Fleet intelligence, we were largely reliant on tactical intelligence sources, such as patrols, our main priority being to watch for any enemy incursions against the beachhead. The Land Rovers were later landed at *Red Beach* to provide an emergency Command Post. Defence Troop provided local defence. Lieutenant

BOLIVIA

BRAZIL

JUJUY

PARAGUAY

San Salvador
de Jujuy

Salta
SALTA

FORMOSA

ASUNCIÓN

San Miguel
de Tucumán

SANTIAGO
DEL ESTERO

CHACO

Formosa

TUCUMÁN

Resistencia

MISIONES

CATAMARCA

Catamarca

Santiago
del Estero

Corrientes

Posadas

CHILE

La Rioja

CORRIENTES

LA RIOJA

SANTA FE

BRAZIL

SAN JUAN

Córdoba

Santa
Fe

San Juan

Paraná

URUGUAY

SANTIAGO ★

Mendoza

SAN LUIS

CÓRDOBA

ENTRE RÍOS

San
Luis

BUENOS
AIRES ★

MENDOZA

La Plata

MONTEVIDEO

SOUTH
PACIFIC
OCEAN

Santa Rosa

BUENOS AIRES

LA PAMPA

Neuquén

NEUQUÉN

RÍO NEGRO

Viedma

International boundary

Province (provincia) boundary

★ National capital

Province (provincia) capital

Argentina has 23 provinces (provincias) and
1 autonomous city (Ciudad Autónoma de Buenos Aires)

0   150   300 Kilometers

0   150   300 Miles

Scale 1:17,000,000

CHUBUT

Rawson

SOUTH
ATLANTIC
OCEAN

SANTA CRUZ

Río Gallegos

Stanley

Falkland Islands
(Islas Malvinas)
(administered by the UK,
claimed by ARGENTINA)

TIERRA DEL FUEGO,
ANTÁRTIDA E ISLAS
DEL ATLÁNTICO SUR

Ushuaia

2 April 1982. British prisoners on the lawn outside Government House prior to repatriation through Montevideo. (Author's collection)

2 April. Port Stanley. Argentinian amphibious commandoes. The soldier on extreme left appears to be armed with a 9mm Sterling, either issued or captured. (Author's collection)

2 April. Port Stanley. A woman carrying a bag of shopping passes a column of Amtraks a few hours after the Argentinian occupation. (Author's collection)

The Argentinian occupation of Stanley. Signs painted on the road advise drivers to drive on the right. (Author's collection)

A Company, 25th Special Infantry Regiment. The inset on the left is the company badge, which includes an image of a soldier standing astride the Falklands. (Author's collection)

Probably Mt Harriet. Argentinian soldiers being fed from field kitchens. The system resulted in some soldiers going hungry. (Author's collection)

Above: Four conscripts outside their peat bunker on Stanley Common. (Author's collection)

Below: 5 May 1982. Ascension. At English Beach, landing craft collected troops after a day of rest and recreation. (Author's collection)

ARGENTINIAN MECHANISED INFANTRY REGIMENT

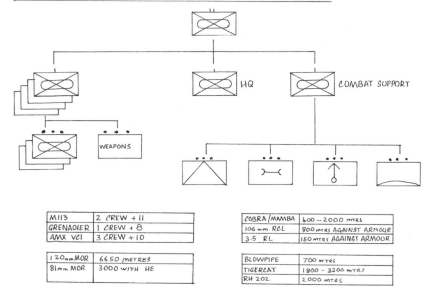

M113	2 CREW + 11
GRENADIER	1 CREW + 8
AMX VCI	3 CREW + 10

120mm MOR	6650 metres
81mm MOR	3000 WITH HE

COBRA/MAMBA	400 - 2000 MTRS
106 mm RCL	800 MTRS AGAINST ARMOUR
3.5 RL	150 MTRS AGAINST ARMOUR

BLOWPIPE	700 MTRS
TIGERCAT	1800 - 3200 MTRS
RH 202	2000 MTRS

Order of battle of an Argentinian Mechanised Infantry Regiment compiled by 3 Commando Brigade HQ Intelligence Section during the voyage to the Falklands. (Author's collection)

HMS *Fearless*. 01.00hrs, 22 May. Defence Troop waiting to land on *Blue Beach*. (Author's collection)

22 May 1982. San Carlos settlement. (Author's collection)

ORGANIGRAMA DE LA CA CDO

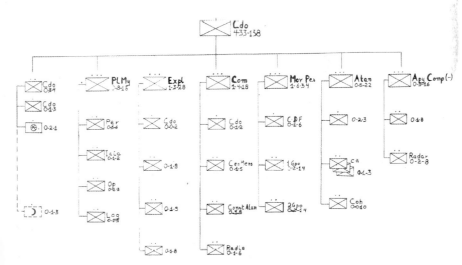

An example of Documentary Intelligence. Organisation of an Argentinian Command Company found in the search of EC *Guemes* HQ at Port San Carlos on 22 May. (Author's collection)

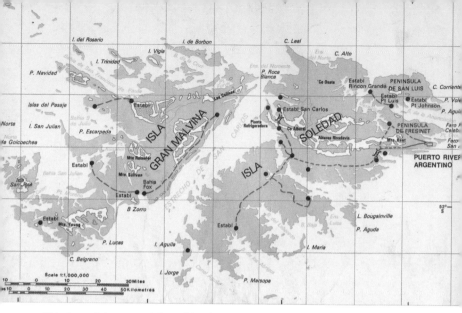

This Argentinian map of the Falklands giving Spanish place names was found at Port San Carlos and was very helpful. (Author's collection)

24 May 1982. HQ 3 Commando Brigade dug in at San Carlos. (Author's collection)

Members of 602 Commando Company captured by the Mountain and Arctic Warfare Cadre at Teal Inlet on 31 May before being flown to the Commando Brigade Forward Interrogation Team at San Carlos. (Author's collection)

San Carlos. The interrogation centre Hotel Galtieri. Marine Smith is the 'doorman'. (Author's collection)

Brigade HQ at Teal Inlet. (Author's collection)

An Argentinian photograph of the captured laser rangefinder. (Author's collection)

NOMINAL OF ARGENTINE FORCES ON THE
FALKLANDS ON 3ʳᵈ JUN 82 (FROM CAPTURED
ENEMY DOCUMENT)

GOB MIL	10
Col	24
CDO CPO Ej V	1
CDO Br 1 IX	8
RI 25	639
RI 8	814
Dest C BI 181	34
Co Ing 9	174
Co Ing 601	228
Arg Com 601	7
B LOG 9	94
HMCR	65
Co Ab Mant Aeron (601)	9
Co PM 181	64
GA ABROT 4	294
GADA 601	465
B Av Comb Ej 601	65
CDO Br 1 MEC X	179
RI MEC 3	917
RI MEC 6	749
RI MEC 7	819
Esc Expl C BI 10	216
Co Ing MEC 10	271
Co Com MEC 10	244
B LOG 10	133
GA 3	215
GA/RI 4	176
RI 4 (-)	326
Co CDOS 601	43
Co CDOS 602	32

TOTAL 7,176

(THIS TOTAL DOES NOT INCLUDE
NAVY, MARINES OR AF TOTALS)

ESTIMATE A TOTAL OF
9½ - 10 THOUSAND TROOPS

Note
a.
b.

Copy of the Army Group Stanley order of battle found in a Combat Team *Solari*
bunker on Mount Kent by 45 Commando on 3 June. (Author's collection)

Serial	Name	Number of Personnel	Comment
1	GOB	10	"Gobiniero" Governor probably GHQ. Located at Government House. Governor General de Brigade M B Menendes.
2	Col	24	No identification.
3	CDO CPO Ej V	1	No identification although "CDO" is probably "Command", "Ej" is Ejercito which is Army and "V" is Roman numeral for figure five.
4	CDO Br I IX	8	"Brigade De Infantera". Probably in Stanley now less 12 Infantry Regiment captured at Goose Green (9 Infantry Brigade).
5	RI 25	639	"Regimentio de Infantera 25", of 9 Brigade. Based at Stanley less ECG captured Fanning Head. (25 Infantry Regiment).
6	RI 8	814	"Regimentio de Infantera 8" of 9 Brigade. Based at Fox Bay. (8 Infantry Regiment).
7	Dest C BI 181	34	" de Cabelleria Blindado 181". Possibly the LTVP 7 unit 181 indicated Army level unit.
8	Co Ing 9	124	"Compania de Ingenerio 9" of 9 Brigade. Detachments at Fox Bay and Port Howard (9 Engineer Company).
9	Co Ing 601	228	"Companie de Ingenerio 601". An Army level unit. (601 Engineer Company).
10	Arg Com 601	7	"Argentina Communicion 601"? Rear link communication unit to Argentina Army level unit.

Serial	Name	Number of Personnel	Comment
11	B Log 9	94	Batallon de Logistique "9 Logistic Battalion" of 9 Infantry Brigade.
12	HMCR	65	Unidentified.
13	Ca Ab Mant Aeron 601	9	"Compania 601". Unidentified but possibly "601 Aircraft Maintenance Company" for army helicopters. Stanley airfield.
14	Co PM 181	64	Compania de Policia Militar - 601 Military Police Company - Army level unit. At Stanley.
15	GA AEROT 4	294	"Grepo de Artilleria - Aerot 4" possibly 4 Anti-Aircraft Group. Probably Stanley.
16	GADA 601	465	Grepo de Artilleria de Defense Anti-Aeria 601 - Army level unit. Probably at Stanley. Elements of GADA 601 had been killed or captured at Goose Green (601 Army Defence Group).
17	B Ar Comb Ej 601	65	Batallon de Avion Combat Ejerito 601. Army aviation unit - possibly equipped with helicopters. An Army level unit.
18	CDO Br 1 Mec X	179	"Commando Brigade de Infanteria Mecanizade" - now at Stanley and probably at full strength (10 Mechanised Infantry Brigade).
19	RI Mec 3	917	"Regimentio de Infanteria Mecanizada 3" - at Stanley. Part of 10 Mechan Infantry Brigade (3 Mechanised Infantry Regiment).
20	RI Mec 6	749	"Regimentio de Infanteria Mecanizada 6" - at Stanley. Also part of 10 Mechanised Infantry Brigade (6 Mechanised Infantry Regt.)
21	RI Mec 7	819	"Regimentio de Infanteria Mecanizada 7" at Stanley. Also part of 10 Mechanised Infantry Brigade (7 Mechanised Infantry Regiment)

Serial	Name	Number of Personnel	Comment
22	Esc Expl C BI 10	216	"Escuadron de Exploracion de Cabellemia Blindado 10" - based at Stanley and probably equipped with PANHARD AML 90 armoured cars. The armoured recommaaisance unit at 10 Mechanised Infantry Brigade. (Armoured Reconnaisance Squadron).
23	Co Ing MEC 10	271	"Companies de Ingeniero Mecanizada 10" - Based at Stanley and part of 10 Mechanised Infantry Brigade (10 Mechanised Engineer Company).
24	Co Com MEC 10	244	"Compania de Communicion Mecanizada 10" - the signals element of 10 Mechanised Infantry Brigade (10 Mechanised Signals ~~Communication~~ Company).
25	B LOG 10	133	"Batalion de Logistique 10". Logistic element of 10 Mechanised Infantry Brigade. (10 Logistic Battalion).
26	GA 3	215	"Grepo de Artilleria 3" - At Stanley and equipped with the Italian 105m Pack Howitzer (3 Artillery Group).
27	GA/RI 4	176	"Grepo de Artilleria/Regimentio de Artilleria 4". Artillery unit organic to 4 Infantry Regiment. This helped to confirm that the ~~three~~ *four* guns captured at Goose Green probably was organic to 12 Infantry Regiment. (4 Infantry Regiment artillery group).
28	RI 4 (-)	326	"Regimentio de Infanteria 4" not at full strength. At Stanley. Part of 3 Mechanised Infantry Brigade (4 Infantry Regiment).
29	Co CDOS 601	43	"Compania de Commandos 601" - Army level Special Forces unit. Had been in the Falklands for some time and had probably patrolled the San Carlos area prior to the landings. (601 Commando Company).
30	Co CDOS 602	32	"Companis de Commandos 602" - Army level Special Forces unit. Recently assigned to the Falklands Islands on 24 May 83. Had already been in contact with the ~~M spAN~~ cadre at Top Malo House. (602 Commando Company). [Mountain and the Warfare Cadre]

13 June, Mount Kent. Intelligence Section prepares their BV for the 'crash move' after the Skyhawk attack. (Author's collection)

ARGENTINIAN MINES FOUND ON THE FALKLAND ISLANDS

Type	Origin	Description	Detonating pressure	Explosive content	Target	Size
FMK 1	ARGENTINA	Plastic	110 lbs	5g	anti-Personnel	3"
FMK 3	ARGENTINA	Plastic	616 lbs	13 lbs	anti-Tank	10"
P 4 B	SPAIN	Plastic	30 lbs	60g	anti-Personnel	3"
C 3 B	SPAIN	Plastic	200 lbs	11 lbs	anti-Tank	11"
P8 33	ITALY	Plastic	17 lbs	1 g	anti-Personnel	3"
P8 81	ITALY	Plastic	330 lbs	4 lbs	anti-Tank	10"
No 4	ISRAEL	Box	17 lbs	5 g	anti-Booby-Trap	5"
No 6	ISRAEL	Metallic	13 lbs	13 lbs	anti-Tank	12"
M 1	US	Metallic	497 lbs	6 lbs	anti-tank	11"

Above: Handwritten list of mines identified in Argentinian minefields. (Author's collection)

Opposite: Pages 1, 2 and 3 of the interpretation of the Argentinian order of battle found in a bunker on Mt Kent by 45 Commando on 3 June. (Author's collection)

Above: 14 June. Argentinian troops retreating along Ross Rd in Port Stanley. (Author's collection)

Below: Marine Tom Priestley of the Brigade Intelligence Section searching the playground for information. In the background is the Intelligence Section BV 202. In common with other buildings in Stanley, ammunition, grenades and human waste covered the ground. (Author's collection)

Above: Stanley. A member of the Intelligence Corps surveys Argentinian prisoners of war waiting to be screened for repatriation. (Author's collection)

Below: Stanley. The Argentinian Officer Commanding 601 Air Defence Battalion negotiates with the author during the repatriation. (Author's collection)

Sketch of six prisoners of war found during a search at the Ajax Bay prison camp. Sergeant Flores, wearing the camouflaged jacket, was 602 Commando Company captured by the SAS in the battle for Mount Kent. Dates of capture are shown. Three were captured at Goose Green. (Author's collection)

Repatriated senior officers are welcomed on their return to Argentina. All had been held until Argentina surrendered unconditionally. (Author's collection)

Metcalfe resisted reinforcement from Brigade HQ staff as 'too many cooks', as he once commented to me.

The Command Post was in its usual structure of several back-to-back BVs forming a cruciform covered by tentage and was already a hubbub of its habitual subdued conversation, radio chatter and comings and goings. I usually only entered whenever I had business with Operations or needed to use the radio. I had been a rear link radio operator on tanks before transferring to the Intelligence Corps and was familiar with the radio procedures. Access to the Command Post was controlled by the Royal Marines Police Troop. The Intelligence Section BV and its 9-foot-by-9-foot frame tent was separate from the Command Post and its entrance positioned at 3 o'clock to the Command Post entrance, which eased navigation between them both at night. A member of the Intelligence Section worked in shifts alongside Operations to maintain the Operations map. When one of the Command Post components, including the Intelligence Section, wanted an activity or information to be entered on the map, the requirement was written on an Action slip and passed to Operations to be logged before being entered using a plastic template on the map. If appropriate, a copy was passed to the Intelligence Section to be entered on our map. One of the marines was always on duty in the Intelligence Section to maintain our maps. Communications Troop, which was the largest element of the Brigade HQ, and Signals Squadron were housed in another cruciform that made up the Communication Centre.

It was undoubtedly a relief to be off the ships, even if it was during the first major amphibious landing by British troops since Suez in 1956. The expected Argentinian retaliation for trespassing on British territory was not materialising and 3 Commando Brigade was consolidating in the beachhead with no interference. The Falklands Citizen Band network was intercepted by a radio operator and we listened as a West Falkland settlement arranged for an Argentinian pilot with a broken arm and badly injured leg to be rescued by Argentinian Search and Rescue. I had refined a habit developed on exercises of eating and sleeping when one could in the knowledge that sessions were likely to be interrupted. Washing and shaving was from a bowl of usually cold water. Meals for officers were provided in a field extension of the Officers Mess known as the 'Greasy Spoon', courtesy of the A Echelon, Brigade HQ and Signal Squadron. The 'Spoon' was usually a good source for an extra tin of rations or, even more welcome, a meal or a slab of cheese.

With about 3,000 troops under his command and faced by about 11,000 Argentinians in three Army Groups based at Port Stanley, Goose Green and West Falkland and his naval logistic support under attack, Brigadier Thompson's preference was to wait for 5 Infantry Brigade. So far, there had been little interference to the landings from Army Group Falklands, which suggested the enemy had been wrong-footed; nevertheless, a raid would destabilise the nearest threat. Early on 22 May, Brigadier Thompson visited 2 Para on Sussex Mountain and discussed the option of raiding Goose Green with Lieutenant-Colonel 'H' Jones, the commanding officer, before 5 Infantry Brigade arrived. This fell into line with the 12 May Orders from Major-General Moore that he was to establish 'moral and physical domination' of the enemy by inflicting as much damage as possible.

There is no doubt that the landing at San Carlos Water had surprised the enemy. In his Intelligence Summary No. 14 dated 6pm on 22 May captured later in the war, Colonel Francisco Cervo, the Army Group Falklands Head of Intelligence, believed that over the next 48/72 hours, 3 Commando Brigade would strengthen the San Carlos Water beachhead and would conduct ground and helicopter reconnaissance and locations so that the twenty Harriers believed to be on the *Atlantic Conveyor* and Electronic Intelligence devices could be landed. In terms of exploitation, he believed that one Commando would land north-east of Murrell (north-west of Stanley) and another at Port Louis in Berkeley Sound and lay siege to Stanley. At the same time, the forces at San Carlos Water would be to break out and advance east by ship and helicopters. He believed an attack would be launched on Port Stanley any time after 30 May with a series of amphibious and helicopter operations supported by electronic deception.

In the late evening, I was informed that 3 Para had captured a prisoner above Port San Carlos. Without doubt, he had spent

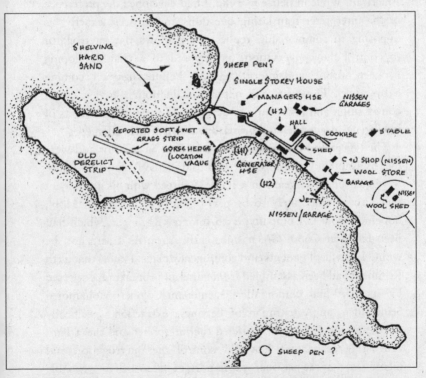

Briefing map of San Carlos and *Blue Beaches One* and *Two* compiled from an interview of a repatriated Falkland Islander. (*See also* the plate section for a captured Argentinian map of the Falklands found at Port San Carlos.)

time at Goose Green and therefore probably had useful tactical information of value to 2 Para. However, my Spanish was not good enough for a detailed interrogation, therefore I proposed to use an interpreter. This method relies on a comfortable relationship between the interrogator, who leads, and the interpreter. I had intended to use Ivor Garcia because I knew he would follow instructions, unfortunately he was still with Y Troop and my second choice of the RAF Flight-Sergeant was not possible because he was on *Norland*.

The third option was an officer who spoke fluent Spanish-American. While in Belize in 1980, I had developed the preference of the interpreter translating questions and answers exactly, as opposing to summarising replies. This allows the interrogator to control the conversation, as opposed to a chat developing between prisoner and interpreter with the interrogator becoming a bystander. However, our natural inclination is to engage in conversation and takes time to develop. The essential elements of intelligence needed related primarily to Task Forces Mercedes.

The officer and I were both flown to Port San Carlos and were met by Captain Orpen-Smellie who told us the Regimental Police were guarding a sergeant in a stable. I agreed with his assessment that he was most likely to be part of the 'Fanning Head Mob', hopefully from C Company, 25th Infantry Regiment, which had been based at Goose Green since early April. As a sergeant, he would know deployments and contingency plans. I knew that 25th Regiment had been assembled from paras and commandos selected by its hard-line commander, Lieutenant-Colonel Mohammed Seinehilden, an Argentinian of Lebanese extraction, specifically to occupy the Falklands. I briefed the interpreter and the 3 Para Provost Sergeant that I would control the interrogation and mentioned that the prisoner was important because of his probable knowledge of Goose Green. Captain Orpen-Smellie gave me a small bag taken from the prisoner.

The interpreter and I then entered the stable and sitting on the ground illuminated by a small paraffin lamp was a swarthy man with Indian features wearing an Israeli-style combat jacket. He stood. He was stocky, his jet black hair was topped by a khaki woollen hat and his face portrayed anxiety. I said nothing as I frisked him and noted the British heavy duty sweater with Colour Sergeant stripes and Royal Marines cloth shoulder titles he was wearing, probably looted from the Royal Marines Barracks at Moody Brook in April. More importantly, this confirmed him to be 25th Infantry Regiment. When I found two photographs of a woman and two children in his jacket pocket, I returned them in his pocket as a gesture indicating: 'Trust me. I am your friend,' and then tipped the content of the bag onto the floor in front of him. As I sifted the items, it included more British Army equipment, including webbing, a pair of Army Northern Ireland patrol gloves, a nylon sleeveless jerkin marked Millets and two US hand grenades. I noted more indications of anxiety. When the sergeant told me his name, through the interpreter I told him I knew he was from Combat Team *Guemes* and that he had breached the Geneva Conventions for the protection of Prisoners of War by stealing British uniforms, presumably from Moody Brook. After about an hour of fruitless conversation, I left the sergeant in the discomfort of the cold and damp stable to contemplate his future and returned about an hour later, but he remained silent. I therefore set out to convince him that it was not in his interests to remain silent – without specifying how, because I had no idea, except that he came from a country where ruthless interrogation was common. When there was then an interruption which required the interpreter to leave the stable, using my limited Spanish-American, I set out to gain his confidence, sergeant to sergeant. I removed the two photographs from his pocket and placed them in front of him and said that I would return them if he contributed to my inquiries. To my relief, he reached out for the photos and admitted to being in the Recce Platoon. He had been at Goose Green for about six weeks. He had been at Fanning Head and in the early morning of 21 May, he and a corporal had been sent to a beach to investigate suspicious activity. When the SBS attacked, the corporal vanished. After laying up throughout the day watching the landings, he decided to return to Goose Green but had been captured near Port San Carlos. With the reward of a mug of coffee and a couple of biscuits, courtesy of the Regimental Police, he used my map to confirm our view that Goose Green was a strongpoint. A 12th Infantry Regiment Company was dug in along Darwin Ridge, an 8th Infantry Regiment platoon was at Boca House and the second 12th Regiment Company was in depth covering the approaches from Lafonia. He did not know where the third one was, except that it had not deployed to Goose Green. He mentioned that the 12th Regiment recruited from northern Argentina and the conscripts were suffering so badly from the weather that stand-to was not practised. Most were occupying two-man, chest-high trenches prepared by sappers from either 9th or 10th Engineer Companies; he did not know which. The settlement airstrip was defended by a company of Air Force cadets and Rh-202s. He described in some detail the defence of the schoolhouse by his company. In the event that Darwin Ridge could not be held, the defenders would filter west towards Boca House and, using the shelter of the beaches, would withdrew across the airfield to Goose Green. The same tactic was also to be used to outflank an attack. The strategy was to expose enemy advancing south down Darwin Ridge to a clear field of fire for the Rh-202s. When he mentioned that a Harrier had been shot down, this confirmed suspicions that Lieutenant Taylor had indeed been hit by ground fire. The sergeant had seen artillery in Stanley and drew a caricature of a 105mm Pack Howitzer in my notebook. He also drew the badges of rank and described the basic organisation of a rifle and support company, the smallest tactical unit being '*El equipo*' (team) of ten men. He described the M2 0.50 Browning as *El Gato*, the Cat. There was no mention of airborne forces at Goose Green.

Although air photographs had given an idea of enemy disposition around the Darwin peninsula, for the first time we were in possession of useful tactical intelligence. When the interpreter returned, the sergeant said to him, 'I didn't realise your friend spoke Spanish.' When I reminded the sergeant his looted clothing contravened the Geneva Conventions, I assured him I would do my best to mitigate any legal proceedings, he replied that the 25th Infantry Regiment Quartermaster issued most of the clothing. Captain Orpen-Smellie agreed to give the prisoner a meal and allow him to sleep.

Since the interrogation had lasted several hours and we were unable to return to San Carlos, Mr Alan Miller, the settlement manager, invited us into his large and well-appointed house. A generator rumbling in a shed supplied power for his modern conveniences that included a refrigerator, washing machine, dishwasher and a Kenwood mixer. I mentioned that his wife in the UK had provided an excellent plan of the settlement, which had proven useful during the planning of the landings. I knew him to be a councillor and a loyalist. Communications throughout the Falkland Islands was maintained using the Citizen Band network, which, as expected, the Argentinians monitored. A daily 'Call your Doctor' service with an Argentinian medical officer had been organised. He had allowed 3 Para the run of the house, which had resulted in the Operations Room and Intelligence Cell being in store rooms. The corridors of the outer house were used for sleeping. The kitchen was a focal point for hot water. Every morning, the wives of an elderly Somerset-born shepherd and a farmhand took a vat of porridge to the troops and, in the evening, soup. Mr Miller said there had been little interference from the Argentinians, except early in the occupation when Major Patricio Dowling, the military security police officer, visited Port San Carlos. Dowling was known to us. Of Irish extraction, reputedly anti-British because of his Irish Catholic background and apparently with red hair, he had led the detachment that had captured Corporal Yorke's Naval Party 8901 section at Estancia after they had evaded capture when Port Stanley fell. Dowling and several military police, presumably 181st Military Police Company, had arrived by helicopter to search for weapons and illegal radios and although Miller co-operated because he had nothing to hide, he had been pistol-whipped, pushed against a wall and guarded by a nervous and frightened conscript. When Combat Team *Guemes* arrived during mid-May, Miller had offered them the Community Hall. He had not experienced trouble from the troops, indeed when their rations failed to arrive, he had supplied food and water. Eventually, we spread our sleeping bags on the kitchen floor.

After stand-to breakfast on a bright morning the next day and knowing that 2 Para required the most recent intelligence, I asked the Raiding Squadron Port San Carlos Forward Operation Base if arrangements could be made to deliver my scribbled report to Brigade HQ at *Blue Beach*.

Visiting the prisoner, the sergeant told me he had a reasonable night and had just finished breakfast. He then mentioned, without prompting, that when I removed the photographs from his pocket, he believed he was going to be shot – such was the shock of capture and the power of suggestion. I took a couple of photographs of him in his uniform and equipment and explained that I would arrange for him to be transferred to a ship holding other prisoners. I thought it was the *Norland* and on board was our Flight-Sergeant. As we shook hands, little did I realise, and I don't suppose he did, that his picture would be flashed around the world's newspapers.

Chatting with the interpreter, he suggested many lives could be saved if there was a Psychological Operations (Psy Ops) programme. At Fanning Head, he had used a loudspeaker in a vain attempt to persuade the Argentinians to surrender but had been disappointed with the results. I was inclined to agree but wondered about the practicality of carting vast amounts of equipment around the Falklands. The other method would be to launch a radio programme broadcasting persuasive news and notices with a flavour of disinformation and misinformation. I was not then aware of our propaganda station *Radio de la Sud-Atlantique*.

About mid-morning, after 3 Para informed me a helicopter scheduled to take me back to San Carlos was due, I was walking to the landing site when there was an outbreak of heavy gunfire and mortars. Stood-to was called and in the Battalion Intelligence Cell, I learnt that a patrol sent out the previous evening had reported enemy and had asked for a mortar 'stonk'. When another patrol sought artillery and mortar support in the same area, it became clear both contacts were a 'blue on blue' (friendly fire) incident. I returned to San Carlos in time for another day of air raids. In one, three waves of aircraft attacking the ships at low level were chased by missiles and tracer, but HMS *Antelope* was struck by a bomb in the aft magazine; which fortunately failed to explode. As the air raids grew in intensity, sooner or later, the ground forces would surely be attacked.

When reports emerged that a pilot seen in San Carlos Water was being rescued and would be flown to San Carlos, I went to 'Busby', the San Carlos helicopter landing site, and met two soldiers, one of whom was wearing a Second World War airborne helmet devoid of any scrim. Assuming they were the escort for the pilot, I briefed them what to do when he arrived and then one of them said 'Can't help you, Staff. I am Captain Coulson.' Initially taken aback and embarrassed that I had not recognised the capable 2 Para

Intelligence Officer, we then had a long discussion on the latest Goose Green intelligence, in particular from the interrogation of the sergeant, until we were interrupted by Lieutenant-Colonel Jones in a hurry to return to 2 Para.

During the afternoon, Brigade HQ was ordered 'Prepare to move' and command and control was passed to Tactical HQ set up in a 9-foot-by-9-foot frame tent attached to a BV parked beside the line of gorse. After dark, 59 Independent Commando Field Squadron plant and diggers then began digging a large trench in a patch of gorse overlooking *Blue Beach*. The night was very dark and was disrupted by a wet wind whipping in from the Antarctic. By about 8pm, Tactical HQ had become stuffy with cigarette smoke and exhaust and soon after I went outside for some fresh air, there was a massive explosion from San Carlos Waters quickly followed by a white fireball, jets of flame and explosions as ammunition detonated, followed by rippling shock waves. What had caused the explosion? Argentinian frogmen? Torpedo? We soon found out. The bomb lodged in HMS *Antelope* had exploded. In the glare of the fires, vessels could be seen alongside the stricken ship and an initial report suggested 97 survivors until it became clear that a steward was the only naval fatality. When it then emerged that a two-man Royal Army Ordnance Corps Explosive Ordnance Disposal (EOD) team attached to 59 Independent Commando Field Squadron had been sent on board by HMS *Fearless,* this concerned Brigadier Thompson because EOD dealt with terrorist devices and safe disposal of conventional munitions. When he asked Major McDonald, who commanded the commando engineers, if it was normal for Army EOD to defuse aircraft bombs on board ships, MacDonald replied it was not normal. Of the EOD, one was killed and the other was very seriously wounded.

In the midst of the reports, the Raiding Squadron San Carlos Forward Operating Base reported that an attempt to extricate a

SAS patrol from near Port Howard had failed again. The patrol had been on West Falkland for about a month and were near their limit of endurance. A LCVP despatched to collect them had been forced to return after encountering worsening weather in Falklands Sound.

When a report then arrived from Port Howard that four camouflaged black-and-white LVTP-7s had been sighted heading toward the Darwin Peninsula, this prompted an urgent discussion. Television pictures of the Argentinian invasion had shown LVTP 7s being used by marine infantry. Large and menacing, they could carry twenty-five infantry, were amphibious and could negotiate swampy, soft ground and beaches with little trouble. But reports immediately after the invasion suggested that the LVTP-7 company had returned to Argentina, although there had been a Commander-in-Chief Fleet report in April that a detachment attempting to negotiate the track from Moody Brook to Estancia had become bogged down and considerable resources were needed to extract them. There had been a pre-D-Day report of an LVTP exiting the south bank of Brenton Lock, north of Darwin, and an observation post reporting a LVPT and troops on an island in the Loch. When Brigadier Thompson asked for my opinion, I advised that while the sighting of the LVTP-7s sailing from Port Howard was important, first, there had been no previous reports of an amphibious vehicle detachment at the settlement; secondly, the Argentinians did not control Falkland Sound; and, third, the sea was too rough and therefore I doubted the accuracy of the report. It was not the first time that we began to doubt some intelligence reports.

The next day at around 3am, it was raining. After command was returned to Brigade HQ Main, I followed Major Chester along a path slippery with rivulets of muddy water splashing down the hill to the Command Post, almost below ground in the pit excavated by the Royal Engineers. It was so dark that all I could see was the illuminated face of his watch. Inside, I met Tom Priestley who took me to the Intelligence Section BV and frame tent in a separate deep trench nearby. As always, our frame tent entrance was located at 3 o'clock to the Command Post entrance to help navigating between the two at night. Bob Birkett and his team had continued to work hard and since there was little enemy activity, all were wisely in their sleeping bags, except for the one marine on duty in the Command Post. Generally, Sid the driver slept in the cab, two squeezed into the BV troop compartment and the remainder were on camp beds in the tent with me and Captain Rowe near the entrance, in case we were required. While it was a squeeze, the numbers generated warmth. Our watches were set on Greenwich Mean Time, 4 hours behind local time. The daylight was short.

7

BREAKOUT

The quantity and variety of documentation captured at Port San Carlos was giving our very few Spanish interpreters/translators a problem, in particular translating terminology and technical terms and assessing accuracy because there was little 'co-lateral' for benchmarking. One interesting pamphlet that was found on almost all the prisoners was entitled 'You *Must* …' referring to behaviour when

CAPTURED BY THE ENEMY

1. **Only give your rank and name** and surrender arms and military equipment.
2. Try to escape.
3. Always wear uniform because if you are caught you could be regarded as a spy.
4. You are entitled to healthcare, food and adequate shelter.
5. Violence cannot be used to force you to divulge information.
6. You cannot be forced to do work that is unhealthy and dangerous and of a military character.
7. A receipt is required for any money and valuables taken from you.

8. You can exercise your right to complain to the Geneva Convention.

WITH PRISONERS

1. Observe faithfully the slogans that his superiors give him, as for the security measures to be adopted with the prisoner

2. Do not forget that your prisoner has the same obligations and rights that you have, including honor and religion.

3. Do not adopt measures that have not been previously clarified with your superiors. Remember that at the time of taking your prisoner, you could find yourself alone and not know what to do

Whoever drafted the document had not included that the Third Geneva Conventions also requires date of birth and regimental number. This is to help identify prisoners. In contrast, British Servicemen were issued with the F/Ident/189 British Forces Identity Card in which the holder was expected to enter, in accordance with Article 17 of Geneva (POW) Conventions 1947, Service number, rank, full name and date of birth and to give no other information. The document came in two parts and the captured serviceman had instructions to give the perforated Part Two to interrogators, so that next of kin could be informed, and 'Give no other information'.

Lieutenant-Colonel Jones had arrived at Brigade HQ on 23 May with his Intelligence Officer, Captain Alan Coulson, in the middle of a morning air raid, and was given confirmatory orders from Brigadier Thompson to raid Goose Green. Brigade Intelligence had watched the defence of the Goose Green stronghold grow from C Company, 25th Infantry Regiment on 2 April to the regimental-sized Task Force Mercedes and assessed its deployment thus:

Screen north of Darwin Ridge.
Recce Platoon

Main defence line Darwin Ridge to the ruins of Boca House.
A Company, 12th Regiment
Platoon, C Company, 8th Infantry Regiment at Boca House covering Salinas Beach.
Schoolhouse strongpoint
C Company, 25th Infantry Regiment
Military Air Base Condor
Two School of Military Aviation companies of cadets providing security and ground defence of the airfield.
Covering approaches from Lafonia.
C Company, 12th Regiment
Reserve.
HQ Company, 12th Regiment
Army and Air Force Artillery.
A Battery, 4th Airborne Artillery. Two Pack Howitzers were being ferried to Goose Green on the Coastguard cutter *Rio Iguazú* when it was attacked in Choiseul Sound by two Sea Harriers on 22 May and one gun was damaged beyond repair. The remaining two arrived from Stanley by helicopter. This left three 105mm at Goose Green.

Two 601 Army Air Defence Group – Two 35mm Oerlikons on the promontory south of the settlement near the godowns.

Six Air Force Rh-202 20mm cannon defending Goose Green Military Air Base.

Engineers
9th Engineer Company had laid minefields covering Salinas Beach, the north end of the airfield, on both sides of the inlet north of the Schoolhouse and between Middle Hill and Coronation Ridge.

By 16 May, intelligence had suggested that at Goose Green 12th Infantry Regiment numbered 382 all ranks, which equated to two rifle companies. Interrogation of a prisoner a week later revealed:

A and C Companies – 130 all ranks each.

Service Company – 120 men.

Command Company – 70 all ranks. Mortar Section had five mortars and Anti-Tank Section had three 88mm Instalaza. There was also a Reconnaissance Section.

The troops were dug in positions protected by minefields.

The missing company, B Company, was later identified to be part of the Strategic Reserve as Combat Team *Solari*. The location of the 4th Airborne Artillery Group had been confusing. On 19 May, intelligence had suggested that it had a presence at Port Howard, or possibly Fox Bay.

The following day, a fuel and ammunition return 'strongly' indicated 105mm howitzers at Goose Green and also evidence of the Group at Fox Bay. Two days later, the PNA Cutter 83 *Rio Iguazu* carrying two Pack Howitzers and other supplies and was forced to beach in Choiseul Sound after being attacked by a Sea Harrier. One gun was recovered. Two more were flown to Goose Green by helicopter. On the 24th, Signals Intelligence indicated that 4th Artillery Group was present at Fox Bay and Port Howard. It was very confusing.

The dawn on 24 May revealed the bright sun rising from the east throwing shadows across the surrounding hills around San Carlos Water – air raid weather. Military logic suggested the Argentinians had forward air controllers and observation posts overlooking the San Carlos Water beachhead watching troops light their cookers for that vital first cup of tea, improve defensive positions and place sandbags or cloth over linked ammunition belts to prevent them glistening in the sun. Blue exhaust smoke curled lazily into the fresh air as BV engines and generators were started to freshen weary radios. Offshore, the grey hulls of the warships contrasted with the dark water and surrounding green hills. The smouldering HMS *Antelope* sent a white beacon high into the blue sky.

Sure enough at about 8.30am, ships hooted, whistles blew and 'Air Raid Red!' was shouted. Positions were manned and then silent expectancy descended. No birds swooped or sang and the wind seemed to take a breath. The roar of a Rapier missile blasting overhead broke the brittle silence and as it streaked toward the valley of the Head of the Bay Brook, we tracked the glare of the exhaust and there they were – four Air Force A-4 Skyhawks in line astern skipping low and fast. It was the first of six raids conducted by the Air Force. Another Rapier streaked out and we watched as guns and missile launchers of the nearest ships swung toward the fast-approaching threat. The slow thud-thud-thud of Bofors multiplied and as the crescendo mounted, the Skyhawks reappeared from behind a low hill, jinking and jiving to confuse the missiles operators and gunners, seeming to target the *Sir Galahad* and *Sir Lancelot* in Bonners Bay in front of us. As three marble columns erupted around the two ships, there was a distant clang and a rusty puff. The Skyhawks then gracefully rose and, banking to port, one – two – three – four, they swept over Ajax Bay and skipped over Sussex Mountains. The firing faded away until once again all was silent. About an hour later, I was standing on the trench lip when an explosion finally broke the back of HMS *Antelope* and she slowly sank, her bows and stern the last to disappear beneath the waves, as did the white beacon. Both LSLs were abandoned until a bomb disposal team checked them out for enemy ordnance.

The All Clear did not for last for long. As another Rapier missile soared toward the valley of Head of the Bay, I jumped onto the trench parapet and saw the distinctive brown and green pattern of three Air Force Mirages streaking low towards San Carlos Water and watched as *Fearless* disappeared into a mass of white slivers spreading over a large area, out of which darted an aircraft chased by a missile, the wings swaying from side to side. As the spray crumpled, the workmanlike lines of the LPD emerged without tell-tale smoke or flames. Incredibly another flight of four aircraft burst from the valley and along San Carlos Waters. Surely this was madness, utter suicide, flying into an anchorage of alert ships already angered by the destruction of HMS *Antelope*? The bay became a network of dazzling glowing flies arching toward the aircraft. Yet more ground-hogging dots magnified into another flight of Mirages, one already trailing black smoke, burst from the chaos and headed towards us. GPMGs were quickly repositioned and we scrambled into trenches as a missile from a ship streaked over Brigade HQ and smacked into the hillside behind and the parapet lips of our trenches suddenly leapt into life as naval gunners tracked the jinking aircraft. We dived for cover – under fire from our side! Other Mirages danced toward San Carlos Paddock, another one trailing black smoke and chased by a missile that agonisingly gained on it – oh so slowly. A blossom of black-and-red smoke mushroomed over the settlement and then another. No parachutes, no large lumps of metal and wreckage falling out of the blue sky, nothing except instantaneous cheering from our trenches, our grandstand. The slow drumming of the Bofors ceased and silence again drifted over San Carlos Water.

The courage of the Argentinian Air Force and Navy pilots operating at their maximum range against a force with modern missile systems was never in doubt. Attacks were pressed with vigour but their inexperience of low level attacks led to bombs failing to detonate. Rumour abounded that our Combat Air Patrol screen defence consisted of two Sea Harriers at any one time and their nearest reinforcement was 30 minutes flying time to the east, out of Exocet range.

When I was informed that *Fearless* was scheduled to leave San Carlos Water to collect Major-General Moore and his HQ Land Forces Falkland Islands, which meant that Intelligence Section 'A' ashore would lose our primary intelligence source until she returned, I hitched a Rigid Raider lift to *Fearless* to develop a contingency plan with Neil Smith. We passed the doomed LSL *Sir Galahad* riding at anchor. Ashore we were spectators but on board *Fearless*, the almost constant Action Stations meant that the ship was tense. In the Gun Room, Neil mentioned that Captain Larken had posted himself in the Gun Direction Platform and was giving running commentaries of the raids, as though it were a cricket match and rumours were circulating that he had persuaded other captains to stay. To my surprise, I found that our Flight-Sergeant was on board; I thought he was on *Norland* interrogating the Combat Team *Guemes* Prisoners of War. However, when he had returned to *Fearless* with prisoner information for the Intelligence Section 'B', he was walking past the Electronic Warfare Office on his way to the Amphibious Operations Room and when he had heard a pilot instruct over his radio '*Vamos a* Fearless! *Vamos a* Fearless! (Go for *Fearless!*), he translated the warning to the Bridge, which gave the ship time to react. He was then 'kidnapped' to translate the intercepted conversations of the pilots. I sought out a naval officer and when I suggested the Flight-Sergeant was required ashore and he should not really have been reassigned without the permission of Brigade HQ, unfortunately, the debate became a little agitated and ended with the officer saying, 'Anyway, I believe the ships should sail and the ground forces should defend themselves.' I banked the comment as one from someone experiencing an unusual situation. I returned to the Tank Deck to hitch a lift and found it filled with sailors from *Antelope*. A radio operator told me he had heard the clang as the bomb hit and when the two bomb disposal sergeants had arrived on board, everyone was assembled on the Flight Deck. After the bomb exploded, damage control parties had tried without success to shore up the damage and when 'Abandon ship!' was ordered, *Fearless* LCUs had taken off survivors. He was expecting survivors' leave. On returning to Brigade HQ, I recommended to Captain Rowe that our Flight-Sergeant be brought ashore as quickly as possible because we needed information on Goose Green from our prisoners.

While the failure or unwillingness of Army Group Falklands to counterattack the landings was significant, in his Intelligence Summary No. 15 dated 24 May, Brigadier-General Daher believed the British needed to solve the threat from Task Force Mercedes before breaking out towards Port Stanley. He suggested that an infantry company could block the approaches from the south or destabilise the threat with an attack by at least an infantry battle group. Other options he believed open to the British included an advance to Fitzroy on the south coast and attacking Stanley through Pony Pass or landing at Teal Inlet or on San Louis Peninsula, north of Stanley. While the Argentinians had a decent air assault capability, so far there was no evidence of them diverting from the strategy of remaining in the strongholds of Port Stanley, Goose Green and Port Howard/Fox Bay and therefore San Carlos Water was safe from counterattack from Goose Green and there was no need to disturb Task Force Mercedes.

The *Atlantic Conveyor*, a merchant ship taken up from trade, was eagerly awaited by 3 Commando Brigade because its reinforcement of 4 CH-47 Chinooks, 6 Wessex helicopters and Lynx to add to the 11 Sea Kings and 5 Wessex already deployed would increase the helicopter capability to shift men, guns and stores. At present, only 4 of the Sea Kings were equipped to fly at night. The intelligence assessment was that if Army Group Falklands identified British interest in Mount Kent, 601 Combat Aviation Battalion had the capability to deliver a useful heli-borne *coup de main*.

25 May was eventful. During the day, the Argentinians circulated a threat assessment suggesting the British would break out of the

San Carlos beachhead, attack Goose Green and use the settlement to advance toward Fitzroy. The seizure of Mount Kent was probable. Amphibious landings were expected at Fitzroy and on the western coast of the San Louis Peninsula. An advance from the beachhead to Teal Inlet was not expected.

At San Carlos, there were more reports of shot-down Argentinian aircrew in several settlements and a curious report of wreckage of a British Sea King found on Tierra del Fuego in Chile. During the night, a SBS patrol found Port Salvador to be empty of enemy and thus Brigadier Thompson could use Teal Inlet to support his advance. A major initiative was to seize Mount Kent as the first step to invest Stanley and when a SAS recce patrol flown to the feature reported it to be unoccupied, this was significant intelligence because Mount Kent dominated the approaches to Port Stanley. In his Orders given on 13 May, Brigadier Thompson had said that if an opportunity arose to advance toward Stanley, he would exploit it. He intended to reinforce the SAS with 42 Commando, a battery of guns and the rest of the SAS, but very wintry weather clagging the whole of East Falkland then prevented further helicopter operations. Nevertheless, the focus on Mount Kent led to the raid on Goose Green being dropped to a lower priority, much to the frustration of Lieutenant-Colonel Jones.

And then at about 6pm, while Brigadier Thompson was holding his regular operational meetings, reports began arriving at the Brigade Command Post indicating the *Atlantic Conveyor* had been sunk after being hit by an Exocet during the afternoon and the several helicopters on board could not be recovered. This was a serious blow. Fortunately, several Sea Harriers had previously been cross-decked to the two aircraft-carriers, a fact broadcast by the BBC World Service in yet another serious breach of operational security. The surviving Chinook that was flying when the missile struck achieved legendary status. HMS *Coventry* had also been sunk.

The sinking spoilt the plans of Brigadier Thompson and the next morning, he and his Staff reviewed the strategic situation and concluded that waiting for 5 Infantry Brigade was the best solution. He had just asked them to examine the feasibility of an overland advance to Port Stanley supported by helicopters when he was summoned to Ajax Bay to take a call from Northwood. Ignoring that Brigadier Thompson was the man on the spot, Admiral Fieldhouse instructed him to mount the Goose Green operation and suggested that more action was required all round. Thompson queried the order. Astonishingly, Fieldhouse advised that recces were not required for the Mount Kent operation and guns were not needed to attack Goose Green. Few who had passed the rigorous Staff College course could make such a ridiculous assessment without being challenged. The instruction also contravened Major-General Moore's 12 May Directive. Brigadier Thompson later said 'I was given a direct order to attack Goose Green, so I sent 2 Para against it.' The Darwin Peninsula and Goose Green had essentially become a self-inflicted prison camp with water on three sides.

Even though the Argentinians had a decent air assault capability, from the information gathered at Brigade Intelligence, there was no evidence that Army Group Falklands was diverting from the strategy of remaining in the strongholds of Port Stanley, Goose Green and Port Howard/Fox Bay. The conclusion was the San Carlos Water beachhead was safe from counterattack. While Task Force Mercedes at Goose Green posed the immediate threat, it had not sallied forth, not even a patrol.

Brigadier Thompson had no alternative but comply with the order and the following day instructed Lieutenant-Colonel Jones that he was to attack, not raid, Goose Green. He could not rely on the four Sea Kings equipped with night-flying capabilities because they were required to support the seizure of Mount Kent, which remained top priority. In relation to approaches to Goose Green, a night landing on Salinas Beach due west of Goose Green had been rejected because of navigational difficulties, and warships were needed to defend San Carlos Water. Marching the 15 miles to Goose Green was the only option. C (Patrol) Company observation posts on Sussex Mountain had been observing enemy activity as far south as Brenton Loch. Another report that a LVTP-7 and about sixty enemy had arrived at Cantera House, at the northern end of Brenton Loch, led to 12 Platoon, D Company, being sent to investigate. It was dropped by helicopter about 2 miles from the house and then took about 4 hours to reach it, such was the difficulties of crossing the pathless terrain. There was no sign of the enemy.

At HQ Army Group Falklands, Colonel Francisco Cervo included in his Intelligence Summary No. 16 dated 27 May:

On 26th May, intense movement of enemy helicopters over the area of Mount Cantera and Mount Usborne has been observed. The artillery fire itself on the area was not answered. Everything seems to indicate that the enemy is politically obliged to launch an offensive action of significance and that the chosen objective is Darwin. The arrival of the Infantry Brigade on board the *Queen Elizabeth* will provide sufficient means for this.

L Company, 42 Commando began to take over the position of 2 Para and Brigadier Thompson assigned a troop of three Light Guns from 8 Commando Battery (nicknamed 'Black Eight') and a detachment from 59 Independent Commando Field Squadron to the 2 Para battle group. Although there were several Army in Brigade HQ who knew the cross-country capabilities of the Scorpions and Scimitars of the Blues and Royals, he did not assign a Troop to 2 Para, even though the Brigade had exercised with a 16/5L squadron equipped with them in the summer of 1981. There was fear that if they bogged down, the distance from San Carlos could be too far for the Centurion tank Beach Armoured Recovery

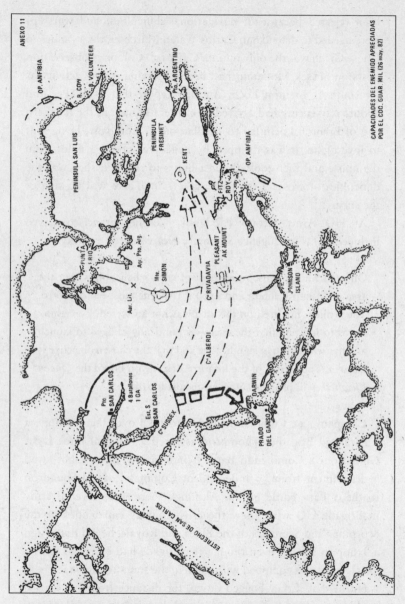

Early June. Argentinian intelligence assessment of British intentions.

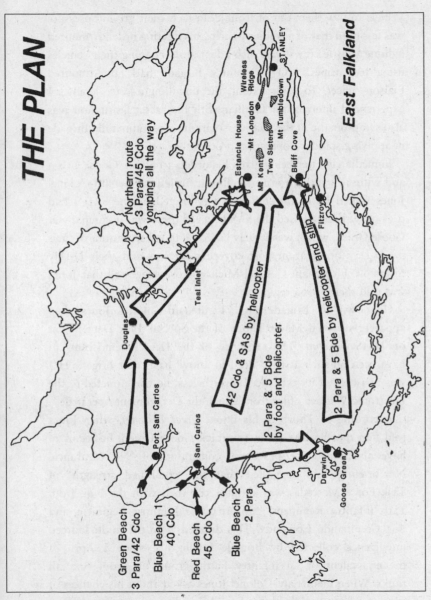

The HQ LFFI plan to assault Port Stanley.

Vehicle to tow them out of trouble. In fact, their ground pressure was less than that of a soldier wearing his fighting order. Armoured fighting vehicle crews were also adept at de-bogging their vehicles using tow ropes. HQ 5 Infantry Brigade had an Armoured Liaison officer. To some extent, the unwillingness to deploy an experienced interrogator familiar with the tactical situation was also symptomatic of the relative isolation of 3 Commando Brigade in applying standard operation procedures.

Immediately after being given his orders to attack Goose Green and without waiting for an Intelligence brief, Lieutenant-Colonel Jones visited HMS *Intrepid* and was briefed by the SAS. I had previously been advised the SAS believed there was a company at Goose Green, which was largely based on the observations of their pre-D-Day observation post covering Darwin and their D-Day diversion. Lieutenant-Colonel Michael Rose suggested that Jones was told there was a regiment.

Unknown to Brigade HQ, Lieutenant-Colonel Jones then apparently visited Major Thorp of the Special Task Detachment on HMS *Intrepid*. The existence of the Detachment seems to have been on such a strict 'need to know' basis that Brigade HQ was unaware of its existence, nevertheless, he was directed to the Electronic Warfare office from which the Detachment operated.

According to Thorp in his book *Secret Listener,* when Jones told him that he was about to attack Goose Green, he seems to have abandoned the peacetime constraints of 'No Clearance, No Briefing' and suggested that the 'combined strength' of Task Force Mercedes was about 1,500 men with the bulk from 12th Infantry Regiment, 2nd Airborne Infantry Regiment and 602 Commando Company. This differed from the multi-sourced intelligence collected by Brigade Intelligence since 2 April of the equivalent of an infantry battle group of about 800 all ranks. When Lieutenant-Colonel Jones asked about his chances of success, Thorp explained that Signals Intelligence was essentially a source available to Operational Intelligence, nevertheless, in giving his views on enemy tactics, strengths and weaknesses, he suggested that the engagement would be the equivalent of a Premier League football team competing against a Sunday pub league team.

Lieutenant Colonel Jones was in a hurry and when he returned to *Blue Beach One* in a Rigid Raider, Captain Rowe was waiting to give him the Brigade HQ intelligence update. A short way into the briefing, Jones suddenly interrupted and asked why he was saying that there were so many Argentines at Darwin and Goose Green when he had just been told that there was probably no more than a company there. Jones then left to find his helicopter, telling a captain who was with him to take the detail from Rowe and follow on. His use of the word 'company' interesting because that is not what Major Thorp had predicted.

The next day, the 27th, there was general relief that 3 Commando Brigade was breaking out of the San Carlos Water beachhead and was beginning its 65-mile cross-country advance toward Port Stanley. 45 Commando 'yomped' (your own marching pace) north-east to Douglas Settlement while 3 Para 'tabbed' (tactical approach to battle) towards Teal Inlet. Mountain and Arctic Warfare Cadre patrols checked out Teal Inlet. 42 Commando was waiting to reinforce the SAS seizure of Mount Kent and defending the beachhead was 40 Commando. Above the grey rain-sodden clouds, the Combat Air Patrol drove off two Mirages who dumped their bombs on Sussex Mountain. Unconfirmed reports of a Canberra being shot down turned out to be incorrect.

About midday, I was instructed to brief about fifty Battle Casualty Replacements (BCRs) who had recently arrived on the LSL *Sir Bedivere*. I joined a Rigid Raider and two officers at the San Carlos Forward Operating Base and we sped to *Red Beach* through a film of oil and debris from HMS *Antelope* drifting on the surface. Passing Sir *Galahad*, we noted the hole carved by an unexploded bomb and, on deck, vehicles peppered by cannon fire.

The Type-12 destroyer HMS *Plymouth* showed evidence of battle damage. After dropping the two officers at *Red Beach*, the Rigid Raider surfed across San Carlos Water to a small bay into which *Sir Bedivere* was tucked to afford some protection. As it drew alongside the rope ladder, I hoisted my 'emergency' pack onto my back, slung my SMG around my neck and was halfway up when the Klaxons sounded 'Air Raid Red Now! Take Cover! Air Raid Red Now! Take Cover!' Looking down, I saw only uninviting green water. Above me, a Royal Marine manning a twin-mounted GPMG mounted on the handrails opened fire and I was drenched by hot empty bullet cases peppering my face and spilling into the sleeves of my smock. Seeing a Mirage streaking low across the water, I scrambled up the ladder, ducked beneath the machine-gun and flinging myself inside the ship, tripped over someone lying on the floor. Then there was a burst of cheering when someone said that an aircraft had crashed into the sea near *Fearless* and the pilot had ejected into the water.

Reporting to the Ship's Warrant Officer, I was taken to the Wardroom where the BCRs were gathered. They had received little news since the landings and so I changed my plan of giving an intelligence brief to instead taking questions and answers. Air raids are unsettling and unnerving and no sooner had I finished when another air raid warning triggered the stampede to Action Stations. On Stand Down, I accepted an invitation to the SNCOs' Mess, however, my request for a shower was not possible because the ship was on water rationing. Another frantic Klaxon, another burst of adrenalin and a pretence to be calm. This was seriously not funny. I had been comfortable tucked into the close confines of *Fearless* but did not like the openness of the LSL; two of them had already been abandoned after being hit by bombs. Nevertheless, the evening meal was served and as I was given a plate brimming with a Sunday roast beef cooked by Chinese chefs, there was 'Air Raid Red! Air Raid Red! Take Cover! Take Cover!' Determined not be inconvenienced by another air raid, I searched for a safe spot and squatted underneath a table eating the best meal since D-Day. The All Clear then sounded. My visit over, I bade farewell in the knowledge that the LSL was leaving San Carlos Water that night. I was halfway down the rope ladder to a Rigid Raider when a Royal Engineer captain asked if I could take a box of empty rifle magazines to 11 Field Squadron RE who were ashore – somewhere! 'Gladly,' I replied, but as he lowered it, its clips caught on the ladder, the lid sprang open and I was again showered, not by hot bullet cases, but by empty rifle magazines, some of which tumbled into the water. 'Never mind,' he said, 'plenty more where they came from.'

The Rigid Raider raced to *Red Beach* to collect two officers urgently required at San Carlos but as we moored alongside the jetty, there was yet another Air Raid Red warning. As the organised chaos of *Red Beach* bubbled, I sat near a sandbagged bunker and noted that everyone was searching the evening skies for the aircraft but none appeared. A party digging weapon pits on the flank of a hill was oblivious to the threat. While I was waiting I met Marine Salmon who had been drafted from the Intelligence Section in 1981; he was a survivor of a minesweeper that had capsized in the North Sea several years before.

The sun was setting as the Rigid Raider softly crunched onto the San Carlos Forward Operating Base. Walking up the hill to the Intelligence Section, I learnt that the pilot of the 'splashed' aircraft, a Skyhawk, had ejected into the sea near *Fearless* and when a Rigid Raider was despatched to rescue him, a crewman drew a large knife to cut him from the entanglements of his parachute. Believing he was about to be stabbed, the pilot reached underneath the waters, hurled his knife into the boat and raised his hands. The crew pulled the pilot into their boat and finding he had injuries, took him to *Fearless* for immediate treatment where he became the subject of fascination when a charismatic Royal Navy surgeon invited relays of guests into the Sick Bay to view their first live Argentinian. The pilot was the first airman flying from mainland bases to be captured and after treatment in the Sick Bay, he was transferred to the Field Hospital at Ajax Bay where he was interrogated by my colleague 'Roo' Rencher. He was repatriated to Argentina where he briefed fellow pilots on his experience of attacking 'Bomb Alley'. Apparently he had been intercepted by the Combat Air Patrol five times.

I had first met Staff Sergeant Robin Rencher when he arrived during a counter-intelligence operation in West Germany in 1973 and I was asked to mentor him. Nicknamed 'Roo', he had emigrated to Australia with his family in the 1950s and after enlisting into the Australian Army, had fought in the Vietnam War and had been at the Battle of Long Tan in 1966. He was wounded in another action and then transferred initially to the Australian Intelligence Corps and then to the Intelligence Corps. He was currently supporting the SAS squadron tasked to raid mainland air bases. The crashed Sea King on Tierra del Fuego was an aborted SAS mission. Its crew and a SAS detachment managed to reach safety in Chile.

8

THE BATTLE OF GOOSE GREEN

When Brigadier-General Parada made another attempt to reach Goose Green by helicopter, the duty Air Force flight commander refused to accept his orders because they had not been authorised by Air Headquarters. Trapped by factional bureaucracy, he signalled Lieutenant-Colonel Piaggi:

> Task Force Mercedes will reorganize its defensive positions and will execute harassing fire against the most advanced enemy effectives, starting from this moment, in the assigned zone, to deny access to the isthmus of Darwin and contribute its fire to the development of the principal operation. The operation will consist of preparing positions around Darwin of an echelon defending the first line and deploying a screen of combat and recce patrols supporting the main operation with harassing fire against Bodie Peak-Cantera Mount-Mount Usborne.

By the morning of 27 May, 2 Para were dispersed among the buildings of a farmstead known as Camilla Creek House about 4 miles north of Goose Green. When the Signals Platoon tuned into the 10am BBC World Service news and the newsreader read,

'A parachute battalion is poised and ready to assault Darwin and Goose Green', there was stunned silence at the enormity of yet another apparent breach of operational security. The comment apparently originated from a member of the Cabinet being careless in a London club. For 2 Para, there were consequences. Lieutenant-Colonel Jones ordered his Battalion to disperse against air attack, which then made co-ordination during the day difficult. Brigade HQ became concerned that if Argentinian intelligence assessed that the Commando Brigade was breaking out in two directions, they would have to redouble their monitoring for indications of a counterattack.

In his Intelligence Summary No. 16, Brigadier-General Daher, the Argentinian Chief of Staff, mentions a breach of security and while he does not expand on the disclosure, he believed that it could be disinformation because no one in their right mind would broadcast an attack. Indeed, he suggests that if the British were being 'obliged' to attack Darwin, the arrival of the 5 Infantry Brigade on the *Queen Elizabeth II* would provide sufficient troops. He speculates that the ship might not be permitted to enter San Carlos Water because it was an icon and therefore troops would be cross-decked to ships east of the Falklands. While he believed the decisive battle would be fought at Stanley, he acknowledged that since the British Task Force had an amphibious capability, it retained the initiative for an assault at a place and time of its choosing.

Lieutenant-Colonel Jones wanted to issue his Orders at 11am, however the message did not reach some of his officers and so it was cancelled. A clash between two C (Patrol) Company patrols and an Argentinian patrol investigating the BBC report then induced further delay. At about midday, three RAF Harriers arrived to support the Battalion, however, forward air control was not available and not only did the bombs miss enemy positions, one aircraft was shot down. The pilot was later rescued. Patrol Company then ambushed a blue civilian Land Rover near Burntside House and captured an officer and three soldiers from the 12th Infantry Regiment Recce Platoon. The absence of an interrogator meant the Battalion was forced to rely on an interpreter inexperienced in interrogation. From these events and other intelligence being analysed at Brigade HQ, it was clear that Task Force Mercedes was alert to the threat from the north.

The delays meant Lieutenant-Colonel Jones was unable to give his Orders until mid afternoon, which placed him under considerable pressure because the company, platoon and section commanders needed time to brief their units. Captain Coulson, the Battalion Intelligence Officer, began by describing the enemy situation that Goose Green was defended by 12 Infantry Regiment with a minimum of three companies supported by three guns and minefields. Using a list of nineteen points, he describe the defence from the general area of Burntside House south to Goose Green. These mainly focused on two companies astride the peninsula to the north of Darwin and a company to the west of Darwin below Darwin Hill. Goose Green School was a platoon position.. The picture south of Darwin to Goose Green was less clear. But time was short and when Coulson came under pressure from Lieutenant-Colonel Jones, he resorted to rattling through the brief so quickly that taking notes was difficult.

Lieutenant-Colonel Jones essentially planned a six-phase night-and-day silent and noisy attack and 6,500 yards advance with the aim of capturing Darwin and Goose by first light next day. Nine hours were allowed for battle preparation and the move to the Start Line and 4 hours for the attack. Jones concluded his Orders, 'All previous evidence suggests that if the enemy is hit hard, he will crumble.' Quite how he reached this decision is unclear. There was no intelligence or evidence to support this as the fight that

Combat Team *Guemes* put up at Port San Carlos on 21 May rather suggested the opposite. Indeed, a 4-hour advance to contact over broken ground against a regiment supported by artillery seems optimistic.

Persistent suspicions that enemy observation posts were overlooking San Carlos Water bore fruit during the day when a gunner with an artillery Forward Observation Officer detachment on a 'shovel' toilet patrol encountered an Argentinian Marine Corps officer hiding behind some rocks. The prisoner was immediately sent to the Forward Interrogation Team at *Red Beach* where it emerged he had arrived with the Amphibious Support Force. When Brigadier-General Daher implemented Plan *Cameleon* to neutralise air defence thought to be north of Mount Usborne, he had volunteered when the Marine Corps was asked to supply a patrol. Shortly after dawn on 23 May, he and ten marines were dropped by helicopter at Chata Hill and lay up for the rest of the day. The next night, the patrol moved east and on reaching Bombilla Hill, spent another fruitless day of observing. The patrol then set off for the high ground of Cerro Montevideo, about 5 miles east of Port San Carlos, but was caught in the open crossing a stream by a Harrier and forced to find a hide. When a recce patrol led by a sergeant reported that he had seen British helicopters with underslung loads, the officer dispersed his patrol around Mount Verde overlooking the beachhead, but was captured while trying to infiltrate British positions. On the same day, two stragglers from the 'Fanning Head Mob' were also captured.

During the afternoon, I was flown to 3 Para Rear at Port San Carlos to interview a senior Falklands policeman and member of the Executive who had turned up with information on Port Stanley. He was 'on the run' and had been living rough on Long Island in Berkeley Sound with several friends armed with weapons and ammunition cached by Naval Party 8901. When he said that a resistance movement had been formed but it was not yet sufficiently organised to tackle the Argentinians, I gently thanked him and mentioned the Commando Brigade had the situation under control. When I highlighted that our principal problem was lack of intelligence about Port Stanley and asked if he knew anyone who might be willing to be extracted and debriefed, he mentioned a former Royal Engineer. I suggested that he make contact and once everything was in place for an extraction, to use the code word 'Rubber Duck' through 3 Para for an extraction. This certainly seemed to please him and although I was a little concerned that I had made a brash offer, I was sure that the SBS would find a solution. He then used my map to locate a company of about fifty soldiers equipped with a 120mm mortar on Long Island, a two-man observation post on Mount Brisbane, north of Berkeley Sound, and said an A-109 helicopter had delivered five soldiers to a radar post north of Stanley. I later sent the information to the LFFI Intelligence Section. A few days later, 3 Para advised they had received 'Rubber Duck', but by then, the Argentinians had sealed Port Stanley.

As the sombre orange skies surrendered to dusk, an air raid warning was circulated. I was walking along the track to the Raiding Squadron Forward Operating Base in the sheep-shearing shed hoping to hitch a lift back to San Carlos when the tranquillity was shattered by the launch of Rapier missiles reverberating around the hills and the distinctive high-pitched scream of fast aircraft. Three crumps from the direction of *Red Beach* at Ajax Bay were followed by the crackle of small arms and heavy explosions. Meanwhile, the Raiding Squadron was ferrying 3 Para up the San Carlos River to the start point for their 'tab' to Teal Inlet, but mist rolled in and another chilly night beckoned. The duty corporal said he had several tasks, in particular, recovering a non-battle casualty to go back to

Port San Carlos, but radio contact with the boat had been lost. Therefore he could not commit another one until he could account for all his Rigid Raiders. Also, the Ro/Ro (roll-on/ roll-off) cargo ship *Elk* was due in San Carlos Water and every available craft was required to unload stores and equipment before daybreak. When he invited me to stay overnight with his detachment, the 3 Para chefs supplied me with a meal. Several hours later, while it was still dark, I was woken by the familiar Johnson outboard engine of a Rigid Raider coming alongside the jetty. Its coxswain reported he had spent some hours waiting for the casualty but when no one appeared and with thick sea mist rolling in, he had returned to base.

Drizzle came with 28 May's dawn. On board HMS *Intrepid*, the Special Task Detachment was alerted to the raid on Goose Green when an automatic frequency scanner intercepted voice transmissions from radios used by Task Force Mercedes. They were something of a surprise because the distance from the ship to the Darwin Peninsula was thought to be too far for the type of battlefield radios used by the Argentinians.

After another decent breakfast courtesy of 3 Para, I boarded a Rigid Raider with the *Sunday Times* correspondent John Shirley and a photographer, both attached to 45 Commando, and Captain David Nicholls, the Brigade Public Relations Officer, on their way to *Fearless* to file a press report about their second day's 'yomp'. When we were about halfway to the San Carlos Forward Operating Base and the ships trumpeted another air raid, the coxswain increased the speed of the Rigid Raider so that it was almost leaping from wave crest to wave crest in a thrilling ride until it crunched hard into a set. I was thrown on my back across the gunwale and sustained an injury that would aggravate me for years to come.

On returning to the Intelligence Section, I learnt that the crumps I had heard early the previous evening were bombs dropped by

Skyhawks attacking *Red Beach* and there had been fatalities. The Flight-Sergeant was interrogating the Marine Corps officer captured by 40 Commando and both spent several hours in a bunker sheltering from exploding ammunition. Fortunately, several bombs had failed to explode. But two were lodged in the ceiling of a room in the derelict refrigeration building identified as an interrogation centre. As the Commando Logistic Regiment recovered stores and supplies amid occasional explosions and the whine of shrapnel and bullets cracking into the darkness, it emerged that a considerable amount of ammunition and stores had been lost. In the second raid, two Skyhawks had pounced on 40 Commando around San Carlos and two members had been killed. Although warnings of the strikes had been given, few people had taken them seriously, after all, the Argentinians had not normally attacked at sunset. It seemed likely the targets had been selected from air photographic reconnaissance.

In the Command Post, I learnt that the 2 Para schedule had slipped and the A Company advance to contact on the left flank had been halted by heavy fire from Darwin Ridge. When Major Philip Neame, commanding D Company, offered to undermine the defence by attacking the 8th Infantry Regiment platoon at Boca House and use the beaches to outflank the defenders on Darwin Ridge, Lieutenant-Colonel Jones told him, 'Don't tell me how to run my battle.' The captured sergeant had said that if there was a necessity to withdraw from Darwin Ridge, the Boca House beaches would be used, leaving the Army and Air Force anti-aircraft guns to dominate the southern slopes of Darwin Ridge. When Major Hector Gullan, Brigadier Thompson's liaison officer with 2 Para, radioed 'Sunray's down', indicating that the Commanding Officer was out of action, Major Chris Keeble, the Battalion Second-in-Command, quickly assumed command. Leaving A Company below Darwin Ridge, he ordered B and D Companies to attack the enemy left flank. The 8th Infantry platoon position at Boca

House was overrun and as D Company headed across the airfield, B Company swung around to the south of Goose Green. As C (Patrol) Company passed through A Company and advanced down the southern slopes of Darwin Ridge toward the airstrip, it came under heavy fire. The 25th Infantry strongpoint at the Schoolhouse was also overrun. The interrogation of the sergeant had again proved accurate.

12 Platoon in D Company was advancing to Goose Green when a white cloth was seen being waved near the airstrip windsock. Believing that Argentinians wanted to surrender and in spite of being instructed to wait by Major Neame, Lieutenant Jim Barry, the Platoon Commander, approached the Argentinians with his radio operator, medic/runner and Corporal Paul Sullivan and his section, to take their surrender. But Argentinians in a nearby trench were less enthusiastic about surrendering and when there was a burst of machine-gun fire from Darwin Ridge, a firefight developed around the trenches during which Barry, Paul Sullivan and a lance-corporal were killed and a para wounded. Paul and I had been in the same section on a six-week jungle warfare course in Brunei. The newspapers inevitably made much of the 'White Flag' incident, however, both sides largely agreed that it was a tragic misunderstanding. More importantly, the incident showed a training weakness: when taking prisoners, prisoners should be instructed to approach.

During the day, two Air Force Pucarás and two Navy MB-339 Aermacchi were ordered to support Task Force Mercedes. Shortly after 4pm, one of the Aermacchi attacking D Company was shot down and its pilot was killed. The Company also shot down one of the Pucarás and captured the pilot.

During the morning, EC *Guemes* who had made it back to Stanley after 21 May and members of the 12th Infantry Regiment Command and Services Company based in Stanley were mobilised as reinforcements and delivered by 601 Combat

Aviation Battalion helicopters to a landing site about 2 miles south of Goose Green. However, only the advance party reached the perimeter during the night. During the late afternoon UH-1H Iroquois helicopters had just collected a second group of reinforcements based around Combat Team *Solari* B Company, 12th Infantry Regiment, and part of the Strategic Reserve, when the deployment was cancelled by Brigadier-General Parada.

When Argentinian intelligence concluded that Task Force Mercedes was facing defeat, Brigadier-General Menendez authorised Pedrozo and Piaggi to decide the best course of action. By the next morning, even though the Argentinian Army code of conduct prevented surrender unless 50 per cent of the force were casualties and 75 per cent of the ammunition had been spent, fortunately, humanity and common sense prevailed and Vice-Commodore Pedrozo surrendered.

The Argentinian Army National Day, usually a time for celebration, also fell on 29 May. From 790 Army and 202 Air Force that compromised Task Force Mercedes, 47 Army were killed, 98 were wounded and 100 were captured during the battle. From a total of about 880 committed, including the reinforcements, about 835 were captured.

Analysing the defeat in Intelligence Summary No. 17, Brigadier-General Daher believed 2 Para had led the advance until 10am when another battalion took over. His tactical analysis was that when the defence counterattacked, support weapons silenced the enemy. The enemy had a considerable number of light mortars, believed to be 60mm. When forming defensive positions, they mined the main approaches. Helicopters had been used to move enemy troops to the flanks and rear of the defence. The British had taken advantage of technology to fight in darkness. Weaknesses included not exposing infantry to risk, and relying on shelling before an attack may be less effective against positions that have overhead cover. The use of helicopters to move troops on the battlefield makes them vulnerable to ground fire. Not only was Task Force Mercedes short of weapons, within a short time after the San Carlos landings, its defensive perimeter had been extended north from 10 miles to 19 miles without additional troops and it had lost EC *Guemes* on D-Day.

The Battle of Goose Green was a hard-won victory. It was also controversial. 2 Para would later write in their Post Operation *Corporate* Report that:

> Throughout the campaign, intelligence and the passage of information was particularly poor ... at battalion level, very little accurate intelligence was received.

In the May 2018 edition of the periodical *The Oldie*, Robert Fox, the journalist embedded with 2 Para, peddled the notion that the Battalion had poor intelligence.

These comment are worth examining. While the Falklands was fought against an enemy about which little was initially known, years of accumulated intelligence practices developed over the decades were largely ignored. Intelligence sources included:

> Commander-in-Chief Fleet intelligence reports since early April.

> The Cable & Wireless telegrams to and from Argentina.

> The Argentinian sergeant. He had been at Goose Green since 2 April, knew the defence and contingency planning.

> Documentary Intelligence that included translations of several documents captured at Port San Carlos, which included the 12th Regiment radio net diagram and call signs and a chart describing the organisation of the enemy Command and Support Company. Media reports.

Lieutenant-Colonel Jones received a verbal intelligence brief at the Orders Group on 13 May and on the 23rd when he was tasked to raid Goose Green and was briefed by the SAS on their diversion on 21 May. However, from the evidence of his Orders, he knew he was facing a regiment. Major Thorp had apparently supplied him intelligence suggesting an enemy force of 1,500. Captain Rowe would have briefed on a force of about 800, which was the most accurate.

On the 26th, Jones received intelligence briefs from two sources, one of which, the Special Task Detachment, was significantly inaccurate. The intelligence that would have been provided by Captain Rowe of HQ 3 Commando Brigade had been constructed since early April, was substantial and, importantly, was multi-sourced, including Document and Prisoner Intelligence. If he was briefed on HMS *Intrepid* that there was a company at Goose Green, then that person was ill-informed. Indeed, the Special Task Detachment persisted in supplying inaccurate information by suggesting that 1,000 reinforcements were committed to the battle, giving about 2,500 all ranks taken prisoner. HQ LFFI Intelligence estimated the strength of Task Force Mercedes to be 1,007.

While it is acknowledged that the events on 27 May resulted in Lieutenant-Colonel Jones giving his Orders later than he had hoped, interrupting Captain Coulson's detailed briefing meant that commanders at all levels lacked intelligence. It is correct that the full defensive layout of Goose Green was not known. This was for several reasons, including poor weather that prevented air photographic reconnaissance and inadequate patrolling before and after the landings. 2 Para later wrote in its post-Falklands report:

The activities of the SAS were particularly frustrating. SAS operations both before Darwin/Goose Green and Wireless Ridge inhibited the Battalion's own patrolling activities and yet no proper debriefing of the SAS was ever made available to the Battalion.

Information acquired from the Argentinian sergeant captured at Port San Carlos proved to be reliable, as did the seven weeks of collation by the Brigade Intelligence Section. I held to the principle that intelligence is essentially advisory and commanders, at any level, take responsibility for accepting or rejecting it. It is a shame that those who reject it often blame the suppliers. The battle had shown that the average Argentinian conscript was prepared to fight. It also exposed the fractures within the Argentinian leadership. In any event, 2 Para had sent a very clear message to Argentina in a tough battle.

9

AFTER GOOSE GREEN

Early the next morning, I was informed that one of the two Pucará pilots shot down during the battle was being flown to San Carlos. Somewhat puzzled about why a pilot should be regarded as a priority over Army officers, given the breakout, I was walking to 'Buzzby' with Ivor Garcia and a Defence Troop Marine when we met 'Roo' Rencher, who resolved the puzzle. Although the wrecked Sea King found in Tierra del Fuego had been involved in a failed SAS insertion, the SAS were still planning to raid an Air Force base in Southern Argentina from which Super Étendards equipped with Exocets were apparently flying and he had been instructed to interrogate air force prisoners and extract as much information as possible. I selected a corrugated hut near 'Buzzby' in which to interview prisoners.

The previous day, Ivor had re-joined us from Y (Electronic Warfare) Troop RM, I think gladly, after providing linguistic support since leaving Ascension Island. The Troop had landed after D-Day and as usual was reporting information to the Command Post where either the watchkeeper or a signaller transcribed it, if relevant, to the Intelligence Section. It was not clear to whom the Special Task Detachment was passing information; it might have been to Brigade HQ on *Fearless*, which was supported by

Neil Smith and part of the Intelligence Section until it landed. Since we were short of linguistic expertise, I had insisted that Ivor must return. Shortly before the Battle of Goose Green, the four heavily laden Land Rovers were making difficult progress along the track south to Darwin, which included the vehicles bogging down, when two marauding Mirages appeared. As one banked and settled down for a low-level strafing run, to the astonishment of the drivers, an order was apparently given to outrun the aircraft. Flight was impossible and as everyone bailed out, Ivor dived onto the soft peat – face-first and 'hit the only blinking stone for miles around costing me my dentures!' Thereafter he was blessed with a gaped-toothed piratical appearance. I warned Ivor that he would be crucial during interrogations and to expect prisoners to test our tact, diplomacy and patience.

When I returned to the Intelligence Section to collect some things, the 2 Para Intelligence Sergeant Colour-Sergeant Morrison and the Argentinian Air Force pilot were sitting on a grassy bank overlooking the Command Post. The pilot was not blindfolded and was wearing a silvery-grey flying suit and a short bomber jacket. Beside him was his white flying helmet with 'Condor' written across the front. Aged about twenty-five years, swarthy with dark, curly hair, he could have been described as disreputable, which was hardly surprising, given he was showing the combined shock of his ejection onto a battlefield in which soldiers were shooting at each other and anxiety after capture.

After he was blindfolded, I led the pilot into the hut and, after shaking hands with him, invited him to sit. With 'Roo' listening at the back of the hut and Ivor interpreting, I invited him to empty his pockets and turn them inside out. He placed some Argentinian money in notes, a marked map showing patrol routes and a bottle of pills and powders onto the ammunition box acting as a table. I then frisked him, removed his empty shoulder holster and silk blue neck scarf and noted that sewn onto his flying suit was the 3rd Attack Group arm badge. I knew his squadron was usually based at Air Force Base *Reconquista* in the Santa Fe region of northern Argentina. The twelve Pucarás had been assigned to Air Force Base Stanley in early April in its normal prime role of providing low-level air support. The squadron had been deployed to Military Air Base *Condor* at Goose Green. He believed that Flight-Lieutenant Taylor had been shot down by an Army 35mm Oerlikon. He claimed that a member of his squadron on an early morning patrol had stumbled upon our landings on 21 May; this was incorrect. His squadron had returned to Stanley in mid-May where he fell ill with 'flu and was grounded, which explained the medication. When he claimed the Air Force Officers Mess was in the LADE office, this did not match our intelligence that the office was very strongly believed to be the centre of Argentinian intelligence operations.

The previous afternoon, he had been briefed to act as wingman to another pilot tasked to attack mortar positions reported to be near Burntside House. During their low-level attack, ground fire badly damaged his aircraft and as he banked towards Port Stanley, it suffered terminal damage and he ejected shortly before the Pucará hit the ground. His parachute had hardly opened when he landed in 'No Mans' Land' and, winded and disoriented, was quickly captured. He believed his leader had been shot down. The pilot claimed that Pucarás were still being ferried to Air Force Base Stanley direct from Argentina and there were regular C-130 Hercules flights to and from Argentina. This snippet was depressing for it was widely believed that the Air Force Base Port Stanley had been put out of action by the bombing. The pilot said he was prepared to attack helicopters, a remark that later horrified a Royal Navy helicopter pilot claiming this was most unfair. Asked about napalm, he said he had not used the weapon but would use it against equipment and stores but not people.

The pilot was the first Argentinian seen by most at San Carlos and while not a picture of an Argentinian Air Force 'efficient fighting machine', he was a source of interest. I was fairly happy with the questioning and handed him over to 'Roo'. We compared notes after he finished and concluded we had learnt little new about Port Stanley except that the runway was still open. I then led the pilot to the San Carlos Forward Operating Base where after an air raid warning, a Rigid Raider took him to the *Sir Percivale*, which had been nominated as the prison ship.

The surrender of Task Force Mercedes meant that, initially, the Commando Logistic Regiment faced a major logistic problem very rarely, if ever, practised on exercises, of assembling, feeding, guarding, treating, providing shelter and evacuating about 1,000 prisoners to safe zones. To add to the problem the *Atlantic Conveyor*, which was carrying material for a Prisoner of War camp, was resting on the bottom of the South Atlantic. Brigade Intelligence also faced another rarely practised requirement of collecting Prisoner Intelligence and searching for items of Documentary and Technical Intelligence. Potentially, the prisoners were a goldmine of information and, ideally, needed to be interviewed while the shock of capture was evident. I did not know if the Ministry of Defence had imposed any restrictions on interrogation, however, in my view, the need for operational and strategic intelligence outweighed political and official proscriptions – provided we remained within the Laws of Armed Conflict and did not do anything silly.

At a meeting with a couple of Brigade Logistic Staff Officers about the issue, Captain Rowe agreed to go to Goose Green and help Captain Coulson select prisoners. When not clearing up the Goose Green battlefield, the prisoners were confined to the settlement sheep-shearing shed, which had 'PW' in white paint marked on its black roof. Fortunately, the suggestion of marching the prisoners to Ajax Bay was shelved. Agreement was reached that prisoners would be flown by helicopter to *Blue Beach* where interrogators would screen out those that were not required and transfer them to *Sir Percivale*. The proposal would be affected by higher-priority operational requirements, the weather and the availability of helicopters.

During the late afternoon, Vice-Commodore Pedrozo was flown to San Carlos in a 3 Commando Brigade Air Squadron Gazelle and was met with due formality by Brigadier Thompson. This, while polite and quaint, was contrary to the important principle of maintaining the shock of capture. He proved to be a ready conversationalist but parried questions intended to extract military information and consequently the interrogation became a battle of wits. Lieutenant-Colonel Piaggi, who was nicknamed 'Kojak' by his soldiers after the US TV detective, was welcomed by Captain Rowe. It soon became clear that he was upset that an airman with little military experience had commanded the Goose Green stronghold, was militarily inept and had not promoted the principle of a unified command. This was our first evidence of the rivalry between Air Force and Army. 3 Commando Brigade had a similar problem. A naval officer had committed 2 Para to the Battle of Goose Green, against the advice of the commander on the spot! That evening, Captain Rowe left for Goose Green, leaving me as acting Brigade Intelligence Officer.

In planning the interrogations of the prisoners, the Flight-Sergeant and I agreed that I would manage the Brigade Forward Interrogation Team while he remained at *Red Beach* managing the Joint Service Interrogation Unit. Our prime Essential Element of Intelligence target was Army Group Stanley. But in spite of the significant source that was now available, it took Brigade HQ some time to remember that prisoners were an important intelligence asset. A Defence Troop section commanded by Sergeant 'Buster' Brown providing guards and escorts had found a stone sheep pen suitable as a reception and holding area and had persuaded 'B' Echelon to give him a tent in which to hold prisoners. Placed in the middle of a paddock around which parts of Brigade HQ were nestled into gorse, logically, it became known as The Tent. The San Carlos Forward Operating Base had been warned it would receive requests to ferry prisoners between *Blue Beach One* and *Red Beach*. 40 Commando agreed to provide medical support. To preserve operational security, prisoners were to be blindfolded except when being interviewed. Unfortunately, the Forward Interrogation Team did not have access to any room and therefore prisoners were seen somewhere private, typically the settlement peat shed.

Early the next morning, 30 May, I was woken by someone frantically shaking me. 'The Boss is still at Goose Green,' said the voice, 'and Major-General Moore is coming ashore with his staff and the HQ 5 Infantry Brigade advance party. Arrange for a briefing map to be put up in the stable.' I struggled into my smock and grabbing my webbing and Sterling walked to the settlement stables in chilly yet glorious early morning sun, along a muddy path hardened by frost, passing fields cloaked in a white blanket. Air raid weather. Offshore, a LCU butted her way to *Blue Beach One*. I was relieved to find that the reliable Bob Birkett had arranged for a map to be erected and had found some chairs. He mentioned that he had ejected some officers who had been 'squatting'. While waiting, I learnt that Tactical HQ would be moving that morning to Teal Inlet.

Major-General Moore, who was wearing a Norwegian Army field cap, and Brigadier Wilson, who commanded 5 Infantry Brigade, strode up the path from the beach followed by a gaggle of officers, most with their trousers mysteriously wet up to the knees. I had the pleasure of renewing acquaintance with a RAF squadron-leader I had last seen in Norway during the winter. After everyone had found somewhere to perch, Major-General Moore explained that he would wear his cap in order to avoid patronising the Green Beret of the Commando Brigade and not offend the Red Beret heritage of 5 Infantry Brigade. Brigadier Thompson returned and after welcoming Major-General Moore and 5 Infantry Brigate then gave his views on the situation. Major Chester, the Brigade Major, then gave the Operations brief that the Commando Brigade was advancing toward Teal Inlet on the northern coast and that the logistic difficulties experienced during and after the landings had improved. The seizure of Mount Kent was crucial. Argentinian commanders had not yet reacted to their defeat at Goose Green. Brigadier Thompson welcomed 5 Infantry Brigade and gave his views on the situation. Major-General Moore concluded by ordering the two Brigade HQs to meet and plan the defeat of the enemy on the basis that 3 Commando Brigade would advance on the northern flank while 5 Infantry Brigade took the southern flank. For those of us who had been ashore for the seven days, this was welcome news.

As I watched the conference, I could not help but observe differences between the two brigades and was reminded of the historical meeting of the Eighth and First Armies in the North African Campaign of the Second World War. Was the Commando Brigade the successor of the 8th Army – scruffy, dirty, probably smelly, and yet proud we had achieved so much in difficult and unexpected circumstances? Were 5 Infantry Brigade the 'new boys' and keen to get on with the job? Formed in January 1982 as successor to 16 Parachute Brigade, its two parachute battalions transferred to the Commando Brigade had been replaced by 2nd Scots Guards and 1st Welsh Guards. Several intelligence reports had emerged that the Argentinians regarded the Guards Division as an elite because they guarded the monarchy. The third battalion, 1/7th (Duke of Edinburgh's)

Gurkha Rifles was already upset because the Argentines had claimed the Gurkha kukri was second rate compared to their machete. On mobilisation in early April, the Brigade had exercised for two weeks at the Sennybridge Training Area, including during a heatwave. It then boarded the *Queen Elizabeth II*, which sailed to South Georgia where the troops cross-decked onto *Canberra* for the final approach to San Carlos Water. This had resulted in the tease 'P&O cruises where Cunard refuses!' Concern was expressed that the Brigade was not acclimatised to the rigours of the hostile environment and South Atlantic winter weather.

Among those in the stable, I noticed a scruffy individual, whom I recognised to be the journalist Robert Fox, pushing himself forward to speak to Major-General Moore. Embedded with 2 Para at Goose Green, I noted the nervousness of a man recently exposed to unusual danger. He described the Argentinian surrender to be a matter of honour, which did not add up considering the tactical situation, and expressed some concern for the civilians at Port Stanley who could be held hostage; they were anyway. Fox was eventually introduced to Major-General Moore, who seemed a little impatient with the self-importance associated with most journalists, and told him that he had landed to take the political pressure off Brigadier Thompson and allow him to concentrate on advancing to Port Stanley. I was relieved by this statement, for the pressures imposed on Brigadier Thompson had been considerable. Every time we saw him go to HMS *Fearless* for another difficult satellite telephone conversation with Northwood 8,000 miles to the north, and with someone who seemed to have little concept of the Brigadier's responsibilities as the commander on the spot, we sympathised.

As the conference was breaking up, I met Major David Burrill, the HQ LFFI SO2 G2. I did not know him, nevertheless, he was the first Intelligence Corps officer I had seen since the autumn of

1981. He handed me some maps for distribution and a useful Technical Intelligence aide-memoire. I took him to the Intelligence Section where, over my first coffee of the day, he said that two Intelligence Corps officers and an Intelligence Section were supporting HQ LFFI at Northwood. They had flown to Ascension with Major-General Moore and his Land Forces headquarters and had then boarded a helicopter in which the pilot searched the north of the island for the *Queen Elizabeth II* when she was, in fact, at sea, 50 miles to the south. En route, General Moore and his Tactical HQ, which included Major Burrill and a small intelligence detachment, cross-decked to HMS *Antrim* for a fast dash to San Carlos Water.

I updated Major Burrill on the intelligence picture and highlighted the apparent unwillingness of Army Group Stanley to sally forth. In relation to the prisoners, I was finding it difficult to impress on the Brigade HQ that the administration of prisoners of war was a logistic problem, with intelligence dipping in and out to select prisoners for interrogation. Interrogations had already proven useful since we had landed. When I explained the Commando Brigade interrogation structure of two centres manned entirely by Other Ranks, he seemed content but acknowledged there was a shortage of interrogators and Spanish linguists. He mentioned that a second Joint Service Interrogation Unit had been assembled in the UK for detailed interrogation but it was not scheduled to be in theatre until third week of June.

During our meeting, Neil Smith and Intelligence 'B' landed from *Fearless,* thoroughly relieved to be ashore. For the first time in nine days, the Brigade Intelligence Section was a single unit. They had been in the same LCU as Major-General Moore and described how when the ramp splashed into water on the beach, apparently the Staff officers looked at the gap between the beach and the ramp with alarm. The coxswain then left his bridge and, with considerable sarcasm, offered piggybacks until Major-General Moore splashed ashore. His staff had no alternative but to follow. It explained the wet trousers. There was another option. Neil knew the coxswain and asked him to nudge the landing craft alongside the nearby jetty and thus the Intelligence Section landed dry-shod.

After Major Burrill returned to *Fearless,* Neil and I discussed our situation and agreed that the performance of the Intelligence Section had been quietly outstanding. Since leaving UK, it had grown from one lacking practical Operational Intelligence experience to one that was applying intelligence principles and providing Captain Rowe with good intelligence in time to be of use. We still lacked some basic intelligence on the Argentinians, such as tactics and habits, however, this should, we hoped, emerge from our guests formerly of Goose Green. Captain Rowe had grown into his role as the Brigade Intelligence Officer and was in regular contact with Brigadier Thompson. We agreed I would transfer my prime activities to managing the Brigade Forward Interrogation Team and then wandered around San Carlos looking for a suitable base. Not far from the house of the settlement manager, we found a farmyard with five rooms, but three were occupied by the Commando Brigade padres, one of whom mentioned he had passed the commando course carrying a crook, instead of a rifle. We set about persuading them, with frequent references to the Geneva Conventions, that our needs were greater than theirs and agreement was reached that we could use their rooms during the day. This left one stable for administration, searching and storing property and report-writing. We named the complex 'Hotel Galtieri'.

In the late afternoon, the heavy beat of a Sea King Commando helicopter was heard. It landed near Brigade HQ and when the naval loadmaster slid open the door, out tumbled three Argentinians, two armed with FAL rifles. Covering them with my Sterling, I ordered them to drop their weapons and lie on the ground and then a couple of Defence Troop, who happened to be nearby, took control of them. The loadmaster handed me a small bag but before I could ask where and how the prisoners had been captured, he gave a cheery wave, shut the door and the helicopter took off. Thus, we knew absolutely nothing about our guests. Defence Troop led them to a track near the house of the settlement manager and carried out a more detailed search. All were very wet, dirty and quivering with the shock of capture and cold. While 'Doc', a naval medic, checked the other two, I cleaned and dressed the wound of the third, who responded with plenty of *'Muchas gracias, señor'*. I needed him to trust me. They were then admitted to 'Hotel Galtieri'.

Two admitted to being from the School of Military Aviation and claimed that after arriving on the Falklands at the beginning of May, they had deployed with a radar beacon after the landings to a position in the hills overlooking San Carlos Water. Their first chief had been a civilian who had been inserted into the area before the Argentinian invasion, until he was replaced by a warrant officer. The detachment had operated a watch system of pairs working 4 hours on duty, 4 hours rest and security, and every afternoon at 2pm, a situation report was radioed to Argentina. The extent of the landings had been a surprise, indeed the warrant officer disappeared. Over the next week, their radio and beacon failed and when their rations ran out, the trio spent three days trying to surrender to British patrols without success until the helicopter had flown over their campsite and landed nearby. On learning about the beacon, I asked the Air Operations desk at Brigade HQ if the aircrew could supply a brief on the circumstances of the capture but this did not materialise. We would have liked to inspect the campsite for equipment and codes but without a grid reference, this was impossible. With similar radar detachments probably posted around the beachhead, it was no wonder the Argentinian air raids had been so accurate.

We were aware that a School of Military Aviation company numbering about 200 all ranks had arrived on the Falklands initially to provide security detachments at Air Base Force Stanley. Most had then been sent to Goose Green to defend the airfield and had quickly been overrun by 2 Para. I suspected that the prisoners could be associated with the lieutenant-commander captured by 40 Commando on 25 May. Although the questioning was generally successful, the circumstances under which it was carried out was disappointing because the padres demanded their quarters and so we were therefore compelled to continue our conversation outside in the dark, just like a conspiratorial meeting, in order impress on them that intelligence was more important than their sleep. The three airmen were later put in The Tent with the two senior officers from Goose Green and transferred to the Joint Service Interrogation Unit at Ajax Bay the next day.

In January 2014 one of three prisoners, Sergeant Oscar Doria Fernandez, was given two crosses by Pope Francis to place in an Argentinian and a British cemetery as a gesture of peace. He had contacted me about four years earlier to contribute to his book on his experiences during the war.

Meanwhile, 45 Commando reached Teal Inlet while 3 Para advanced to positions overlooking Smoko Mountain. In the middle of a firefight between the SAS and a 602 Commando Company platoon, 42 Commando managed to secure a foothold, at last, on Mount Kent. The weather had turned much colder, accompanied by sharp overnight frosts. San Carlos was muddy but at least the air raids were less frequent. During the day, Brigade HQ began its move to Teal Inlet. Command was transferred to Tactical HQ and Brigade HQ 'B' was ferried first by landing craft to Port San Carlos. As I watched the heavily overloaded Intelligence Section BV wobble down to the beach and onto the LCU, I was somewhat disappointed that I might not enter Stanley. On the profit side, the padres checked out so we converted the stables into a decent interrogation centre that included an office/accommodation and three interview 'rooms', one of which doubled as a detailed search area with tables and chairs, lights and blankets for blackout. Defence Troop could always be relied on to scrounge a few necessities. The Tent had been taken and so we transferred the holding area to the peat shed. The Royal Marines Police left one of their number, Marine John Smith, to help with the prisoners. Apparently, he had survived a freefall parachute jump when both parachutes failed to open fully and claimed that he had a photograph of him bouncing 10 feet when he hit Mother Earth. An expert scrounger, he successfully filled our parlour by exchanging souvenirs, such as helmets, with sailors on board the warships for rations. He had specific instructions to prevent journalists entering 'Hotel Galtieri'.

When the defence of the Brigade HQ and Signals Squadron (Rear) was re-organised after the departure of the main body and I was placed in command of the sector encompassing the settlement manager's property and the surrounding area, Sergeant 'Buster' Brown of Defence Troop and I surveyed the sector and allocated stand-to positions. B Echelon, Brigade HQ and Signals Squadron undertook to provide food and drink for the prisoners. We were also grateful for the kindness of Lieutenant Jackson, of the 3 Commando Brigade Air Squadron, who often dropped in with fresh and tinned food and ensured that neither we nor our guests ever went hungry.

Helicopters continued to fly small groups of prisoners to San Carlos, however, we rarely knew when they were *en route* until they arrived. Among the steady trickle was a signals lieutenant, unearthed by Ivor Garcia, who claimed he knew little of any tactical value and then admitted to being the only cypher officer at Goose Green. A strong-willed 12th Infantry company commander reinforced by a keen sense of national identity, he became more relaxed when he was persuaded that being difficult was largely self-defeating. He supplied useful information on the structure of an infantry company. Company commanders were first-lieutenants and each company consisted of infantry, recce, anti-tank and support sections. He commented that at Goose Green, he usually had enough time between British attacks to withdraw, regroup, evacuate casualties and resupply with ammunition before the next attack. Infantry sections were built around two five-strong fire teams equipped with a 7.62mm MAG machine-gun. At the conclusion of the questioning, the lieutenant scribbled on a piece of paper that he thought 1,250 troops had attacked Goose Green. I crossed out his figure and wrote '650'. He smiled ruefully.

During the mid-afternoon, a Wessex helicopter landed with Sergeant Bob Dilley, the 45 Commando Intelligence Sergeant, and five prisoners captured by the Mountain and Arctic Warfare Cadre at Top Malo House during the morning. Bob briefed us that the five, a captain, a lieutenant and three sergeants, were from 602 Commando Company and had been trapped in the House. One of the Cadre had said to one of them, 'Never in a house!' Although we still had several Goose Green prisoners, the new prisoners were Special Forces, most likely had been in Port Stanley recently and were in good health and were worth a conversation. Bob warned that the lieutenant, a big man and apparently the toughest, was vocal and had advised his colleagues to stick to number, rank and name. An examination of their property revealed nothing of significance. A tough confrontation was expected, after all, they were Special Forces. However, after about an hour, the lieutenant began to shake and I was sufficiently concerned to summon the 40 Commando Medical Officer, who pronounced him fit. When, within an hour or so, he again complained of heart palpitations, the Medical Officer and I agreed the last thing we wanted was a dead Argentinian in an interrogation centre and so he and the captain, who was resisting, were transferred to the peat shed. We loudly thanked the two officers for the co-operation.

By dark, we had dealt with all the other prisoners, except the three sergeants. We had not eaten since breakfast and neither had the sergeants and so we invited them to a supper of compo rations scrounged by Marine Smith. Before long we were drinking coffee with them, talking soldier to soldier. They relaxed and said their parent arms were infantry, armoured and medical, all were volunteers who had completed commando training and had been awarded their green berets ten years previously. We learnt it was the practice in the Argentinian Army for suitable individuals to be given commando training and then to be posted to conventional units until summoned for commando operations. 602 Commando Company had been assembled the day after the British landings and consisted of a headquarters and three platoons. It had been attached to HQ Special Forces for four days of briefings and retraining before being flown to Air Force Base Port Stanley by a C-130 Hercules. This piece of intelligence was not unexpected. The sergeants described how as they filed from the aircraft, it was loaded with casualties. After a week of familiarisation and patrolling in Port Stanley, the Commando deployed its three patrols in a tripwire screen roughly from Teal Inlet south to Mount Simon. The sergeants had been on Mount Usborne. We could account for two platoons. One had nearly prevented the SAS from occupying Mount Kent and the other had been trapped at Top Malo House. It seemed likely the other was to the south. The sergeants were critical of their officers and said they had been badly briefed and were ill-informed about the Falklands. They admitted the British were formidable and that their mission had been a complete disaster. One described the Argentinian Army organisation and added, after all, we knew it anyway. Not everything!

The interrogations resolved another query. The Special Task Detachment had suggested that 602 Commando Company had been at Goose Green but this now seemed most unlikely and we wondered if there had been a mistranslation of the Spanish word *'commando'* also meaning 'command'. Sometime after midnight, we finished the meal and the sergeants were escorted to the peat shed. The night was chilly but clear with a bright moon and frosty grass crackled underfoot. After fetching the captain and the lieutenant, I led the five to the Forward Operating Base where a Rigid Raider was waiting to take them to *Red Beach*. On the beach the Lieutenant asked if he could say a prayer before being shot. 'Don't be so bloody silly,' I replied, 'get into the boat and bugger off!' He had not impressed me.

The neutralisation of 602 Commando Company was important because the north to south tripwire had been breached and Army Group Stanley was now blind on their northern flank. The advance of 5 Infantry Brigade along the coastal, southern flank would be a distraction and diversion.

On 1 June, we again lost Ivor Garcia when he was transferred to the prison ship *Sir Percivale*. This left the Flight-Sergeant as the only interrogator at *Red Beach*. Ivor found about 400 prisoners, many from Goose Green, guarded by a weak guard force and virtually wandering all over the ship. He immediately reduced the planning of incidents by forming the prisoners into mixed squads of conventional forces and Special Forces and officers and other ranks and organised a programme to register them. An Argentinian naval officer helped and between them they unearthed several officers giving false details. Most of the prisoners were later transferred to the *Norland* for repatriation.

By 2 June, the management of the Goose Green prisoners became confusing when HQ LFFI instructed that all of them were to be flown direct to the prison camp at Ajax Bay. Some pilots had been directed to the *Sir Percivale*. At 'Hotel Galtieri', life had become a question of survival. We were short of almost everything, in particular rations, however, fortune favours the bloody-minded and Marine Smith was doing an excellent job. I decided to review the interrogation results with Major Burrill on *Fearless*. During the usual stimulating conversation with Major Southby-Tailyour at the San Carlos Forward Operating Base while waiting for the coxswains to finish breakfast, we debated the future of the Falkland Islands and agreed it would be bleak if there was opposition to modernisation; the absentee landlord feudalism of the 'camp' ranches needed to adopt modern agricultural techniques. Eventually, a Rigid Raider was ready. I went to the Gun Room expecting to find LFFI Intelligence but found Flight-Lieutenant White in solitary splendour. He said the Section had moved to the Ship's Intelligence Office alongside the Amphibious Operations Room. I gave him the insignia and scarf of the Pucará pilot and hoped it would cheer him up. And then, when I went below to the Chief's Mess for breakfast, the duty chef treated me like the Prodigal Son. As I sat down at a table, I heard 'Good morning, Nick' but was too involved with loading my spoon to notice. 'Good morning, Nick!' with a little more emphasis this time and when I looked around to see who was interrupting my feast, I was delighted to see four Intelligence Corps friends. It was good to have a chat with colleagues. They described the few weeks with Major-General Moore at his HQ in Northwood and seemed slightly bemused by the militarism of the ship, the constant Action Stations and the mind-shattering klaxon warning of air raids.

Breakfast and chat over, I went to the Amphibious Operations Room, now occupied by HQ LFFI staff, and met Captain Tolley, who told me not to worry about my unshaven and dishevelled appearance as it would remind HQ LFFI staff officers that we were at war. Major Burrill then arrived and I explained that the Commando Brigade had captured about 1,100 prisoners since landing. Since I was keen to retain a Commando Brigade Interrogation Team, we agreed that Bob Dilley and Ivor Garcia should screen prisoners at *Red Beach* and select those suitable for transfer to 'Hotel Galtieri'. He would arrange for HQ LFFI to take responsibility for the administration of prisoners on *Red Beach* and *Sir Percivale*. After a luxurious shower and a shave, too bad if the air raids came, I bade farewell to Flight-Lieutenant White; a year later he was killed when his aircraft crashed into the sea. When a Rigid Raider arrived, the coxswain mentioned he was short of fuel and asked if I had seen any 'loafing' jerrycans? Indeed I had and we were soon heading out into San Carlos Water fully fuelled.

I returned to 'Hotel Galtieri' in time for a mug of tea and then, to my utter amazement, the door opened and in walked a stocky Intelligence Corps sergeant. A shrewd and expert Spanish linguist, we had both been in Belize in 1980 during which he often stayed in my flat in Punta Gorda while involved on a sensitive project. With him was a RAF Regiment flight-lieutenant, who had seen service in the Indo-Pakistan War and with the Royal New Zealand Artillery in the Vietnam War. He spoke Spanish-American, which was good news, and had completed a three-day Tactical Questioning course, as opposed to the normal five days. He later wrote a book about his Falklands experiences entitled *Her Majesty's Interrogator*. Both had been involved with the South Georgia prisoners on the *Tidespring*. Their arrival meant that the prospects of handling the prisoners was considerably better than they had been in the morning. We just needed prisoners who could describe the defence of Stanley.

As dusk fell, a member of the Brigade HQ and Signals Squadron Rear Echelon, dug in near 'Hotel Galtieri', reported that he had intercepted a Citizens Band conversation between an Islander and an Argentinian official in Port Stanley. We listened as a person living in

Hill Cove on West Falkland reported to the official that two shepherds had found another Argentinian pilot with a broken leg and a badly damaged shoulder, sheltering in a derelict hut. He had been shot down three days earlier and was refusing to move in case he was betrayed and was insisting on Argentinian recovery. I asked Air Operations if there was any chance that the pilot could be rescued, without success. The priority was to support the advance to Port Stanley.

3 June was another miserable day with persistent freezing rain and a cold southerly wind. Soon after seven o'clock, prisoners were brought to 'Hotel Galtieri' from Goose Green, Captain David Charters and a warrant officer, both Intelligence Corps and HQ LFFI Intelligence, arrived with orders from Major Burrill that the three of us were to review prisoner problems being experienced at *Red Beach*. After the obligatory intellectual discussion with Major Southby-Tailyour while waiting for a Rigid Raider, we began our review.

Red Beach was the organised chaos of any logistics area and was crammed with equipment, boxes and crates, some of which were intact, others were spilling their contents onto the boggy grass and muddy road. Landing craft and Mexeflotes motorised rafts discharged their cargoes onto the beach or a concrete ramp. Helicopters rattled overhead with underslung loads while lorries and Land Rovers splashed along muddy tracks. Engineering plant tore at the earth, widening tracks and digging pits in which to store ammunition.

Part of the prison camp outside the derelict building had become a muddy barbed-wire compound with five leaky tents straining in the wind and a pile of discarded Argentinian uniforms on the ground. The search-and-holding area inside was warm and dry. We found Ivor Garcia sitting against a wall chatting to some prisoners, one of whom was a doctor. He said he was having all sorts of problems and that the Commando Logistic Regiment Provost Staff was hopelessly understaffed to manage the numbers, having lost one killed during the bombing of Ajax Bay. A GPMG was aimed at the door to deter a breakout and two unexploded bombs from the air raid were lodged in the ceiling of one of the rooms earmarked for the prisoners. Everyone tiptoed past the room. Medical Squadron and the Surgical Teams were using some of the accommodation originally allocated for prisoners to house the wounded. More room would be required when Port Stanley was assaulted. The worsening weather and threat of air raids ensured that every available person was seeking adequate cover. Rations and water for the prisoners were in short supply.

On a small hillock was the quiet, sorrowful cemetery of temporary graves, each marked by a simple inscribed cross, and a Union Flag. Seeing a group of Royal Marines on the beach, I instinctively wandered over to see them meeting a jackass penguin that stood about 2 feet offshore with oily muddy water gently lapping its webbed feet. It was nodding like some old man. It had been adopted and named 'Marine Galtieri'.

As I was waiting to hitch a lift to *Blue Beach One*, a launch from *Canberra* chugged to the dilapidated jetty and two women stepped from it, the hint of perfume wafted past me – the scent of femininity amongst the chaos of war. They were quickly surrounded by excited medical officers, so I assumed them to be doctors or nurses sent ashore to assess the wounded for transfer to the ship's Sick Bay. A rubber Gemini then arrived and we bounced over the wavelets and arrived at the San Carlos jetty just as a LCU was unloading a 2nd Scots Guards company, heavily laden with weapons, ammunition and packs. Since they were wearing helmets, I asked if an air raid warning was on and was told no. Suddenly out of the mass, I heard, 'Ah, Intelligence Corps. Hello!' I looked around to see a person introducing himself as the Officer Commanding 81 (5 Infantry Brigade) Intelligence Section. We had a brief chat and as he was whisked away by another officer, I undertook to visit him as soon as possible, circumstances permitting. Again, it was comforting to meet another member of my Corps.

When 5 Brigade was mobilised, its staff were briefed at Northwood and given a considerable quantity of basic intelligence that included Argentinian capabilities, recognition manuals and terrain information. But its primary source of operational information was the media and when formal situation reports did emerge, they were usually out of date, however HQ LFFI believed the Brigade had the latest information. Poor communications en route delayed signals.

When I returned to 'Hotel Galtieri', the Flight-Sergeant had been questioning the seven prisoners and had sent four to the peat shed holding centre to await transfer back to *Red Beach*. The remaining three were two artillery officers and an Air Force sergeant-major. With the Flight-Sergeant interpreting, I questioned the sergeant-major. Immaculately turned out with a small pack on his back and carrying a suitcase and a brief case, he was swarthy, moustachioed, and seemed perfectly at ease. He claimed he was a clerk and that his presence on the Falklands was a big mistake, particularly as he usually worked at Air Force Base Comodoro Rivadavia despatching troops to Stanley. He was checking the payload of a Hercules C-130 when its ramp shut and the aircraft took off. On landing at Stanley, he then helped administer the arrival and departure of aircraft and therefore he probably knew the identification of some units flown to the Falklands. The imposition of the Exclusion Zones meant that most flights had been flown at night. After a few days, he had been posted to Goose Green to manage the military post office. Prisoners who have worked in unit clerical offices and post rooms are of considerable value and since we were still piecing together the Task Forces Mercedes order of battle as a benchmark for Army Group Stanley, he was worthy of a more detailed chat. But when he became resistant, I inspected his briefcase for any levers and found two English-made dolls, two calculators and some personal letters and suggested that he had been looting, thereby contravening the Geneva Convention.

He insisted he had purchased them. I was certain he knew more and sent him to the Joint Service Interrogation Unit at *Red Beach*.

While the Flight-Sergeant took one of the artillery officers, a lieutenant, I took the other, a captain. The interpretation skills of the flight-lieutenant needed to be tested and so I briefed him that I required exact translation and he was not to engage in conversation. The captain was to focus on me. Little was known about him, although his rank probably meant he was the commander of the 4th Airborne Artillery Group sent to Goose Green. When brought into the 'interview room', he could hardly deny he was airborne; he was wearing his wings above the left hand top pocket of his jacket and a red beret. As the interview progressed, the flight-lieutenant began to indulge in conversation with the captain. In order to regain control of the interrogation, I dispensed with the flight-lieutenant and began a conversation with the captain in English and my limited Spanish, but to each question or statement, he replied, 'You are an English gentleman. You know I cannot answer that question'. Indeed I did and was about to conclude the interrogation and send him to the Joint Service Interrogation Unit when two Defence Troop marines asked if they could check the blackout of two ceiling windows. Since they did not have a ladder, they piled two chairs on top of each other, flicked a coin and the loser began to climb the precarious contraption. Inevitably, it collapsed burying the Royal Marine under the chairs. Unperturbed, the pair then used a rickety ladder they had found but it broke. I could hardly contain myself and neither could the captain. There is one technique known as the incompetent approach, the aim being to convince a confident prisoner that he is superior to the interrogator and will therefore make mistakes as he demonstrates his superiority. It is particularly useful with Special Forces. The demeanour of the captain noticeably relaxed as we watched the unintentional comedy and, over a mug of coffee, he became more amenable and admitted he was the battery commander. When I mentioned that British gunners had been impressed by the handling of the guns at Goose Green and that counter-battery fire had been difficult, he relaxed further. Significantly, he had no knowledge of the 2nd Airborne Regiment being at Goose Green. However, when he admitted he had visited Port Howard, this cleared up the several reports of airborne artillery unit at the settlement one day but not the next day. Before sending the two prisoners to *Red Beach*, the Flight-Sergeant and I agreed they were both worth another conversation. Since the Flight-lieutenant appeared reluctant to acknowledge expertise he did not have and the necessity for discipline in the interrogation room, he was better deployed with the Joint Service Interrogation Unit.

Meanwhile the war continued. The Commando Brigade was advancing toward Port Stanley. Mount Kent and Mount Challenger were firmly in the hands of 42 Commando. Army Group Stanley had not counterattacked from their Outer Defence Zone. The Commando Logistic Regiment was establishing the Brigade Maintenance Area at Teal Inlet and flying stores and equipment forward. On the southern flank, 5 Infantry Brigade was having all sorts of problems consolidating at Fitzroy. J Company, 42 Commando, which was mainly the former Naval Party 8901 and under temporary command of 2 Para in 5 Infantry Brigade, captured nine evaders from Goose Green in Laconia. All were evacuated to *Red Beach*. An Argentinian C-130 was shot down by the Combat Air Patrol. Persistent rumours abounded that naval officers did not approve of shooting down the regular Hercules to Port Stanley 'milk run' because the aircraft were unarmed. I thought it an affront to allow any enemy aircraft to fly to and from the mainland.

10

TEAL INLET

Early on 4 June, Captain Charters arrived at 'Hotel Galtieri' and said that Bob Dilley, an interpreter and I were to rejoin HQ 3 Commando Brigade at Teal Inlet and over the next three days were to identify an Argentinian officer ranked major or above willing to take surrender terms to Brigadier-General Menendez. I was a little confused about this plan as several such officers had been captured at Goose Green and grabbing a major from a unit defending the Outer Defence Zone was most unlikely. He also mentioned that the Essential Elements of Intelligence required by HQ LFFI included enemy dispositions, unit identifications and an assessment of morale of the Argentinian marines. I was to radio a daily report, including 'nothing to report', to HQ LFFI. The order essentially meant that the Brigade Forward Interrogation Team moved forward.

Soon after I had radioed Bob Dilley at *Red Beach*, the Brigade Air Squadron advised me a helicopter was due within the next 20 minutes, but as I was about to leave 'Hotel Galtieri', six RAF appeared commanded by a flight-sergeant, who identified them as Spanish linguists from Gibraltar. The resource was urgently needed but they were hopelessly ill-equipped for life under either the stars or canvas and so I sent them to reinforce our

Flight-Sergeant at the interrogation centre at Ajax Bay and help with the residue of the Goose Green prisoners as we anticipated more prisoners during the assault on Army Group Stanley. Since I needed to replace the flight-lieutenant, I asked the flight-sergeant to select one of his men to join me at Teal Inlet. As I waited at 'Busby', the cold rain was penetrating by the time a Gazelle settled on the grass. I had placed my kit on to the back seat when the pilot asked if I would sit in the back and watch for marauding Pucarás approaching from his rear blind spot and then he lifted the helicopter a few feet and, at low level, flew to Port San Carlos, and picked the track to Teal Inlet churned up by the Brigade HQ BVs. Hugging the low valley of the San Carlos River, we skipped over the moorland slopes, scattered flocks of sheep, and on reaching Teal Inlet, the pilot banked hard right and landed in a nose-up combat approach in a field near a small wood. Wishing the pilot good fortune, I climbed out into the bitterly cold wind and snow flurries hurtling in from the south and gave him the thumbs-up All Clear.

The Intelligence Section was tucked in the wood, alongside the Command Post, as usual. It was good to be back. Neil Smith said the drive from Port San Carlos had taken 16 hours and it had been beset with overloaded BVs bogging in the soft ground. When I reported to Captain Rowe in the Command Post and advised him of my orders, we agreed the initiative, while commendable, was far easier said than done. He then briefed me on the intelligence picture and said that Brigadier Thompson intended to assault the Outer Defence Zone on 6 June and had given his commanding officers their objectives:

3 Para – Mount Longdon.
45 Commando – Two Sisters.
42 Commando – Mount Harriet.

Since Brigade HQ was under orders to move, he suggested that I attach myself to the Royal Marines Police Troop located in one of the settlement sheep-shearing sheds. I knew most of them anyway and after a warm welcome, was shown to my 'room', an empty pen on the upper floor.

The once-tranquil settlement of Teal Inlet was now a busy port, airport and logistics centre called the Brigade Forward Maintenance Area. The Rear Area was *Red Beach* at Ajax Bay. A routine had developed that when a LSL arrived offshore, its consignment was transferred onto motorised Mexeflote that crunched onto the beach near the jetty. Eager Beaver forklifts then distributed the stores to collection points along a track.

Inevitably, some crates and boxes had broken open, however, there was no need to guard them as front line demands were top priority. During the day, a constant stream of helicopters flying to and from the east were directed by ground marshals to their consignments. The loadmaster leant out and dropped a hook on a rope to a soldier standing on or near the consignment who caught it and hooked it to the net. After jumping off, he signalled to the marshal that all was ready and then the helicopter took the strain, rose, and leaning forward flew to the hills to the east.

Evening meals from a field cookhouse were usually followed by a game of 'clag', a version of Nomination Whist, with the Royal Marines Police huddled around a candle or, less likely, a paraffin lamp.

The game is believed to have originated in the Royal Air Force during the Second World War as an acronym for 'Clouds Low, Aircraft Grounded', and was played by aircrews waiting for suitable flying weather. Letters from home were major tonics to morale, as they had been for centuries, and one day, I received three, admittedly three weeks old, and a Red Cross parcel containing confectionary, biscuits and a homemade fruit cake, which I shared with the Royal Marines Police.

When the BBC World Service blundered with yet another serious breach of operational security by announcing that 'Teal Inlet is HQ of the force attacking Stanley', Brigadier Thompson was furious. Argentinian intelligence had been focusing on 5 Infantry Brigade assembling at Goose Green for its advance to Stanley via Fitzroy, and yet the BBC were reporting activity to the north. The destruction of 602 Commando Company, poor weather and inability to fly air recce suggested they had lost sight of the Commando Brigade.

There was some uncertainty about the makeup of the Outer Defence Zone. We had lost the information disseminated by Commander-in-Chief Fleet, however the tactical gap was filled, to some extent, by Y (Electronic Warfare) Troop and the Special Task Detachment. It was about this time that the civilian engineer attached to the Troop wanted to conduct an operational field trial of his prototype jamming by attacking Army Group Falklands communications and sought the assistance of the Special Task Detachment for a linguist. However, in his book, *Secret Listener,* Major Thorp describes that he was unwilling 'to help some engineer play with his toys' by releasing a linguist and claims his unit was swamped by intercepted messages yet to be analysed. Thereafter whenever Y Troop, to whom he reported, asked for a linguist, he was disinclined to release any on the grounds that they worked a shift system and were catching up on lost sleep.

Although the Royal Artillery had been using CL-89 'Midge' surveillance drones since the 1970s and had deployed them with 94 Locating Regiment in West Germany, distrust about its robustness when operating in a harsh environment was a factor in not deploying them on Operation *Corporate.* However, 29 Commando Regiment was supported by the *Cymbeline* Mark 1 mortar location and area surveillance radar, fitted to helicopter-transportable two-wheel trailers. The reduction in intelligence surveillance and acquisition assets therefore meant that units were forced to scavenge for information, but not one prisoner was 'snatched' from the Outer Defence Zone and none were seized in patrol clashes. It therefore meant that the tactical questioning resource at unit level and interrogation at Brigade level was not being exploited. Royal Engineers played a key role in identifying minefields and other obstacles.

On the left flank, 3 Para reduced the 10-mile round-trip from their forward company at Estancia to Mount Longdon by establishing a patrol base near the Murrell Bridge about 2 miles south-west of their objective. This allowed D (Patrol) Company to spend more time investigating the objective but, on 4 June, the bridge was compromised and shelled. Two days later, a 601 Commando Company section forced two patrols that had met at the patrol base to withdraw. The Battalion then adopted a three-day patrol programme of one night approach, second night on reconnaissance and third night returning to base. The patrol base was checked during the evening of 8 June, but there was no sign of several items lost in the attack. A platoon scouting a position was detected by a RASIT ground surveillance radar on Mount Longdon.

In the centre, careful liaison between 45 and 42 Commandos prevented 'blue on blue' contacts. On 4/5 June, a Recce Troop patrol and a commando engineer section covered 12 miles in 16 hours plotting enemy positions and checking for mines; none were found. The next night, the Troop installed an observation post on Two Sisters, but within about 24 hours it was forced to withdraw during a clash with a 4th Infantry Regiment section and a detachment of Marine engineers exploiting mist and rain to lay mines. When the shooting stopped, a Marine engineer sergeant and a Royal Engineer commando sergeant agreed a local truce so that the enemy could recover their four dead. A fighting patrol crossing the open ground between Mount Kent and Mount Challenger forded the Murrell River; however, the defence of the enemy sector had been reinforced by 601 Commando Company and the National Gendarmerie and the patrol became involved in a tough battle. At risk of being cut off, it withdrew under accurate artillery fire.

On the right flank, 42 Commando had succeeded in gaining a firm foothold on the undefended peak of Mount Kent and suffered six days of freezing weather, the temperature dropping to minus 12 degrees Centigrade. When the Commando seized Mount Challenger and Mount Wall and outflanked the 4th Infantry Regiment, the Argentinians withdrew to Mount Harriet and counterattacked Mount Wall. In a patrol clash on 3 June, Recce Troop lost a laser rangefinder. Mount Wall was recaptured within 24 hours. The ground to the west and south of Mount Harriet was strongly suspected of being mined, and so it proved. A patrol checking a bridge south of the feature took 7 hours to evacuate a seriously wounded Royal Marine. The following night, a 59 Independent Commando Engineer Field Squadron troop and 42 Commando Assault Engineers cleared a path through the minefield south-east of Mount Harriet. A patrol near the Stanley–Fitzroy track ran into mines and while a casualty was being evacuated, the remainder infiltrated the western slopes of Mount Harriet but were spotted by an Argentinian patrol. The probing of the southern slopes of Mount Harriet convinced 42 Commando to attack from the south. A patrol found positions from which Milan Troop could dominate the Stanley road and protect the Commando right flank from interference by the two armoured car squadrons listed as part of Army Group Stanley.

While wandering around Teal, I came across the temporary grave of Sergeant 'Kiwi' Hunt, of the SBS, killed on 2 June. After the seizure of Mount Kent, a patrol screen consisting of G Squadron SAS, the SBS and Mountain and Arctic Warfare Cadre were tasked to dominate the general area of Mount Vernet, which is roughly halfway between Teal Inlet and Port Stanley. Brigade HQ and the

SAS agreed a SAS 'shoot to kill' zone south of and including Mount Vernet and circulated the details to HQ LFFI and HQ 5 Infantry Brigade. When helicopters delivered the SBS and the Cadre several miles from their planned landing zone, the Cadre were suspicious and headed for high ground to confirm the position, but was unable to advise the SBS of the error. My colleague 'Roo' Rencher had briefed G Squadron that there were no known friendlies in the 'kill zone' and consequently when the SBS patrol was seen, it was assumed to be enemy and ambushed. Sergeant Hunt was leading and was killed. An immediate consequence was that Brigade HQ appointed a Patrol Master.

After one of my daily radio conversations with LFFI Intelligence, I had an amiable chat with a Commando commanding officer in which he asked about my role. I explained that I had several. Currently it was to find an officer prisoner willing to take terms to General Menendez. I outlined that the role of Brigade Intelligence was to collect sufficient information from a variety of sources and agencies in time for Brigadier Thompson to plan and fight his battle. When, for instance, his Commando was engaged with the enemy, Brigade Intelligence looked into the middle and far distance for threats, such as a counterattack or reinforcements that might affect his battle.

When I asked how many prisoners his unit had captured and he replied that his orders were to kill as many of the enemy as possible to reduce their will to fight, I suggested that dead men tell no tales. Prisoners are important intelligence sources. The capture and handling of captured enemy personnel and suspect civilians was very rarely practised on exercises and the penalty for this lack of expertise was emerging. A couple of prisoners could have probably given substantial information and saved time and effort, particularly as air photographic reconnaissance had been severely reduced by poor weather and other priorities. I mentioned that I had been conducting counter-intelligence since 21 May in order to protect the rear of the Brigade from interference by civilians sympathetic to Argentina. While it is easy to criticise the relative lack of intelligence, the amount collected was sufficient to breach the Outer Defence Zone and thereafter it was a matter of a gritty infantry tactical battle.

By 6 June, Brigadier Thompson believed he had enough information to issue Orders the next day for the Brigade attack two days later, but HQ LFFI was unable to assure him that 5 Infantry Brigade would be ready because of the difficulties it was experiencing as it advanced on the southern flank to Fitzroy.

Bob Dilley arrived with one of the RAF linguists, a corporal, who claimed that he had been 'kidnapped' by LFFI Intelligence and had been sent to HQ 3 Commando Brigade to beef up our linguistic capability. While appreciating his linguistic skills as a Spanish interpreter, we actually needed Spanish-American speakers. And then Private 'Ali' Ciasco, a tough Belizean serving with the Commando Logistic Regiment, was detached to Brigade Intelligence. The Brigade Forward Interrogation Team now consisted of Ali, the RAF corporal and me. The LFFI Joint Service Interrogation Unit at *Red Beach* sifting the last of the Goose Green prisoners consisted of the Flight-Sergeant, the Flight-Lieutenant, the Intelligence Corps sergeant and five RAF linguists from Gibraltar. Ivor Garcia was still detached to interpret during the repatriation of prisoners to Argentina.

The poor weather that had prevented both sides conducting air photographic reconnaissance broke on the 7th with bright sun and blue skies – and the associated risk of air raids. The Argentinian 1st Air Photographic Group had been active throughout the war and about midday I joined a group of Royal Marines looking upwards and saw, outlined against the blue sky, a white trail climbing towards an aircraft flying very high. Then there was a white puff. I later learnt that HMS *Exeter* had shot down a Learjet with a Sea Dart. It was one of four aircraft on a line-abreast sortie photographing San Carlos Water and Falkland Sound.

On 3 June, a 45 Commando patrol commanded by Lieutenant Andy Shaw was checking a position on Mount Kent and found plenty of evidence of a hurried departure in the form of abandoned clothing and equipment. A check of a bunker revealed that it was the command post of Combat Team *Solari* (B Company, 12th Infantry Regiment). During the Battle of Goose Green, it was deployed to reinforce Task Force Mercedes. No measures had been taken to destroy or protect documents and in the bunker there were three important documents. Although dated early April, they were still valid and were essentially an intelligence coup. An analysis of the documents revealed the following:

The Strategic Reserve Operation Order.
A significant number of helicopters had been allocated, presumably from 601 Combat Aviation Battalion, to the Reserve. There was no indication that the helicopters would fly at night and a 50% loss was expected on any mission. The enemy had already lost several helicopters and the assumption was made these would be replaced. Included in the Order was a list of locations to which they may be deployed, code words, nicknames for places, and the rationale for deployments.

Map Showing Regimental Boundaries in Port Stanley.
This was of great value and showed the inter-regimental sectors with nicknames for the sectors and the boundaries between them. The map presented the Intelligence Section with an opportunity to revisit the 1966 Ordnance Survey map of Stanley showing the layout of the town and defensible buildings in the event of fighting in a built-up area.

The names and strengths of the Argentine Army units in Stanley.
The list gave the shorthand unit titles and total establishments. Marrying to full titles was not too difficult. It gave a total of 7,176 all ranks.

The documents arrived at Brigade HQ and were analysed to be a major Documentary Intelligence find for several reasons. (*See* plate section.) It largely confirmed that the Argentinian Army order of battle given at the Orders on 13 May on HMS *Fearless* was accurate. It also proved the accuracy of the Cable and Wireless intercepts and provided first-hand co-lateral to information supplied by Northwood. Taking into consideration the Air Force and Marine Corps, an estimate of 10,000 all ranks in Army Group Stanley was concluded. The find also largely solved the conundrum surrounding the Strategic or Z Reserve, which had been registered in at least three places. The force had been formed primarily to reinforce Army Group Stanley and consisted of the 4th Infantry Regiment defending the Outer Defence Zone on Two Sisters and Mount Harriet, 12th Infantry Regiment at Goose Green and the 4th Airborne Artillery Group with its 105mm Pack Howitzers.

On 8 June, Captain Rowe interrupted the council-of-war between Major-General Moore and Brigadiers Thompson and Wilson on *Fearless* and briefed on the Documentary Intelligence find. In relation to the defence of Stanley, the enemy situation deployed thus:

Mount Longdon	one 7th Infantry Regiment company.
Mount Harriet	one 4th Infantry Regiment company.
Two Sisters	one 4th Infantry Regiment company.
Wireless Ridge	two 7th Infantry Regiment companies.
Mount Tumbledown	5th Marine Infantry Battalion
Estimated thirty-nine 105mm Pack Howitzers.	

In spite of the inevitable tension between the certainty of some intelligence and the ambiguity of unevaluated information, which was hardly surprising given the time at sea, restrictions on 'need to know' and the lack of intelligence when the crisis emerged in March, the principle of attacking with the intelligence that was available prevailed, as opposed to waiting for more. The agreed strategy was:

Phase One – 11/12 June.
3 Commando Brigade to seize the Outer Defence Zone.
3 Para to seize Mount Longdon.
45 Commando to capture Two Sisters and then exploit to Mount Tumbledown.
42 Commando, supported by the Welsh Guards with two 40 Commando replacing the losses suffered at Port Pleasant, to attack Mount Harriet and be prepared to support 45 Commando.

Phase Two – 12/13 June.
5 Infantry Brigade to seize the southern sector of the Inner Defence Zone
Scots Guards to capture Mount Tumbledown.
1/7th Gurkha Rifles to capture Mount William.
3rd Commando Brigade to seize the northern sector Inner Defence Zone.
2 Para capture Wireless Ridge.

Phase Three – 13/14 June.
3 Commando Brigade to capture Sapper Hill, enemy positions south of Stanley and the town, the airport and trap the enemy against the eastern beaches.

Brigadier Thompson was keen that if the opportunity arose, 42 and 45 Commandos were to maintain the momentum by exploiting towards the Inner Defence Zone and attack Mount Tumbledown. But there was little intelligence on the eastern slopes and therefore the attack would be advance to contact, supported by the intelligence collected so far.

The Orders broke up with reports of the disastrous air attack on the two LSLs in Port Pleasant. It later emerged that Brigadier Wilson had wanted to land his 5 Infantry Brigade in force at Fitzroy but had been prevented doing so when HMS *Fearless* and *Intrepid* were declared to be politically sensitive capital ships and were prevented from landing troops in the right numbers, in the right place, at the right time, ready to fight – as had happened at San Carlos Water.

The consequence was that on 8 June, two LSLs, *Sir Galahad* and *Sir Tristram*, had been caught by Argentinian aircraft while unloading troops and supplies on a clear day. During his daily evening briefing, Sergeant 'Buster' Brown said that during the 5 Infantry Brigade operations, *Fearless* LCU *Foxtrot* 4 had been sunk by a bomb, killing six crew from the *Fearless* 4th Assault Squadron, including Chief Petty Officer James, who was a member of No. 2 Chief Petty Officers Mess.

Two days later, I was woken by the familiar chatter of Chinese and learnt from a senior rating with the men that they had been providing laundry and tailoring support on board one of the RFA ships and had become anxious about the bombing of the ships. My understanding was since they were not Royal Navy, they were not obliged to put themselves in harm's way. During the day, our linguist airman returned to HMS *Fearless* with toothache to visit the dentist and took several documents to deliver to LFFI Intelligence. Brigade Tactical HQ moved into the settlement manager's house in the afternoon and took command as Main HQ left Teal and headed east into the dripping mist that was blanketing the cold and sodden 'camp' to a new position on the western slopes of Mount Kent.

That night, in probably the most daring patrol of the war, a strong 42 Commando fighting patrol diverted the attention of the 4th Infantry Regiment while two Mountain and Arctic Cadre patrols of Royal Marines infiltrated through the enemy positions and established hides on Goat Ridge close to the sheep track that ran from Mount Harriet over Two Sisters to Murrell Bridge. Over the next 24 hours, the Cadre plotted Argentinian positions and activity on the eastern slopes and withdrew the following night. The ground held by the 7th Infantry Regiment on Mount Longdon and Wireless Ridge was almost impossible to recce. During the evening of 9 June, in a radio conversation with Captain Rowe, he said the Brigade was dominating its areas of tactical responsibility, however, no prisoners had been captured. The lack of a skill that should have been practised·but wasn't was still hampering the ability to paint an accurate picture of the defence of the Outer Defence Zone.

So far, Army Group Falklands had failed to take advantage of opportunities to disrupt the British. The San Carlos Water beachheads had not been attacked because the landings were considered to be a diversion for an attack nearer Stanley. The occupation of the strategically important Mount Kent had been opposed only by a small commando unit, indeed the performance of the Special Forces Group had been inept. When 5 Infantry Brigade found themselves in disarray at Port Pleasant, Army Group Stanley rejected a plan suggested by 4th Infantry Regiment on Mount Harriet and Two Sisters to attack the Port Fitzroy beachhead. A document captured after the Argentinian surrender showed that Army Headquarters in Buenos Aires had examined the feasibility of launching a co-ordinated counterattack named *Operation Mailbox* planned for 15 June:

Task Force Reconquest in Fox Bay to attack Darwin and secure a drop zone west of Goose Green for the delivery of the 4th Airborne Brigade, which was the National Reserve.

5th Infantry Regiment at Port Howard to cross Falkland Sound and attack the Amphibious Operations Area at San Carlos Water.

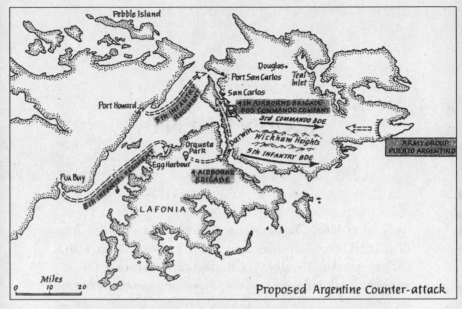

Operation Mailbox showing Argentinian counter-attack proposals.

The Amphibious Commando Group to parachute onto Wickham Heights and threaten the flanks of both British brigades.

The newly raised 603 Commando Company to harass enemy lines of communications and logistic centres.

Army Group Stanley to counterattack the British advance to Fitzroy.

But the Air Force was uncertain that it could gain and hold sufficient air superiority to allow delivery of the 4th Airborne Brigade and the Army was concerned about its inexperience in amphibious warfare. Instead, Brigadier-General Menendez was instructed to counterattack. By 10 June, Major-General Moore judged everything was ready and Brigadier Thompson issued his confirmatory orders for Phase One.

11

MOUNT KENT

Early on 11 June, a Royal Marine Police passed a message from Brigade HQ that Bob Dilley and I were to re-join Brigade HQ. Packing my kit, I walked to the helicopter landing site and wedged myself in the back of the Gazelle. Bob would follow on the next sortie. With the co-pilot and passenger (me) on constant lookout for marauding Pucarás and A-109 gunships, the pilot skimmed low over the sunny moorland, swerved in and out of gullies and headed towards a deserted slope dotted with small green patches about 3 miles west of the rocky summit of Mount Kent and about 6 miles west of the centre of two features that make up Two Sisters. There was no movement and when I asked the pilot if he had the correct map reference, he checked his map. Yes, he said, and then I saw figures moving around the green patches, which turned out to be camouflage nets covering the BVs. Even the tell-tale antennae and radio masts were almost invisible. I got out, gave 'thumbs-up' thanks to the pilot, and then as the Gazelle rose it bent the grass still tinged by the silver frost of the previous night and bounded back toward Teal Inlet. Apart from the clatter of the disappearing Gazelle, the peaceful scene was only interrupted by chirping birds announcing the warmth of the winter sun to the east. Even the motors of the usually annoying BV generators were lost in the stillness.

The Brigade HQ position of camouflaged BVs, trenches and sentries manning GPMGs was widely dispersed across the hillside. To the north, smoke from distant fires at Estancia trailed upwards and beyond that, the cold Salvador Waters twinkled in the wintry sun. About 3 miles to the south-east was Two Sisters. To the north-east was a 29 Commando Regiment battery, occasionally spitting a wisp of grey smoke, followed by a bark and swish as the shells careered towards their targets. Another battery was about a mile south-west of the position. Sometimes incoming shells crested the slopes but no one seemed too anxious. A Sea King Commando clattered across the plain, swept over Brigade HQ, dropped onto the flanks of the dewy mountain and deposited some 2 Para, weighed down with weapons, ammunition belts, bergens and radios, re-joining the Brigade from Fitzroy.

I found the Intelligence Section BV. With Bob arriving about an hour later, we were almost at full strength, with the RAF linguist yet to return from seeing the dentist on *Fearless*. When I recognised a Welsh Guards officer who had been on the Jungle Warfare course in Brunei in 1979, he said he had lost most of his Mortar Platoon as casualties on the *Sir Galahad* but blamed no one. He had been attached to Brigade HQ as the Welsh Guards Liaison Officer for Phase One. Over a breakfast of baked beans, apple flakes, a Rolo, and nuts and raisins, washed down with a cup of cocoa, Neil brought me up to date. Clean fresh water was in short supply. Fortunately, I had filled my two water bottles at Teal but, sooner or later, I would be scavenging from rivulets with the associated risk of an upset stomach, in spite of purification tablets. All vestige of embarrassment of a 'shovel patrol' had disappeared. Battlefield latrines are no respecters of rank or religion. Those at San Carlos had been a grand affair of an enclosure shielded from the wind with six balance poles, but here it was behind a rock with performers not infrequently subjected to a hail of small pebbles from passing helicopters.

I spent a little time trying to acquire some tentage to give interrogation some privacy, unsurprisingly without much success, given the priority of moving men, ammunition and rations. My normal point of contact in B Echelon had apparently been on the *Sir Galahad*. While familiarising myself with the position, I visited HQ 59 Independent Commando Engineer Field Squadron to review the lack of good intelligence of enemy mines and minefields, in particular the scarcity of information beyond the Outer Defence Zone. A suggestion that troops should run across minefields, as opposed to slow and difficult breaching, had raised a few eyebrows. A couple of prisoners would probably have answered our questions. Fortunately, Roy Packer had photographed some mines captured at Goose Green and had distributed copies to the three attacking units.

Stand-to was called shortly before dusk and as night fell, silent and cold with Southern Hemisphere stars gleaming in the clear sky, a white carpet of frost soon covered the slopes. And then the silence to the east was broken by the rattle of small arms fire, the crump of explosions as the artillery opened fire and drifting flares split the darkness. The battle for the Outer Defence Zone had begun. Listening to the Command net, it soon became clear that the 7th Infantry Regiment company were giving 3 Para a stiff fight on Mount Longdon and then suddenly the key turned in the lock and the battalion slowly advanced. The 4th Infantry Regiment company on Two Sisters was defeated by 45 Commando.

To the south, 42 Commando outflanked the defence of Mount Harriet from the south and overran the 4th Infantry Regiment Company and Regimental HQ in a battle regarded as a classic night action. During this battle, Captain Rowe was with Brigadier Thompson and the Tactical HQ when the

29 Commando Regiment Cymbeline mortar-locating radar twice indicated several helicopters flying from Port Stanley towards Goat Ridge. The number indicated the Argentinian Strategic Reserve responding to a contingency plan. Once a significant British force approached Goat Ridge, it would be counterattacked by 601 Combat Aviation Battalion. 42 Commando was ordered to stand-to, however, no one could see or hear enemy helicopters approaching the ridge.

As dawn emerged, bright, clear and frosty, the Commando Brigade had overrun the Outer Defence Zone and Phase One was complete. The intelligence priority was to collect information for Phase Two but when Argentinian artillery began shelling the three captured objectives, this prevented intelligence search teams being pushed forward to search for documents and Technical Intelligence. It also meant the unit intelligence officers had less opportunity to select prisoners for interrogation, the priority being to evacuate the wounded to the field hospital as quickly as possible and the prisoners to the LFFI prison camp established at Fitzroy. Again, Defence Troop provided escorts and guards and selected a stone sheep pen as a holding area. Captain Larken's steward had somehow smuggled himself ashore and was working in the 'Greasy Spoon' Officer's Mess where he supplied soup and biscuits. Medics were on standby to treat the wounded and ill.

Only 42 Commando was able to send prisoners to the Brigade Forward Interrogation Team. The first prisoner was an artillery Forward Observation Officer, a captain. His escort, a warrant officer, also brought a trace showing details of Argentinian artillery registration locations. It showed that the unit was thinking about battlefield intelligence. Brian Dodd immediately started producing copies for distribution. Deciding it would be useful to have a gunner to help plot enemy positions and ask technical questions, I was going to the 29 Commando Regiment

Command Post to see their intelligence officer when I met Brigadier Thompson, 'How is it going?' 'Fine, sir. I am asking the gunners if they could help with interrogation.' 'Good idea. We don't have much time!'

Unfortunately, the Regiment could not produce an officer, but appointed one to be available, so I returned to the prisoner to find that he had been blindfolded and was sitting on the ground facing across the plain to Estancia. When I removed his blindfold, he admitted he was angry and humiliated to be a prisoner and claimed he had ditched documents and maps after capture, which, if correct, was a nuisance. Nevertheless, he confirmed the organisation of the 3rd Artillery Group and that he was the forward observation officer usually attached to the 3rd Infantry Regiment. This regiment was deployed along the coast of Port Stanley and when pressed about why he had been captured on Mount Harriet, he eventually admitted that he had been visiting a friend. While it may have been an unfortunate decision to be in the wrong place at the wrong time, it seemed likely that he had been liaising with the 4th Infantry Regiment forward observation officer. He claimed that 3rd Infantry Regiment was supported by six 105mm Pack Howitzers.

A lieutenant-colonel whose regiment had been destroyed during the night was dignified. Shock of capture betrayed anxiety. A search revealed a personal diary containing personal and operational information and a second one, bound in beautiful leather, listing a day-by-day log of events compiled by his adjutant. When his regiment arrived in early April, it had marched to Mount Wall where his men had suffered badly from the chaotic logistic system and the weather. In late April, the regiment was withdrawn to defend the centre and southern flank of the Outer Defence Zone. He could account for the two rifle companies on Two Sisters and Mount Harriet but claimed to be unable to tell us anything about the third one, A Company, except he believed it had been detached soon after landing to the Strategic Reserve. On his right flank was 7th Infantry Regiment. The composition of the ground had made digging-in difficult.

In the middle of the interrogation, a helicopter landed about 100 yards away and out spilled a large gaggle of excited war correspondents armed with notebooks and cameras at the ready and eager for a story. They were escorted by a Royal Navy commando-trained lieutenant-commander. Journalism had a habit of undermining interrogation, unless it is journalists conducting them as interviews and since lives were at risk, supported by Sergeant 'Buster' Brown and two marines from Defence Troop, I approached them and emphasised that the prisoners probably had important information and therefore, they, the journalists, were not welcome. When I asked 'Buster' to ensure that none of them came any further forward, I was expecting the usual objections about freedom of the press. I was astonished when they remained by the helicopter. A couple of years later, the lieutenant-commander and I were instructors in the same unit.

After the interruption, I continued my conversation with the lieutenant-colonel and it became apparent that the Argentinian threat assessment was an attack from the south along the axis of the Darwin to Fitzroy track. The Commando Brigade assault from the west was something of a surprise, particularly as all the activity had been to the south-east at Fitzroy. The patrolling west of the Outer Defence Zone had been regarded as a distraction. Annoyingly, he refused to answer any questions on Argentinian deployments around Stanley.

A lieutenant quickly proved amenable and I decided to allow an inexperienced tactical questioner to open the interrogation, but when he forgot everything he had been taught and opened with: 'You spikate English, me no spikate Argentinian and if you no answer, I make you answer!' Time to take over. The lieutenant was a cheerful character and was appalled to find he had been assessed as the 4th Infantry Regiment Intelligence Officer. His problem was that when captured, he was carrying a radio and a leather satchel containing intelligence-related documents. He claimed that the documents had been delivered by a sergeant from Port Stanley the previous night. He claimed he commanded the .50-inch Machine Gun Platoon and was the son of a serving general. As the afternoon gave way to evening, I felt the prisoners had more to give and since I did not wish them to collude, I arranged for them to be escorted individually by helicopter to the Joint Service Interrogation Unit at Fitzroy. Bob Dilley escorted the lieutenant-colonel. 'Buster' Brown thought he could use a captured radio, so I gave it to him.

One item found by 42 Commando was a British-manufactured laser rangefinder in working order. Enemy pilots had shown they were prepared to press home low-level air strikes, even when the odds were stacked against them. Privately, Neil and I believed the rangefinder had been left behind by a British patrol, however, inquiries established all rangefinders could be accounted for. And then, the forward air controller attached to 42 Commando arrived at the Intelligence Section and mentioning he lost a rangefinder on Mount Harriet during a patrol clash on 3 June, he said he could identify his because he had put two bullets through the body. Since he had been part of the Air Intelligence section, this was worth milking and so Neil and I examined the rangefinder, turning it this way and that, back to front, and murmured agreement that either it was not the missing rangefinder or he must have missed because it was intact and undamaged. Eventually, we gave way and returned it to him on the promise of a pint.

5 Infantry Brigade had been expected to launch Phase Two after dark but when Brigadier Thompson returned from visiting units in his brigade, Major-General Moore and Brigadier Wilson, commanding 5 Brigade, were at his headquarters seeking a

24-hour delay so that 5 Brigade could have more time to prepare its night attack across ground it had not seen. When the proposal was agreed to, Brigadier Wilson accepted the offer of the Mountain and Arctic Warfare Cadre to guide the 5 Brigade units to their start lines. While this was disappointing because it meant the Commando Brigade would continue to be exposed to artillery fire for a further 24 hours, 5 Brigade was still recovering after the traumatic events of 8 June. After dark, I had my first meal and drink of the day. By midnight, another frost had laid a white carpet across the slopes.

The next morning, 13 June, was bright. Increased helicopter movement relating to Phase Two meant that inexperienced navy pilots had been drafted in to move troops and some were mistaking Brigade HQ as a gun position or something similar and were landing nearby, only for Colonel Tim Secombe, the Deputy Brigade Commander, to furiously use his stick to shoo them elsewhere.

About midday I was brewing a mug of tea when 'Air Raid Warning Yellow!' was broadcast from the Command Post. We had heard it before, so there was no great urgency as whistles were blown, GPMGs were manned and troops sauntered to trenches and weapon pits. And then, after an urgent 'Air Raid Red! Air Raid Red!', I saw an aircraft hurdle over the saddle of high ground to the east, followed by another, and another, until there were seven dark-brown-and-green aircraft roughly in line astern. This was not a normal British tactic and then, as they banked towards us, I recognised them as Skyhawks. Sid, our driver, crouched behind the coaxial GPMG on his BV roof was joined by Ali Ciasco as the No. 2, feeding the ammunition belt. As I scrambled up the seemingly endless slope to the trench dug by Dick Birkett, the Skyhawks, their cockpits glinting in the weak sun, were rapidly closing in. And then two black dots somersaulted from the lead aircraft. Dick was already in the bottom of the trench and as I hauled out his fighting order and dived on top of him, both bombs exploded in a burst of whistling stones, rocks and shrapnel. Peeping over the lip, I saw the following Skyhawks – low, dangerous and menacing – open fire, the rapid cackling of their 20mm cannons carved the earth with high spouts of grass, stones and small rocks. GPMGs opened fire and, after a Blowpipe missile exploded between two aircraft, there were more loud bombs in quick succession. Cursing that I did not have my steel helmet, in an act that some psychiatrist would be able to explain, I pulled my windproof hood over my head. The aircraft screamed overhead and were gone, their shock waves dislodging the rocks, stones and earth of the sangars, flattening grass and whipping antennae. Figures emerged from the earth to survey the damage and watched as four aircraft headed towards the east. Three banked to port – back to our position. One appeared to be trailing thin smoke. Again low and fast, the menacing Skyhawks approached. Neil, who had ignored the first warning, came panting up the slope toward Dick's trench and with a mighty 'Watch out! I'm joining you!' hurled himself on top of Dick and me, driving the wind out of our lungs. Cannon fire again threw up dirt, stones, grass and rock splinters and then they were gone. In spite of the violence of the attack, the only damage was to two Gazelles. As wisps of smoke curled lazily from the bomb craters, 'Doc', the Navy medic, trawled through the position seeking casualties; there were none. And then an officer standing on a rock outside the Command Post shouted. 'Next time there is an air raid, don't shout, "They're over there and coming this way." You must give aircraft, type and from which direction, for instance, "Four Skyhawks approaching from the north." Otherwise no one knows what to do!' It made very good sense and then somebody asked, 'Which way is north, sir?' 'Over there!' stuttered the officer, flinging his arm dramatically to the west. He had a point, however, air raids were rarely practised on exercises.

And quickly the stories circulated, most substantiated. Brigadier Thompson and his RMP escort, Corporal Dean, had taken cover when a bomb landed 35 metres from them but did not explode. Neil, on hearing the first bomb explode, threw himself out of the BV onto the ground, saw a helmet and jammed it onto his head, only to find it was still firmly attached to a pack. Sid's GPMG had a stoppage after two rounds. Ali Ciasco's boot had been clipped by a bullet. A Land Rover near our BV had been laced by cannon fire and the window cockpit of a Gazelle had been shattered. Tom Priestley was in the briefing tent preparing it for the Phase Two Orders when it was shredded by the 'grapeshot of pebbles'. Several chairs he had scrounged were damaged.

The attack was significant because judging by its accuracy, Brigade HQ had been discovered – either by Electronic Warfare direction-finding, air photographic analysis or pilots identifying the position from observation of the glare of the helicopter cockpits. Since there was a possibility that the Argentinians could realise the significance of the attack, Air raid warning *Yellow* was ordered. About half-an-hour later, a translated intercepted ground-to-air message from a pilot was passed from Y (Electronic Warfare) Troop: 'Ninety-three now! Ninety-three now!' It made absolutely no sense until we checked a captured Argentinian map and found that the nearest artillery battery was circled with the figure '93'. The pilots had probably seen the helicopters.

The weather deteriorated during the afternoon and light snow laid a carpet across the 'camp'. Another Air Raid Red was sounded and, this time, the dash to trenches was conducted with greater urgency. Motivated by the first attack, I had identified a stone run as a shelter and watched, no doubt, with some interest by several Royal Engineers, I began heaving rocks and stones aside and within a short time had built a sangar, a task that in peace conditions would have taken hours. I was joined by the *Observer* correspondent John Shirley. Although suspicious of him as a journalist, we chatted until the All Clear was given.

With Brigade HQ compromised, Major Dixon ordered a 'crash' move, but the timing could not have been worse. Phase Two was imminent and it was essential to have good communications with 2 Para for its attack on Wireless Ridge and with 5 Infantry Brigade for the assault on Mount Tumbledown and, if the opportunity arose, to be ready for the Phase Three advance into Port Stanley. The air raid had added urgency to the move and although the weather had closed in and more snow scurried across the plain straight at us, another 'Air Raid Red! Air Raid Red!' saw the BVs scatter, a Wessex take cover in a gully and everyone seek cover behind rocks and in folds of the ground. GPMGs and rifles were cocked. This time we were ready and as two aircraft burst from the base of yellow snow-laden cloud, 'Fire!' was followed almost immediately by 'Cease fire! Cease fire! Mistaken identity!' as two RAF Harrier GR3s did a smart about-turn and darted back into the shelter of the low clouds, waggling their wings as they disappeared. A 'blue on blue' was defensively agreed, however, there was also agreement that it was a case of friendly aircraft when not needed, and being absent when needed.

As the wintry dusk fell across the 'camp', Tactical HQ moved into a gully about 500 metres from Main HQ and prepared to take command; Neil allocated Scotty and Scouse Atkinson to join Captain Rowe with it. The Main HQ column then set off east cross-country intending to cross the Murrell River and move to a new position on Two Sisters, now occupied by 45 Commando, but things began to go wrong. Movement across the tussock grass was stop – go – stop – go and, as a consequence, several overloaded BVs, including the Intelligence Section's, shattered the shear pins between the prime mover and the tow. Colour-Sergeant Prescott and his Light Aid Detachment of mechanics were soon busy repairing the vehicles. Each time the column stopped, a defensive cordon was formed. The Murrell proved too deep to cross and as the column headed north toward Murrell Bridge, it stopped and deployed into defensive positions as two jerky headlights split the night from a vehicle grunting along the east–west track. No one moved except for weapons being gently cocked. After the vehicle, a Land Rover, had passed, the column picked up the track toward the bridge. The moon had risen and really was like 'a ghostly galleon tossed upon cloudy seas' as thin clouds brushed across its face. On reaching the track, the column headed east to Port Stanley and passed through a small lake of shallow water.

Almost to our front, 2 Para supported by the Blues and Royals were attacking the remainder of 7th Infantry Regiment on Wireless Ridge. I later learnt that the Battalion was on its Start Line when Lieutenant-Colonel Chandler, who had taken over from 'H' Jones, was given a marked map captured on Mount Longdon. It had arrived from Brigade HQ and showed a minefield astride his planned axis between his Start Line and the objective of high ground to the south nicknamed *Apple Pie*. It was a little late to do anything about it so he ordered the attack to begin. On our right, 2nd Scots Guards were attacking the 5th Marine Infantry Battalion on Mount Tumbledown. Artillery and mortars crumped, machine-guns rattled and tracers carved long, shallow arcs in the darkness. Flares floated eerily in the swirling mists and smoke.

With the whine of BV engines betraying our presence, the column motored slowly along in the dark but as it crossed another drift, the BV in front of ours capsized onto its side. We stopped to give assistance. At the next drift, our BV slid off the ford and slowly keeled over into the dark, cold water. I had the misfortune to be sitting on the side onto which the vehicle had capsized and saw nothing but dark water creeping up the front and side windows as the BV settled. On top of me was Brian Dodd and on top of him was Sid, struggling to open his door. I had visions of gradually being soaked by the freezing water and then Sid shoved his door open and we clambered out. The Light Aid Detachment recovery BV reversed into the stream and passed a towline which righted our vehicle and after a couple of minutes, we were jolting along the track across dark countryside of tussock grass dusted with snow punctuated by exposed puddles of water and mud. As the column then left the main track and headed south up the distinctive sheep track towards Two Sisters, a strong, cold wind, barrelling in from the sea, whipped the snowflakes on the windscreen. The wind-chill gradually decreased. During a short halt, the crescendo of the battles on Wireless Ridge behind us and Mount Tumbledown in front cut through the darkness. Moody Brook was suffering badly from shelling and a big fire was raging. Air Force Base Stanley was being shelled from warships and there were several loud explosions. A Casevac Scout helicopter clattered up the valley behind us. Suddenly, the street lights of Port Stanley below spluttered and illuminated. It was an incredible moment. There was our objective that we had come 8,000 miles to liberate.

The length of the column began to reduce with breakdowns and associated lack of spares. The need to feed the BVs carrying the Command Post radios meant a couple were drained of fuel and left behind with their crews. As the surviving BVs ground along the track, the town lights still glittered. More snow fell. Our BV fuel gauge showed fresh air but somehow Sid persuaded it to ignore its thirst. At another halt a Royal Artillery major complained about our brake lights. 'Mount up! Move now!' and again the BVs crunched along the track. When the major's vehicle broke down, we were unable to help. We caught up with the column as it reached a small flat plateau below the eastern summit of Two Sisters and lined up alongside a high bank. White camouflage nets were thrown over the vehicles and standing patrols with GPMGs covered all-round defence. The 7-mile journey had taken 13 hours. I snuggled deep into my sleeping bag alongside the BV and was soon asleep in spite of the racket of battle.

When 'Stand to' was given about 2 hours later, low grey clouds were sweeping across a bleak, icy and colourless landscape. Not even the sea far to the south twinkled. I had run out of water and broke the ice of a frozen pool. I had drunk worse in the jungle, so this would do, but it was foul. I had not eaten since breakfast the previous day and after a tin of warm baked beans followed by a tin of apricots, I climbed a hillock clutching my cup of hot coffee and saw Port Stanley below, beyond Sapper Hill, which was being laced by machine-gun tracer and thumped by artillery and mortar fire. Wireless Ridge was quieter than Mount Tumbledown. The distant airport was wreathed in dark smoke.

As 'Prepare to move' was ordered, Sid's BV was obviously still thriving on fresh air so we reduced its weight by walking, our fingers crossed it would not splutter to a halt. Tom Priestley and I were chatting when he pointed to four men emerging from rocks on a ridge about 500 yards to our right. Since no friendly forces were reported to be in the area and therefore they must be enemy, the column stopped, all round defence was adopted and a couple of machine-guns fitted to BV roofs covered the rocks. When the Intelligence Section was instructed to investigate, this came as something of a surprise. Nevertheless, Neil divided us into two detachments of three, one controlled by him, the other by me. Quick orders and then in the knowledge there was enough suppressive fire from the BVs, we skirmished across a stone run and up the slope to the figures. Fortunately, they turned out to be a Forward Observation Party attached to 2nd Scots Guards who had been supporting the attack on Mount Tumbledown during the night. They were uncertain about the BVs but had recognised our uniforms. About 30 minutes later, the column dispersed on the high and gently sloping grassy flanks of a valley. The wind howling from the south across the plain was the messenger of snow and sleet sweeping in from the sea. Fuel was again redistributed to keep the Command Post BVs running. A gun battery across the valley suddenly erupted into a frenzy and crushed a counterattack launched from Moody Brook against 2 Para.

About an hour later, 2 Para was reporting columns of Argentinian troops withdrawing into Port Stanley. Brigadier Thompson was keen to pursue, however, Major-General Moore instructed that both brigades were to exploit no further than the 39 easting of the racecourse on the outskirts of Port Stanley. As brigades advanced, it became apparent that 2 Para had breached the limit of exploitation by turning their radios off, except for one found by Brigadier Thompson who ordered them to stop. By mid-afternoon, it was clear the Argentinians had lost the will to fight and 'Weapons tight' was ordered unless in self-defence. We could now go home and 'Where's the transport?' was asked by more than one wag. Using a Command Post radio, I contacted Captain Rowe, who was with Brigadier Thompson and a small Tactical HQ, suggesting that Ali Ciasco and I move forward to help with any Spanish language issues and also commence an operation to collect intelligence before the Argentinians destroyed documents.

I do not recall great elation that the war was over, just relief. It had all started seventy-four days previously. Most seemed to know someone who had been killed or wounded and there was great sympathy for the families of husbands, fathers, sons, brothers and lovers killed on a tiny island 8,000 miles from home. At least it had been a war without the stain of atrocity.

Conditions on Two Sisters deteriorated dramatically. Most of us only had dehydrated Arctic rations, but water was scarce. Fuel was still being drained from the BVs. When a Royal Marine mechanic from the Workshop Squadron of the Commando Logistic Regiment asked if he could buy some paper for his last hoard of tobacco, I had none as I did not smoke so I sent him to Neil who shared a packet of cigarettes with him. We also heard that Tactical HQ, which included Scottie and Scouse Atkinson, had run into a minefield and the Artillery BV leading the convoy had been damaged by a mine. The Royal Artillery major was seriously injured and was kept warm overnight by his driver, Gunner Ince, by lying alongside him.

A ceasefire was eventually agreed and then Major-General Moore sent a signal to the Task Force:

HQ LFFI PORT STANLEY. IN PORT STANLEY AT 9 O'CLOCK PM FALKLAND ISLANDS TIME TONIGHT THE 14 JUNE 1982, MAJOR GENERAL MENENDES SURRENDERED TO ME ALL THE ARGENTINE ARMED FORCES IN EAST AND WEST FALKLAND, TOGETHER WITH THEIR IMPEDIMENTA. ARRANGEMENTS ARE IN HAND TO ASSEMBLE THE MEN FOR RETURN TO ARGENTINA, TO GATHER IN THEIR ARMS AND EQUIPMENT, AND TO MARK AND MAKE SAFE THEIR MUNITIONS. THE FALKLAND ISLANDS ARE ONCE MORE UNDER THE GOVERNMENT DESIRED BY THEIR INHABITANTS. GOD SAVE THE QUEEN. SIGNED JJ MOORE.

Although the Argentinian surrender breached the Argentinian Army code of conduct stating surrender was illegal unless more than 50 per cent of the men were casualties and 75 per cent of the ammunition had been spent, the following terms were agreed:

Argentinians units to retain their flags.

Officers to remain in command of units.

The surrender ceremony to be private.

Argentinian officers to retain their pistols in order to protect themselves.

Prisoners to be repatriated in ships supplied by the Task Force.

I returned to our snow-covered tent erected by Neil to find the mechanic curled up in his sleeping bag. I crawled into mine and looked forward to going back to England. Two-thirds of Operation *Corporation* had been successful; only the reoccupation of Southern Thule remained.

12

THE LIBERATION OF PORT STANLEY

As 15 June dawned, grey and cold with frequent snow squalls that hurtled from the ocean and charged across the 'camp' blanketing our position, we listened to the radios. Shortly after a Sea King had delivered a net full of fuel jerrycans to replenish the thirsty BVs and Main HQ assumed command from Tactical HQ, Ali Ciasco and I were instructed to report to Captain Rowe, who was on the outskirts of Port Stanley. A couple of hours later, a Sea King emerged from the gloom and its loadmaster squeezed in those required by Brigade HQ – about twenty with all our kit, 'standing room included'. The helicopter rose in a swirl of snow and plunged to the landing site at the racecourse on the western outskirts of the town where a Royal Marine gleefully warned us that we had landed in the middle of a minefield and recommended we follow the white mine tape in single file across the grass to Ross Road. As the column turned right toward Port Stanley, a waddle of penguins, no doubt relieved that tranquillity had returned, gathered on the foreshore and watched as we plodded past towards the evidence of the fighting. The former Army Camp and the Seaplane Hangar had been shredded by shelling, wrecked Argentinian lorries and jeeps were scattered on both sides of the road and some Argentinian peat bunkers among shell craters had collapsed. On the outskirts, paras were making themselves comfortable in some abandoned buildings. Two dead Argentinians lay beside each other on a grassy area near the Battle of Falklands Islands Monument, their tattered greyish uniforms flapping in the wind. I briefly searched them. The one on the right lay straight, his lifeless arms to his side; the other lay with his right arm across his face, his left raised in supplication. Nearby a cannibalised Argentinian Coastguard Sea King helicopter was parked at the base of a steep grassy bank near Government House.

On the outskirts of the town, we traced Captain Rowe to Sullivan House, the Colonial Secretary's house, where he told us that we were to be detached to the LFFI Intelligence and Security function being assembled by Major Burrill. He mentioned there was no power in the town, and the water filtration plant had been damaged by a shell.

Leaving our bergens with him, we continued along Ross Road, crossed the ceasefire line marked by barbed wire at the edge of the town manned by the Blues and Royals and entered the 'Argentinian' side. There were no lights of any sort. I had expected to see masses of bonfires as the Argentinians burnt documents and generally vandalised streets and houses, as defeated armies not infrequently do, however, the town was peaceful, the only movement being 'bricks' of para patrols using their urban techniques refined in Northern Ireland. Outside the building listed on my map as the Town Hall, when we met Captain Charters and an Intelligence Corps sergeant, I had failed in my ambition to be the first Intelligence Corps to enter the town. Captain Charters had been tasked to co-ordinate intelligence operations in the town, in particular Documentary Intelligence searches of enemy HQs. He mentioned that when HQ 10th Brigade had been searched, he was relieved that its Operations map mirrored the HQ LFFI

Intelligence map. He had requisitioned the LADE office, next-door to the Town Hall, as our base. This evoked a keen sense of justice done because it was strongly suspected to have been used by the Argentinian intelligence and security to collect information prior to their invasion and now we were about to use it for our purposes. I was pleased when he said that our RAF Flight-Sergeant and Bob Dilley were also in the town and then warned that since 2 Para were patrolling the town, a self-imposed curfew seemed advisable.

The Argentinian prisoners had been assembled into several large buildings and warehouses. In spite of the undoubted patrolling expertise of 2 Para, Port Stanley was full of armed enemy soldiers some of whom most probably were hard-line officers, bitter and angry at their defeat. Indeed, the officers had been allowed to keep their sidearms, apparently to protect themselves from soldiers angry at the surrender. Since we were going to be based in the town, I needed a more powerful weapon than my rather weather-beaten SMG. Outside the Town Hall, which was being used as holding centre, I met a Royal Marines Police Troop sergeant who had the same ambition and we persuaded two conscripts to hand over their FAL semi-automatic rifles and ammunition. We also obtained a 7.62mm MAG general purpose machine gun, a box of linked ammunition and some grenades.

When Captain Charters tasked me to search the Secretariat on Ross Road West, Ali left to brief Captain Rowe on where we were. I recognised the building from a photograph showing an Argentinian flag flying from its flagpole, but the headquarters of LFFI and 3 Commando Brigade were moving in, and several Falklands Islands civil servants back at their desks made searching for Argentinian material a little difficult. The next task was Government House and as I walked to it in the gathering gloom of another cold dusk, I met Ali and we made our way up the long driveway. On the front lawn where the British prisoners had been gathered in April, Argentinian soldiers were liberating food and drink from two containers. The House lies in the shadow of some trees and was decidedly spooky. Reliant on the narrow beams of our issue torches, at an annex door at the back, we felt for wiring indicating an improvised explosive device and entered and then got lost inside. We walked around to the front and successfully entered through the conservatory. The inside was too dark for a detailed search, however, we briefly examined several rooms on the ground floor, all of which were in a good state of repair. In a large room furnished with an impressively large wooden desk and several comfortable chairs, I found several interesting documents suggesting the office had been used by Brigadier-General Menendez, the Argentinian governor. I assumed it had been the office of HM Governor and made a mental note that a more detailed daylight search would be necessary. Next door was a conference room that had been converted into an Operations Room. On the walls were pinned Argentinian maps, orders of battle diagrams and air photographs. These I removed. In a small room containing a teleprinter were cable and wireless telegrams and a shredder surrounded by masses of paper. I found Ali in the conservatory the next day stuffing grapes into his jacket. Years later, I learnt that before Governor Rex Hunt had vacated the building in April, Mrs Hunt had considered spraying the fruit with insecticide. Fortunately, she did not.

The fine drizzle that had persisted since our arrival in Port Stanley had turned into cold, penetrating rain. On our way back to the LADE office, we went to the British Antarctic Survey House on Ross Road, about 100 yards from Government House where the LFFI Intelligence Section was billeted, to deposit the material gathered so far. After passed through the ceasefire line, I picked up a crate of a dozen bottles of red wine from one of two open shipping containers containing food. An Argentinian squatting on the grass seemed to be suffering from dysentery. Captain Charters turned up at the LADE office and I briefed him that it had been too dark for a detailed search of Government House and suggested the building be declared 'no entry' until further notice. He then suggested we needed transport. Some Argentinian vehicles had already been commandeered while others were beyond repair with smashed engines and torn wiring, however there was a column of abandoned Panhard AML 90 armoured cars in Philomel Street. I gingerly tried to start two without success. Several prisoners in a house occupied by the Argentinian HQ 3rd Brigade could not help and we had no idea where the troopers from the two Armoured Car companies were. Captain Charters then went to the Secretariat to receive orders and returned saying that there were none, however, Captain Sale of HQ LFFI had apparently frowned upon my looting of the wine. Since we were very short of rations, I undertook to scrounge some food from one of the Commando Brigade HQ and Signals Squadron echelons, but when I arrived at the ceasefire checkpoint, the Royal Marines Police were in control and a sergeant advised me his orders were that once anyone had crossed into the 'British' Sector, that person would not be permitted to return to the 'Argentinian' sector. This induced a ridiculous argument, due to fatigue, with me insisting that the intelligence base was in the 'Argentine' sector and we needed to float between both sectors. The sergeant eventually allowed me to cross, however, I could not find the echelons and returned to the 'Argentinian' sector without any problem, empty handed.

Royal Marines Police Sergeant 'Buster' Brown then informed me that Captain Sale wanted to see me at the Secretariat. Assuming it was something to do with the wine, I decided to plead guilty to the charge of looting and that my mitigation was that looted wine was better than bad water and it was a first-time offence. However, he did not mention it and explained that the next day the prisoners in the town were to be rounded up and either confined to warehouses or be marched to the prison camp at Stanley Airport. Prisoner repatriation had been negotiated and a tactical questioning centre was required to select 500 Special Category, who would be held until Argentina surrendered without conditions. They would be interrogated by the Joint Service Detailed Interrogation Unit, which was expected to land at Ajax Bay about 20 June. Since this was a HQ LFFI operation, a liaison officer and a guard force would be supplied and the Falkland Islands Company contracted to supply vessels to ferry the prisoners to the ships. Our estimate was that about 11,000 all ranks from the Army, Air Force and Navy had been captured. During the day, columns of Argentinians, some heavily laden, were being escorted to Stanley Airport by J Company, 42 Commando, some of whom had been members of Naval Party 8901 captured in April. Resistance was minimal, indeed one elderly couple asked that we be gentle with the conscripts, 'After all, they're so young and confused.' I was not entirely surprised by this display of maternal concern. The lack of fight among the rank-and-file prisoners had already been noted. Many of the conscripts were in a poor physical condition, largely through neglect by their officers to ensure their welfare. There was also growing concern there would be a medical emergency unless the *Junta* agreed to the repatriation of the Prisoners of War.

When I returned to the LADE office, we took advantage of our self-imposed curfew to inspect our accommodation. The ground floor consisted of a large reception area, the office of the former Argentinian consul, a small kitchen, a toilet and a store room. All were clean and warm, which was a welcome change from the darkness, cold and wet of the last three weeks. Upstairs was a communications room full of teleprinters and in a room that had been locked were two high-powered military radios not normally associated with booking internal flights. When we found a large bronze statue of the Argentinian hero Martin Herrera in a store room, I persuaded my colleagues that it should be presented to the Intelligence Corps Officers and Sergeants Messes to display on alternate 14ths of June to commemorate this remarkable victory.

Unfortunately the displays never happened. There was also a suggestion that the statue should list those Intelligence Corps who took part in Operation *Corporate*.

We barricaded the entrance of the LADE office, agreed a contingency plan to defend ourselves with our recently acquired weapons, split into two groups of three and tossed a coin. Bob Dilley won and defended the high ground of the upstairs, while my section was downstairs and the first line of defence with the MAG and grenades. After a meal fortified with the red wine, we loaded and cocked our weapons and the machine-gun, primed several grenades and promptly fell asleep,

The next day, the 16th, dawned weak and watery bright. I had not slept well, not because I was lying on the floor, but because the office was too warm! Breakfast was a simple affair of tinned beef burgers and a cup of coffee. The town water works, damaged by a shell during the later stages of the fighting, finally failed. The toilet would not flush and illness at best and disease at worst surely beckoned. The proprietor of the Upland Goose Hotel refused to let us fill our water bottles with clean water and indicated a couple of rather unhealthy looking barrels. The hotel was full of journalists and had figured in several intelligence reports as possibly an Argentinian officers' mess. Fortunately, a kind couple across the road offered us their water barrels, which looked considerably more drinkable.

The previous evening, the Argentinian occupation of West Falkland was dismantled when HMS *Avenger* moved the Fox Bay garrison to Ajax Bay. Three *Intrepid* LCUs escorted by HMS *Cardiff* collected the troops from Port Howard. The fourth LCU collected the marine infantry and others from Pebble Island. The total was about 1,900 prisoners to add to those captured at Goose Green. During the morning, *Canberra* entered San Carlos Water and embarked about 1,200 prisoners held at Ajax Bay and confined them to cabins; 100 Welsh Guards and some

RAF provided the guard force. HMS *Andromeda* took a large consignment of stretchers and blankets for Argentinian wounded during the Phase Two and Three battles. Major Burrill was concerned to find Brigadier-General Menendez on *Fearless* had not been kept in isolation, instead he had been allocated a comfortable cabin complete with a drinks cabinet well stocked with whisky and was being treated as a guest who was permitted visitors. Less than impressed with this naval hospitality, he had him transferred to the prison camp at Ajax Bay.

As I scouted the town the next day searching for a tactical questioning centre, I noted dug-outs, many reinforced by large bales of wool and corrugated iron, some excavated in gardens and others underneath vehicles. Some empty houses had been broken into and were in a deplorable state while others had the notice '*Prohiba de Entrada*' (No entrance) posted outside them. Some had been designated as air raid shelters by the town civil defence committee. The streets were littered with discarded military equipment – helmets, combat jackets, webbing and 'flak jackets', mostly in good condition. Several abandoned box-bodied signals trucks had not been touched. The Falkland Island Defence Force Drill Hall seemed to have been used as a supply point and resembled a chaotic supermarket with tins of food, meat, fruit salad, vegetables, coffee, sugar and milk. I began to wonder why Argentinians soldiers at the front had gone hungry. British Second World War helmets and 1937 webbing lay scattered on the floor and in a storeroom were sub-aqua equipment, diving knives broken in half, aqualungs and masks scattered on the floor. Several wet suits had been damaged beyond repair. Another room was filled with boxes of candles, batteries, gas cylinders, cookers and footwear – including fishermen's thigh boots. In a small office was an US Army collapsible bed and a desk with school registers on it. Outside in the mud and among burnt clothing was a small incinerator, probably used as a field kitchen.

The Junior School on John Street seemed to have been occupied by Argentinian Special Forces and was generally clean and undamaged. Desks and chairs were neatly piled into a storeroom and drawings and paintings remained pinned on the wall, indeed a picture of the Queen still hung over a blackboard. The main hall of the Senior School at the junction of Villiers and John Streets had been taken over by the Brigade Intelligence Section and Air Defence Troop. Prisoners had cleared it of rubbish, including a sangar used as a toilet. Years later, Tom Priestley told me that when he checked out the Colony Club, he had used basic techniques to search for improved explosive devices and had found a full-size snooker table covered in rubble and dust and night vision goggles, maps, grenades, ammunitions and rations and some wine in a couple of containers. He left the cheap 'plonk' and was welcomed back to the Intelligence Section like the prodigal son. He then collected some ration packs. When the Royal Marines Police later visited the School and asked if anyone had any bottles they should not have, everyone looked suitably innocent. When he made a second trip to the containers, he advised a Royal Marines Police patrol that he was looking for the Special Forces prisoners and asked the patrol if they could speak Spanish. Nothing more was said. I checked out the Falkland Islands Company offices opposite the East Jetty and quickly identified that it suited our purposes. There was a large square giving access to the public jetty from which prisoners could be transferred to the repatriation ships. Two large, dry warehouses could be used as assembly points. Three prisoners and I then converted six offices for screening and tactical questioning and cordoned off an assembly area into an 'unsanitised' area for those yet to be screened and a 'sanitised' for those waiting to be escorted to the jetties.

And then the inevitable happened. Captain Charters told us of a change of plan! I wryly remembered the parting words of Brigadier Thompson at the Sunday conference in Plymouth, three-and-a-half months' earlier 'Keep smiling, stay flexible'. Apparently, the practicalities of administering the prisoners were likely to be very difficult and repatriation was seen to be the optimum solution; however, Argentina was still reluctant to allow British ships to enter her waters and therefore there were no arrangements to administer repatriation of troops. Captain Charters then said that 600 Special Category were required until Argentina formally surrendered and listed them as commanding officers, pilots, intelligence officers, Special Forces, field security police, military police, radar and communications, artificers, bomb disposal teams, air defence and missile operators and aircraft ground crew. An urgent Essential Element of Intelligence from the Royal Engineers was the identification of minefields and locations of improvised explosive devices. Captured combat engineers and pioneers who gave their parole to make areas safe would be paid and administered by our sappers.

Canberra was expected after dark. Over an evening meal, we divided into two groups, A Watch led by me and B Watch by the RAF flight-lieutenant. I was a little concerned because he had apparently found billets in the town and would not be immediately contactable. Argentinian negotiators had been instructed that all columns were to be commanded by an officer and all equipment except for uniforms, a spoon and washing kit was to be jettisoned before embarking, including the sidearms of Argentinian officers. Hostility was expected from officers and senior other ranks and I believed the risk of retaliation or being taken hostage was high. That said, I had noted the lack of fight and animosity among the lower ranks and had no fear about walking among them, indeed they proved to be useful sources of information. Every prisoner was to be asked his name, rank and military occupation or unit and if he did not fit into the Special Category, he would pass through to a search team provided by the Royal Marines Police and later the Royal Military Police, for a detailed search. The small courtyard outside the British Antarctic Survey offices at the head of the jetty would be used to hold Special Category until such time as there were enough to be flown to the prison camp at Ajax Bay. HQ LFFI had been assured by the Falkland Islands Company that its vessels would transfer the prisoners to the repatriation ships.

After dark, *Canberra* and two warships anchored in Port William. 3 Para Company reinforced the guard force. At about 8pm, as the weather deteriorated into squalls of snow whipped up by a vicious wind from the south, A Watch was sheltering in the courtyard of the British Antarctic Survey small office adjacent to the jetty when Royal Marines escorted the first group of about 200 Argentinians, apprehensive, silent, weary and wet. Some were hobbling. There was still no power in Stanley and the only light was being provided by the captured Argentinian Coastguard cutter *Islas Malvinas* tied up to the public jetty. Of some concern was that the Globe Hotel near the jetty had a bar and was serving troops.

With the Falkland Islands Company motor coaster *Forrest* and three *Canberra* launches providing a shuttle service, a routine soon emerged that when a column arrived, the Watch commander briefed the senior prisoner about all equipment that was to be jettisoned and that the prisoners were to form three files facing the jetty. At the order '*Nexta!*' the prisoner stood in front of the three screeners and answered the questions '*Como se llama? Grado? Unidad? Empleo en las fuerzas armadas?*' ('Name, rank, unit, employment in the armed forces?'). Depending on the answer, it was either '*Adios! Hasta la vista!*' for repatriation or '*Alla!* (Over there!), pointing to the British Antarctic Survey office if identified as Special Category.

The last time that the British had handled so many prisoners was in Suez in 1956 and, to some extent, we were unprepared for some reactions. An angry Army lieutenant claiming to be the son of a general refused to surrender two pearl-handled silver Colt .45 automatics in his holsters and hurled them into the water declaring in English 'No bloody English are going to have these!' One suspects they are still there along with other weapons and equipment. A corporal handed me a large sheath knife presented to him by his colleagues inscribed with his April promotion date on the blade. An officer gave me his Colt and ammunition, which I retained for personal protection. A corporal commented that it had been 'a boring war'. The survivors of 601 and 602 Commando Companies, distinctive in their green berets and disruptive pattern US uniforms, were collectively more mature than the infantry. Some wore combat waistcoats. They were directed to Special Category. I later learnt, not surprisingly given the lack of illumination, they had smuggled in parts of a pistol but were betrayed by other prisoners. The 601 Company Commander, a major, stood silently beside us, tough and nationalistic.

During a short respite waiting for a boat, an Army lieutenant wearing Marine Infantry camouflaged trousers told me in good English that he was 4th Infantry Regiment, had been on Mount Wall and had withdrawn to Mount Harriet. His platoon had been subject to air attack and had clashed with British patrols. The weather had been poor and although ammunition was plentiful, the food trailer for central feeding often failed to arrive and consequently, when soldiers went hungry and morale dipped, it required considerable effort to persuade them to remain in their positions and not scavenge for food. He was less than forthcoming when I challenged him about accounts of field punishment, including being staked to the ground with rope and bayonets. The 42 Commando attack from the south of Mount Harrier had not been expected because British patrols had been probing from the west, nevertheless he praised his men for fighting, if only, he admitted, to survive. During the final stages of the battle, he had led survivors past Royal Marines reorganising and joined 5th Marine Infantry Battalion on Mount Tumbledown and two nights later had fought against 2nd Scots Guards. He was complimentary about their battle skills. His main lesson was that while a conscript army is inferior to professional soldiers, it should not be taken for granted that conscripts will not fight. He considered that some of his equipment was superior but struggled to give examples. He believed that the regular use of helicopters to transport troops was a mistake because of the number lost. His men should have been fitter. The lieutenant was disappointed with the performance of the senior officers, in particular their not contesting the San Carlos landings. He believed that the Argentinian Army would learn from the war and next time, with a wry smile, he said the British would not find it so easy. As he followed his men onto the coaster, we shook hands. Thereafter I noticed that junior officers generally cared for their soldiers, middle-ranking and senior officers less so. The commanding officer of the 6th Mechanised Infantry Regiment commented, 'The sixty days in foxholes destroyed the will to fight.' He was selected as Special Category.

Among others repatriated were the Army engineers who had kept the airport runway open and the gunners of the 3rd Artillery Group who had provided valuable close support but failed to spike their guns. 601 Air Defence Artillery Group had fired on friend and foe. The gunners from the 101st Artillery Group had been flown by C-130 on 12 and 13 June with four CITEFA F3 155mm howitzers and were repatriated within the week. Two guns delivered on the last night were captured with their muzzle covers still in place. A request from the major commanding the 10th Armoured Recce Company that his men return with the unit guidon was agreed. Prisoners kept asking for water, but there was none because the water filtration plant had been damaged.

About midnight I received message from the jetty that the crew of the *Forrest* were refusing to sail because they had completed their shift and the relief crew had not appeared. There had been no warning and alarmed at the prospect of the repatriation slowing down, I searched for the HQ LFFI liaison officer without success.

Apparently, there was a celebratory dinner with Major-General Moore, somewhere. I therefore I asked the crew if they would make a final trip while I sorted out the issue, again without success. While I was muttering something about having left my family to liberate the Falklands, the relief crew tottered onto the jetty, but they had been drinking at the Globe Hotel. About 20 minutes later, a conscript slipped and fell into the freezing water between the jetty and hull of the coaster and was dragged out by his lieutenant and myself just before its black hull crunched against the jetty. The soaking soldier was confused, even more so when I wrapped a woollen Argentinian poncho given to me by a prisoner, around his shoulders. '*Muchos gracias, señor,*' he said grasping my hand. Shortly afterwards, A Watch handed over to B Watch and we went to bed cold, wet, hungry and thirsty but in a warm building.

About 8am the next day, I returned to the jetty to find it still crowded with prisoners and a small pile of automatic pistols on the ground near the Royal Marines Police searchers. I was intrigued by fire hoses snaking from a standpipe to a smoking house and also a 40 Commando troop with fixed bayonets. What had happened?

The Flight-Sergeant told me that some civilians and soldiers, apparently 3 Para, drinking in the Globe Hotel had decided to sort out Argentinians waiting to be screened, but the prisoners they chose were mainly from the 7th Infantry Regiment, which largely recruited from tough working class neighbourhoods of Buenos Aires. During the Battles of Mount Longdon and Wireless Ridge, some paras reported the enemy using the language of 1930s Hollywood gangster movies.

A tense situation escalated when several smoke grenades were thrown and the handbrake of a Panhard armoured car was released and directed at the prisoners. The prisoners added to the chaos by setting fire to the Globe Store, which resulted in the Stanley Fire Brigade attending – cheered on by British and Argentinians alike, but their hoses were either rotten or had been stabbed and fountains of cold water soon drenched the mob. Further disorder erupted when three Argentinian lieutenant-colonels heading three columns barged through the waiting files and demanded to be repatriated as a priority.

The situation was becoming increasingly fraught. Our RAF Flight-Sergeant was not entirely proficient with Colt .45s and was unloading one taken from an officer when he had an accidental discharge. The bullet hit the road and whistled into the darkness. As silence immediately enveloped the square, he cheerily piped up, 'Sorry about that, chaps!' The situation was restored and the repatriation continued. This was the only serious breakdown of discipline throughout the repatriation.

About 100 Special Category collected during the night were escorted to the racecourse and flown to Ajax Bay by helicopters, including the Chinook that survived the sinking of the *Atlantic Conveyor*. The disruption and several other lesser challenges to the repatriation led to Brigadier-General Jofre, who commanded 10th Infantry Brigade and had been appointed as the Argentinian repatriation senior representative, being summoned by an officer from HQ LFFI. When he claimed that he could not to speak English and sent a major and a captain to represent him, Jofre was instructed that he and both officers were to be available at all times.

As the loading of *Canberra* continued, more interesting prisoners passed: the medical orderly claiming to be a fully qualified doctor who had a conversation in fluent German with a couple of colleagues; the English teacher with the surviving former pupils of his class from a Patagonian school, some with Welsh surnames; the trumpet player who entertained with a tune; the English-speaking conscript who did not want to return to Argentina and interpreted for us until the repatriation was complete. There were twenty dog-handlers from 181st Military Police Company who arrived with their huge, well-groomed and noisy Alsatians, which led to a suggestion the dogs should be transferred to the British Army, but all failed the entrance examination to 'sit', until someone helpfully commented the dogs understood only Spanish; they were also repatriated. An officer wearing a tattered jacket said that he had been caught in the open during an air raid and it had been shredded by shrapnel. A conscript was allowed to keep his helmet because a bullet had entered in the front and exited from the back, without harming him. As a group of Air Force gunners passed, I confiscated an item that a prisoner claimed to be a piece from a Sea Harrier. A captain kept his compass because it was a present sent by his wife. Of some interest to the Protestants among us was the range of religious objects, from rosary beads, bibles and statuettes to several infantrymen carrying a large statue of the Virgin Mary. British soldiers using Argentinian ration packs sometimes found a rosary inside, presumably from a packer. Of some interest was the number of padres.

It was inevitable that the jetty became clogged with prisoners waiting to be ferried to the *Canberra* and then, about midday, the situation was made worse when a member of the *Forrest* crew brought a message from the *Canberra* Royal Navy Liaison Officer that the limit was 4,167 prisoners. The message came without warning and so we presumed there had been a communications breakdown between the Royal Navy Liaison Officer on *Canberra* and HQ LFFI. There was still no sign of a HQ LFFI liaison officer. Among the 300 screened prisoners on the jetty was a group of naval officers and ratings, including one on a stretcher with severe trench foot and in the windswept square were columns waiting to be screened. For some reason, the 40 Commando troop had also fallen out and all that remained were the three screeners and the Royal Marines Police searchers. It seemed to me that the repatriation process had essentially collapsed. As the most senior person on the spot, I found a Commando Brigade staff officer and asked him to alert HQ LFFI that there was a problem at the jetty and arranged a lift for him in a Blues and Royals Scimitar. Having heard nothing for about an hour, I walked to Sullivan House to find it empty except for Brigadier Thompson at a desk upstairs. I told him the problem – *Canberra* full, repatriation controlled by HQ LFFI but no liaison officer and no communications and the 40 Commando guard force fallen out. He was not happy and radioed HQ LFFI and very firmly saying that, 'The prisoners are your problem. Come down and sort it out – now!' The Commando Brigade had responsibility for the security of Port Stanley and he asked that I keep him briefed on the repatriation. I then hitched a lift back to the jetty and halted any further repatriation. About half-an-hour later, Colonel Ian Baxter, the HQ LFFI Deputy Assistant Adjutant and Quartermaster-General, then arrived, 'Now, what is this all about, Staff?' I replied with some impatience, 'I have about 800 prisoners awaiting screening, 500 screened on the jetty ready to board, including a stretcher casualty – but *Canberra* has reached its limit, the guard force has fallen out and there is no HQ LFFI liaison officer. Me and my team are knackered. What are your orders?'

He assessed the situation and issued a stream of orders. 'Put the Special Category in the BAS offices. Return to the remainder in the godowns. And don't panic, Staff.' While resisting the insinuation of his last comment, my patience had worn out and I reminded him that responsibility for the repatriation of the prisoners lay with HQ LFFI, not an Intelligence Corps NCO. The role of the screeners was, solely, to select 600 Special Category prisoners. About an hour later, Lieutenant-Colonel Stevenson, a tall Royal Marine, arrived as the HQ LFFI liaison officer and was really helpful.

The next morning, HQ LFFI advised that parts of a rifle had been found among some Special Category transferred to Ajax Bay. At the jetty, evidence of organised resistance by Argentinian officers had been detected including masquerading as conscripts, smuggling bayonets, knives, parts of weapons and other equipment and being a nuisance – much to the annoyance of the conscripts. Reinforcements to the screening teams allowed us to exploit the little love lost between officers and conscripts by mingling with the columns to gather intelligence so that resistance could be undermined, sabotage of the repatriation could be detected and dropped documents, equipment and weapons could be collected. In my Watch, I mingled with the prisoners, supported by Ali Ciasco loitering behind me with a loaded rifle and listening for clues of disruption. Unfortunately, the flight-lieutenant did not appreciate that mixing with prisoners in a friendly fashion produces results, particularly when the penalty is not repatriation.

No sooner had the prisoners waiting on the jetty been returned to a warehouse than we were warned that the *Norland* was due into Port William the next night. As evening was swiftly approaching and the night promised to be foul, both Watches gathered in the LADE offices for a meal from Argentinian rations of baked beans and corned beef. Strange to be eating food made in Leeds from Argentinian rations! About an hour later I began to feel most unwell, queasy, sweaty and with a splitting headache, nevertheless there were prisoners to be screened. At about midnight, as the Argentinian auxiliary *Bahia Paraiso* was due to embark repatriated prisoners, B Watch arrived and it was with some relief that while walking back to the LADE offices, I vomited. I suspected dirty water and immediately feeling better, drank the last of my good water and did not eat for the next 24 hours.

The next morning, 18 June, we learnt that President Galtieri had resigned, thanks to intervention by the International Committee of the Red Cross and the Brazilian and Swiss Governments, and the *Junta* had given *Canberra* safe-conduct to Puerto Madryn, about 650 miles north-east of Port Stanley. She was escorted the next day to a berth and, within 3 hours, the prisoners had disembarked, the senior officers were treated to a near heroes' welcome and the remainder were quietly packed into buses and driven to barracks. *Norland* arrived at Port William and that night embarked 2,047 prisoners, whom she also ferried to Port Madryn.

The townspeople were beginning to emerge from their houses, nevertheless, Port Stanley was in a sorry state, without water and disease threatening both armies and the civilians. The Globe Store was still burning and the streets and square leading to the public jetty were littered with heaps of discarded equipment and clothing being picked over by British soldiers searching for souvenirs. HQ LFFI therefore instructed that prisoner working parties were to clear the town of the abandoned equipment, the mass of ammunition littering the roads and that the dead were to be buried. The only prisoners to be left in the town were the casualties in the field hospital in one of the warehouses.

In between the repatriation, LFFI Intelligence mounted a counter-intelligence operation to investigate the extent of Argentinian subversion and infiltration before and during the occupation. This type of operation had originated as part of the Intelligence Corps field security strategy first developed in 1914 at the beginning of the First World War and was designed to protect the Army from subversive and covert resistance. It was known that several residents with known or suspected Argentinian sympathies had been evacuated to Argentina shortly before the surrender. Among those investigated by a Polish-speaking intelligence Corps warrant officer were nine Polish seamen who had jumped ship from a trawler before the Argentinian invasion.

I was tasked to interview a Falkland Islander who had been employed in the LADE offices as a secretary before the Argentinian invasion. Shown into a neat living room in a house owned by her father on the southern outskirts of the town and given a most welcome mug of hot tea by her sister, I was conscious of my filthy uniform and hoped that the fact that I had not showered for a fortnight was not too obvious. The secretary said that she and her young daughter had returned to Port Stanley three months before the invasion. When she said her estranged husband was a serving Royal Marine whom she had met when he had been a member of a previous Naval Party 8901 and was now drafted to 42 Commando, I speculated that her connection to the Naval Party had probably been a factor in her being employed with LADE. I advised the increasingly distraught lady that I was investigating the extent of Argentinian intelligence gathering in Stanley and that her employment in the LADE office would give considerable insight. The interview progressed satisfactorily for about 2 hours until two Harriers flew low overhead. She began to shake and weep and it was then that I began to appreciate the strains under which the citizens of Port Stanley must have lived, in particular those living near Argentinian positions on Stanley Common. Three women had been killed nearby by a British shell during the final battle. I therefore concluded the interview and undertook to let her husband know that she and their daughter were safe.

As I was returning to the LADE offices, I met a column of prisoners being escorted to the airport by Marine Fletcher. As a member of 42 Commando, he had been a skiing instructor on the Arctic Warfare Training course in Norway. He told me he had enjoyed the experience of war but now just wanted to go home, as we all did. At the rear of the column, I noticed an Argentinian sergeant armed with a pistol and asked him to hand it to me, reminding him that under the surrender agreement, only officers were permitted to carry weapons – for personal protection. He refused on several occasions and then I raised my Sterling. Still he refused and it was only when I cocked my gun that he unbuttoned his holster, drew out the pistol, ejected the magazine and as he pulled the working parts to the rear, a shell jumped out. He then handed the weapon to me butt first. I said 'Gracias' with some relief and we shook hands. Before returning to the LADE offices,

I decided to tempt fate by having a beer at the Upland Goose Hotel but was confronted by the scrawled hand-written notice sign 'Out of Bounds to Troops. By Order Magistrates'. It was a little ungrateful. I later bought a can from the Globe Hotel, which now sported the sign 'Globe and Laurel', courtesy of paint provided by the Commando Logistic Regiment.

The *Bahia Paraiso,* the Argentinian naval auxiliary involved in the scrap metal merchant incident on South Georgia and now a hospital ship, arrived to collect sick and wounded prisoners. Having been warned of her arrival the previous day, I had visited the Argentinian field hospital in a warehouse to check with the senior medical officer if there were any shirkers among the patients. The approximately 400 casualties included amputees, those who had been blinded, had stomach wounds and, in a corner, those with psychiatric conditions. One could not help but admire the commitment of Argentinian and British military medical staff and the few civilians tending them. When the ship arrived, an Intelligence Corps sergeant and the flight-lieutenant screened stretcher cases at the field hospital at Stanley Airfield while my team at the jetty dealt with wounded in Port Stanley. The International Committee of the Red Cross had been monitoring the repatriation throughout. I had first met the Red Cross shortly after Goose Green when they visited the prison camp at *Red Beach* and recommended prisoners should retain their steel helmets, which was an eminently sensible solution because the beach was a main stores base and the prisoners were housed not far from ammunition dumps and had been bombed. I had found their representatives to be impartial to the extent that on more than one occasion they had judged against Argentinians complaining of ill-health or with an urgent need to return to Argentina. The senior representative was a very pleasant Swiss who spoke good English with a French accent. When an Air Force doctor and his medical assistants arrived with the first batch, the wounded were mostly gunshot- and shrapnel-wounds casualties, those with burns and several stretcher cases, a conscript with a serious head wound and three with gastro-enteritis. There was also an unusually large number of aircrew, including a civilian pilot, claiming to be wounded or ill. We were suspicious and after having a short conversation with the senior Argentinian medical officer who confirmed he had been pressured into harbouring the pilots, I informed the Red Cross who watched as we selected several aircrew as Special Category and sent the remainder to the prison camp at the Airport.

When a captain complaining of heart problems asked to see the Red Cross, I advised its representative who then asked a female doctor to conduct an assessment. She carried out a rather public consultation and confirmed the officer had a genuine complaint and recommended he be admitted to the *Bahia Paraiso* sick bay as a matter of urgency. While searching the medical bag of a medical officer, I found a concealed 9mm pistol. Fortunately the Swiss representative had been watching and when I showed the weapon, in a very public display, he singled out the Argentinian, threatened to remove the retained status of the medical officer and reminded him that his job was to save lives and not to encourage further loss. To be honest, I suspected the doctor had been pressured into the attempted smuggling.

By this time, a detachment from 160 Provost Company, Royal Military Police, attached to 5 Infantry Brigade, were sharing the searching responsibilities with the Royal Marines Police. In spite of frequent warnings to Brigadier-General Jofre and the prisoner column commanders, the searchers were still finding parts of weapons, bladed instruments and souvenirs. Something had to be done and when a 3rd Infantry Regiment conscript attempted to conceal a hacksaw and a knife in his boots, the officer commanding the military police decided that an example must be made to deter further breaches of the repatriation agreement. He therefore summoned Jofre and his two liaison officers and explained to the three officers through an interpreter that what was about to happen was entirely their fault. He then conducted a strip search of the anxious young soldier down to his underpants and then gave Jofre a public, expert, old-fashioned sergeant major dressing down emphasising that breaches of the ceasefire agreement were intolerable and that, in future, prisoners caught with prohibited items would be dealt with severely, as would Jofre for not co-operating. When the tearful conscript was dressed, the military police gave him a mug of tea and took him to the jetty. The threat seemed to work, for a little while later I found a dumped pistol near a column.

We had nearly finished the repatriation when a British major sporting French parachute wings above his left breast pocket of his incredibly clean combat jacket and wearing full webbing included a pistol, bayonet and large hunting knife arrived, 'Who is in charge here?'

As I looked round, the screeners stopped while the Royal Marines Police carried on searching. 'I suppose I am, sir. What can I do for you?' I replied. He said that he had very recently arrived and was tasked to organise the repatriation with his team of sixty-nine and a computer. He introduced a Royal Engineer warrant officer of Gibraltarian extraction. I was somewhat irritated, nevertheless, a break would be welcome and so I suggested that he set up on several 40-gallon oil drums on the jetty and then stood to one side with my Watch. Apart from the warrant officer, none of the others could speak Spanish and soon the jetty became a mass of chattering Argentinians clutching boarding cards, which they gave to a soldier before they boarded a coaster waiting to ferry the prisoners to the ship. And then the threatening heavens opened and as wet snow fell, the warrant officer mentioned that the ink in his pens had frozen and the pencils didn't write on wet paper. 'Where can we go?' he appealed. When I advised him there was nowhere except the warehouses, the major and his team left the jetty. I learnt later the team was part of a HQ LFFI organisation commanded by a full colonel tasked to administer the prisoners and run the prison camp, indeed it had practised handling prisoners on exercise prior to employment. Unfortunately, the prison camp was floating around a hold of the sunken *Atlantic Conveyor* and several thousand prisoners had already been repatriated.

By the afternoon, the bright early morning had disintegrated into sweeping cold rain and snow and a penetrating westerly wind. Warned that another ship was due in, Bob Dilley and I were tasked to check the Grass Trials Unit on Stanley Common for intelligence. Mindful of mines and booby traps, we kept to the stony track and noted the disorganised network of water-filled craters, trenches and shelters and naval and air bombardment craters. It was little wonder that some Argentinian soldiers admitted they had abandoned their positions and sheltered in Stanley. We passed one of the four impressive 155mm CITEFA howitzers and white mine tape fluttering around a battery of 105mm Pack Howitzer under flapping camouflage nets and surrounded by empty shell cases glinting in the muddy gun pits.

Suddenly, there was a tap-tap-tap coming from a nearby house. I knocked on the door and it was opened by a lady. Beside her stood a small girl with big brown eyes watching us apprehensively. The woman invited us into the small and dark front room, which was freezing from the cold wind sweeping in through a broken window pane. She told us that the house belonged to her father, who was the Falklands' oldest inhabitant, and that he had been evacuated to England in April. I remembered him from video recordings and advised the child that 'Grandpa is safe in England.' This brought smiles to their faces. The woman said that the house had been requisitioned by the Argentinians and she was repairing it but she was apprehensive about cutting peat because of mines. Bob and I checked the house and garden for booby traps and discovered several Tigercat missiles in the garden shed. I advised the woman not to touch anything outside until Royal Engineers had cleared the area.

As part of the LFFI counter-intelligence operation, the next day I interviewed a senior Falklands Island Company manager in his office. From conversations with Falkland Islanders during the advance to Port Stanley and the townspeople, there was considerable resentment at the perceived collaboration by the Falkland Islands Company with the Argentinians. Indeed, managers had been photographed at a reception given by Brigadier-General Menendez in early April to celebrate the Argentinian 'liberation' of the Falkland Islands. However, throughout the occupation, the manager was in the near-impossible predicament of balancing the thin line between collaboration and keeping the Falkland Islanders supplied. He claimed in his defence that he thought it sensible to work with the occupation authorities and thereby ensure the islanders were adequately supplied. He believed he had been correct in his dealings with the Argentinians and produced settled requisition forms for the use of equipment, the coasters and material in order to prove they had paid for Company resources. Interestingly, he mentioned that everyone knew the Naval Party 8901 strategy because their plans rarely changed; it was a classic example of a breach of operational security. As I concluded my interview, he asked if I could arrange for the local radio to announce the company had not collaborated; I said I would try.

That evening, the 25th Special Infantry Regiment swaggered onto the square. Although formed specifically for the Argentinian occupation, it had been deployed piecemeal. C Company had fought at Port San Carlos and Goose Green. The commanding officer, Lieutenant-Colonel Seineldín, and his adjutant, both wearing green commando berets, ignored the Argentinian liaison officers. After I had briefed them about the items to be jettisoned at a given command, those with a problem doubled out and lined up on the road. It was a far larger group than other regiments and as an interpreter and I passed along the ranks, each man came to attention, gave his rank and name and described his problem. The adjutant translated, however his version often differed markedly from my interpreter and thus most queries were rejected. The adjutant confirmed the regiment had defended the airfield and had been subjected to considerable naval gunfire and air attacks on Air Force Base Stanley. No one had been killed and a few had been wounded. He denied that the two officers who had been with C Company at Port San Carlos were in their column. During the searches, the unit war diary was found with a soldier.

The next day the second Joint Service Interrogation Unit landed at *Red Beach* with the primary role of interrogating prisoners captured during the fighting and those selected as Special Category. A day later, I was walking to 42 Commando at the European Space Research Organisation Agency complex near Moody Brook to see if the husband of the LADE secretary had deployed, when a a colour-sergeant driving a captured Mercedes Unimog offered me lift. He had been the acting Company Sergeant Major of Naval Party 8901 and had been captured. As we passed a 29th Commando Regiment battery, he said, 'They won the war for us.' I agreed. Indeed, the following message had been intercepted on 13 June:

> British artillery has complete dominance over Argentinian artillery. The British are firing at and hitting targets on the extreme edge of Stanley. About 140 men have been hit by shrapnel. No more men should attempt to go because the losses will be too terrible.

I found Lieutenant de Jaeger, the Intelligence Officer, and when I told him about my conversation with the secretary, he said that her husband was in Plymouth and undertook to send a message that his wife and child were safe. He gave me some airmail envelopes for her.

Before returning to Port Stanley, I walked across Moody Brook Bridge, which had been reported as destroyed, to the shattered remains of the Royal Marines Barracks. On the slipway were two undamaged Bosun sailing dinghies, in a field was a small multi-barrelled rocket launcher and on a track was an abandoned Iroquois helicopter. The area was littered with water-filled craters and shrapnel and fluttering white tape and red signs displaying the skull and cross bones and the word 'Mina'. Above, Wireless Ridge was silent and to the south across Stanley Harbour the white houses of the town glistened in the sunlight.

Meanwhile the repatriation was nearing its end. I was with the escort taking a group of about 100 Special Category to the racecourse with a small Royal Marines escort when 2 Para approached four abreast, linked ammunition belts draped around shoulders, along Ross Road and entered Stanley Cathedral. Traffic was halted. Best to wait, so I invited my column to sit on the grass to let them pass. Years later at a function at Eton College, I met the Battalion padre, Reverend Cooper, and recounted the chaos the Battalion had caused. As 3 Commando Brigade began to assemble, in contrast, 45 Commando, weighed down by heavy packs and equipment, silently filed into town to board the RFA *Sir Percivale* tied up alongside the Falkland Islands Company jetty for a well-deserved rest that included a shower, a meal provided by the ship and some beers. As they waited to board, the Royal Marines mingled with some prisoners. The Commando Logistic Regiment arrived. It had kept the Brigade supplied in spite of the difficulties of the terrain and lack of transport. The Medical Squadron had tended a high percentage of the 777 wounded. The unsung Brigade HQ and Signals Squadron also gathered. The Command Post had been operational since 2 April.

On 22 June, before HQ LFFI set up in Government House and the return of Governor Hunt, Captain Charters tasked me to carry out a detailed search, this time in daylight. I was struck by the colonial style of the building and its similarity to Flagstaff House in Victoria Barracks, Hong Kong, which had been the former residence of the Commander-in-Chief, British Forces. I had handed its keys to a Hong Kong civil servant when the barracks closed in 1978. Government House was still surrounded by white mine tape. Apart from the bullet holes from the 2 April battle, in my opinion Brigadier-General Menendez and his staff had generally respected it, no doubt encouraged by Mr Don Bonner, the driver and butler to Governor Hunt, who had visited every day during the occupation. This time, I entered through the door to the annex and encountered a few HQ LFFI Staff officers and signallers establishing their headquarters in the former Argentinian Operations Room. They agreed to leave while I conducted a more thorough search, during which I removed a map covered by a trace showing Argentinian deployments and the silhouettes of British aircraft. Among ships marked with a cross as 'sunk' was HMS *Invincible,* which was incorrect. On another wall were briefing notes about British units with the SAS listed as based at Aldershot, as opposed to Hereford. Again sitting at the large desk in the Governor's office, I noted everything seemed to be in a good state of repair and that the habits of the previous occupants had been honoured. For instance, English popular paperbacks lined a bookcase and references on Colonial administration were placed neatly in a glass-fronted wooden cabinet.

I was surprised that radios and cypher equipment in the Communications Room had not been damaged or destroyed and consequently, I arbitrarily filled a postbag with message sheets and cryptographic tape. A registry contained classified documents, which I also bagged. Four post bags of mail, mostly from junior ranks to addresses in Argentina, were all franked with a 'Las Malvinas' stamp. A dealer later told me the find was worth about £10,000! I checked lounges, a games room containing a snooker table, the upstairs bedrooms and bathrooms and the servant quarters in the annex. I deposited the postbags with the LFFI Intelligence Section.

In 1985, while visiting the Ministry of Defence to help a Staff officer to draft an answer for a Member of Parliament on his inevitable allegations of the mishandling of Prisoners of War, I was shown several sacks labelled 'Falklands' on a table in a store room and asked if I knew anything about them – indeed, I did! I had been searching the building for a couple of hours when more HQ LFFI staff arrived. Among the first facilities needed was a toilet for Major-General Moore and I recommended something suitable to an aide. Civilised toilets were at a premium and there was still no running water in the town. The British Army was back!

During the day, the naval transport *Almirante Irizar* arrived in Port William to embark the balance of the prisoners. Among the final batch assembled in the single Falkland Islands Company warehouse was the 5th Marine Infantry Battalion and two soldiers with gastro-enteritis on stretchers. Distinctive in their disruptive pattern combat uniforms and black berets, they regarded themselves as an elite. During the screening at the jetty, Brigadier-General Jofre's portly driver and his senior clerk, both Army, arrived. Both had probably thirty years' service between them, but were despised by the marines. The adjutant hissed '*Ejército!*' (Army!) and spat in disgust. The two were closely screened and allowed to embark. The adjutant was the last to go through. Fed up with his arrogance, I asked a Royal Marines Police searcher to conduct a thorough search. When he finished, I asked the adjutant in conversation what he thought of the army. Again, he spat. 'I am Army,' I told him. 'But your hat?' he replied nonplussed, pointing at my cypress green Intelligence Corps beret, which was lighter than the commando green of the Royal Marines.

A Royal Engineer officer brought the officer commanding 10th Engineer Company, who had been trying to subvert paroled Argentinian sappers into not co-operating with Royal Engineers marking minefields and lifting mines; he was transferred to the prison camp at Ajax Bay because it was evident he had information of value but was disinclined to share it. On the other hand, an engineer lieutenant had proven most helpful on several occasions and apparently later wrote to his wife praising the British. He was repatriated.

In general, considering their national pride, captured officers were easier to manage than expected. Most accepted the inevitability of capture. Several senior officers were adamant that Argentina would return, some said within twenty years, others within five and one within the year, which did seem a little unrealistic. Most accepted that while the defence had been numerically superior, they had been defeated by experienced and well-trained troops. Some suggested that the concentration of counter-insurgency and internal security operations had blunted readiness for a conventional war until reminded that the British had been involved in counter-insurgency and internal security since 1945.

Most criticised the conscript nature of their Armed Forces and commented on the respectful relationship between British officers and other ranks. Junior officers seemed to have genuine concern for the men and in several instances witnessed their men being screened before embarking themselves. One officer who had been led to believe that Harrier raids, destruction of the helicopter force and poor roads had prevented regular distribution of supplies to his men on Two Sisters blamed inefficient and ineffective logistic support. Virtually all the career warrant officers and senior NCOs expressed considerable dissatisfaction with their senior and middle-ranking officers and had little patience with the conscripts. Most conscripts looked upon the war with the stoicism I had witnessed in Belize. Some were well-educated and they included university graduates. Those defending the Outer Defence Zone had experienced bad weather conditions and apart from those suffering with foot aliments, most seemed in a reasonable state of health. Most looked upon captivity with a laid-back philosophy typical of conscripts through the ages. They had no interest in international events, except for football and rugger, and looked forward to discharge. How they would be received in Argentina was not yet known.

By the time the last of the Argentinians had left the Falkland Islands, 11,848 had been repatriated by teams of NCOs and one officer; 595 all ranks had been retained as Special Category. Thirty-five engineers and 200 other ranks had been given parole. A few civilians were captured. A typically arrogant television war correspondent who was selected as Special Category complained loudly, as expected, until it was explained that firstly, captured war correspondents must be treated as prisoners of war and, secondly, he had a story no other journalist would have. Two priests named by several conscripts as propaganda experts slipped through the net. A substantial amount of equipment was captured including 12 Panhard AML 90 armoured cars, 7 Tigercat missile launchers, 3 155mm L3 and 10 105mm Pack Howitzers, 15 Oerlikon twin 35mm and 15 Rh 202 20mm air defence guns and a Coastguard patrol boat; and 11,000 rounds of 105mm and 4 million rounds of 7.62mm ammunition, to name a few items. Clearing the minefields, some of which were marked, remained a task – and it still is.

During the afternoon, 'Dutch' Holland warned me that the entire Intelligence Section was scheduled to embark on HMS *Fearless* that night and I was not to worry about being left behind. I was aware a couple of colleagues who had been on deployment since April were transferred to Ajax Bay by HQ LFFI to help the recently arrived Joint Service Interrogation Unit. They would remain deployed until Argentina formally surrendered in mid-July. Nevertheless, there was time to relax and I joined an Intelligence Corps colleague for a walk around the town, now largely cleared of the detritus of war and with more evidence of the townspeople. Our first port of call was to identify the warehouse where two cans of beer per man were being issued, a most welcome gift courtesy of the Ministry of Defence. While the town cemetery at Ross Road

East told the history of Falkland Islanders through the headstones, across the road was an Argentinian temporary cemetery of hastily dug graves and wooden battlefield crosses with the name of the occupant inscribed in black ink. But rain had washed away the shallow topsoil to expose boots and a stiff hand. It was a sad place and I wondered if their relatives would be permitted to visit their graves. They would. A total of 237 Argentinian war dead are buried in the military cemetery near Darwin, some of whom have yet to be identified. We continued along the road toward the Argentinian State Oil Company compound. Organised rows of tents of various sizes had sprung up everywhere. A Royal Engineer plant tractor was slipping and sliding in the glutinous mud but no one seemed concerned. We came across pipes laid on blocks of wood, used in an attempt to deceive air photographic interpreters; certainly there had been reports of artillery along this stretch of the coast.

At about 7pm, 'Dutch' told me my attachment to LFFI Intelligence had been terminated and that I was to ensure that I boarded the ship. He would field any demands for me. I set out to rejoin the Intelligence Section at the LADE offices but was delayed by an officer seeking some answers about the repatriation. When I arrived at the LADE office, Neil, who was making sure that nothing had been left behind, said that we were to embark from the public jetty, the Intelligence Section had already left and he was making sure the entire Section left. The key issue was to board a ship! We collected all our kit and walked along Ross Road to the public jetty, now cleared of rubbish, where the beachmaster said the Intelligence Section was listed not on *Fearless* but on the *Canberra* and the others were catching a helicopter to the ship. I had virtually lost all sense of time and a cruise on a luxury liner seemed a good way to end this crazy adventure. Elements of the Royal Marines Police and the Communications Troops were also waiting for a landing craft on the jetty, the scene of so much activity and drama during the week, now curiously quiet and well lit. A landing craft approached out of the darkness and after we clambered on board, the coxswain set course towards Port William, picked up speed and headed for the liner, no longer blacked out. A cold wintry gust swept flurries of snow across the well deck in farewell.

The Intelligence Section later told us when the beachmaster said they were listed on the *Canberra* and should catch a 'petrol parrot' (helicopter) at the racecourse, a distance of about 1,800 yards from the jetty, they 'yomped' the distance and waited for about 15 minutes until flown onto the rear Flight Deck.

13
HOMEWARD BOUND

The landing craft came alongside the rusty white hull of *Canberra* and we clambered up a rope ladder to a large port that led into the luxurious warmth of the main restaurant where checkpoint allocated our cabins. To our surprise, we found that kitbags or suitcases we had left on *Fearless* had been transferred to the ship. Neil, Mick Marshalsay and I were given the three-berthed D74, D deck, port side. Mick would join us in two days when the remainder of Brigade HQ came on board. Neil and I were guided to our cabin, back into the lap of civilisation, where we dumped our kit and went on the search for food – old habits die hard! We checked the Pacific Restaurant and since there were no signs of life; we were about to leave when some stewards appeared. When they learnt we had just boarded, one of them disappeared and returned with a tray laden with bread rolls and apples and then, beckoning us to follow him, he took us to the main galley where he extracted a large plate of lamb chops from an oven. Like a pair of medieval barons, we plundered the plate. Thanking the stewards for their generosity, we returned to our cabin to sort out our kit, packed the clothing that we had worn for the last four weeks into our bergens and had that most important luxury, an endless, hot-water, invigorating shower. Later, the engines rumbled into life and the ship left Port Stanley and headed to San Carlos Water to collect 40 Commando.

Canberra entered San Carlos Water the following day. It was as I remembered it early on D-Day, for a few minutes – peaceful. It was difficult to believe that three weeks ago its tranquillity had been shattered by the noise, death and destruction of sudden and furious air raids challenged by the regular clatter of guns and lattices of angry tracer pursuing low-flying Skyhawks and Mirages screaming low above the waves.

Today, the chilly green water was disturbed by occasional white horses leaping from wave to wave, and was surrounded by serene, yet sombre, green hills and the distant white houses of San Carlos overlooking the two *Blue Beaches*. Oily wisps of grey smoke from around the refrigeration plant at *Red Beach* floated into the sodden skies amid a front of rain creeping down the hillside and lashing the sea into a frenzy. A Type-21 destroyer, its hull rusty and grey, slowly patrolled the inlet, a wisp of exhaust curling from its blacktopped funnel. From its bridge, a signalman blinked a message to the ship. Two orange bobbing buoys marked the grave of HMS *Antelope*. I was unlikely to forget the shattering explosions when she blew up. A chill breeze blew along the deck.

During the night of 24 June, *Canberra* returned to Port Stanley to collect 42 Commando and others from the Commando Brigade. The next morning dawned bright but chilly, but who cared, because the navigator would set a course north to UK. Then a tannoy broadcast a call for anyone who had been to Moody Brook Barracks since the surrender to report to the bridge. Yes, I had and therefore made my way to the Bridge and was pointed at a radio where someone who identified himself as 'Holdfast', (Royal Engineer) wanted to know about minefields in the area. I described the taped-off area near the bridge over the stream and that I had searched the barracks without any undue difficulty. I had not noted any evidence of minefields, such as disturbed earth and taped areas. When I finished, a watchkeeper gave me a tour of the Bridge, which was most interesting. During the day, as Brigade HQ and more units embarked, some by helicopter to the Flight Deck, others by landing craft and some by trawler, some concerns, apparently, were emerging that P&O could contravene Department of Trade regulations governing the maximum number of passengers. Eventually, the problem was resolved, with all lifejackets issued.

Among the new arrivals was Ivor Garcia; how wonderful to see his toothless grin again. He told me more of his adventures since I had last seen him. Ordered to join the LSL *Sir Percivale*, which had been detailed as the prison ship after the Battle of Goose Green, he found about 400 prisoners guarded by an inadequate and inexperienced guard force. Using the knowledge that he had accumulated about prisoner handling since joining the Intelligence Section, he recommended that the Special Forces and officer prisoners be deterred from engineering a mutiny by mixing them with other officers. Little documentation had been forwarded with the prisoners and so he and an Argentinian naval officer listed those on board. It was fortunate that Ivor monitored the documentation because he learnt some Army officers were giving false details while others were exchanging their ranks, insignia and names with each other and with some of the conscripts, who proved to be useful sources for Ivor. The rationale of the prisoners was to create a chain of communication, however, Ivor found that the other ranks who were not interested in being bullied into causing disruption and ensured that each prisoner supplied their correct details. When the prisoners were transferred to the *Norland* to be repatriated to Argentina, the officers were placed in upper deck cabins and the NCOs and conscripts on the lower decks, which essentially severed the chain of command between the decks. Ivor then gathered sufficient intelligence to prevent a mass breakout when he intercepted officers tapping Morse code on their cabin walls and fed in false or garbled messages. By 7 June, a week after the Battle of Goose Green, *Norland* had embarked over 1,000 prisoners of all Services and all ranks captured since 21 May, but only half had been registered and searched. Ivor then helped administer the remainder, a tricky and lengthy process eased by his ability to speak Spanish. Five days later, as the ship sailed into the estuary of the River Plate bound for Montevideo to repatriate the prisoners through Uruguay, Garcia translated for the captain and handled ship-to-shore communications with the Argentinian and Uruguayan authorities and warships. He said that while the officers received a warm welcome, the other ranks were whisked away to a cold and unwelcome reception.

At dusk, *Canberra* weighed anchor and headed north, her bows arrogantly pushing aside the South Atlantic rollers, seemingly with complete disregard for their power and majesty; she dipped and rose with far more grace than HMS *Fearless* could ever manage. The 8,000-mile voyage to Plymouth was scheduled to take 18 days at an average speed of 20 knots per hour. Shortly after leaving, an announcement was broadcast the ship would be docking in Portsmouth because her draught was 4 feet too much for the Plymouth Sound and it would take 7 hours to disembark; this was something of a disappointment, nevertheless, we prepared to enjoy the cruise.

As usual I settled into a routine: 7am roll off my bunk for a luxurious and unrushed shave and a hot shower, followed by breakfast in the 'joint' officers and SNCOs' Mess, the single sitting in the baronial Pacific Restaurant, normally used by the high-end paying passengers. The SNCOs invariably sat on the mezzanine ranging down both sides of the well. The joke was it was to ensure the officers did not misbehave! Four of us sat at the same table – me with Neil, Mick Marshalsay and WO2 Pete Gill, when he managed to get up for breakfast. Pete was a Commando-trained Royal Signals technician who had lost virtually everything on the *Sir Galahad* at Bluff Cove. While describing the bombing, he mentioned that some Royal Marines who knew the layout of the LSL guided the soldiers through the smoke and darkness to safety. Our table was always served by a young but initially sombre waiter whose real name we never discovered, so we nicknamed him 'Big Wal', which apparently caught on with his colleagues. Sometimes he was late serving us, he said because he got up late but we were in no hurry. Breakfast usually consisted of cereal, fruit juice, bacon and eggs, sumptuous bread rolls and tea. After weeks drinking from plastic mugs, the china cups and saucers were a little dainty.

After breakfast, I spent an hour or so reading a book in the Meridian Room, which had been designated as the Warrant Officers' and Sergeants' Mess, often still untidy after the antics of the night before. I had finished *The Rivers of Babylon* at Teal Inlet and among the well-stocked library of books sent by well-wishers in UK, I particularly enjoyed *Solo* by Jack Higgins. After midmorning coffee at about 10.30am, I turned up in an area designated at Brigade HQ to help draft Brigade Intelligence aspects being assembled by Captain Rowe for Brigade post-Operations Report. I also drafted a report for the Intelligence Corps. Both were initial thoughts and written without much consideration to the political consequences, in other words 'gut feeling'.

Lunch at 12.30pm consisted of a relaxing meal of soup, a main course, a sweet and cheese and biscuits and was followed by a siesta in our cabin. However, as the weather improved, that changed to a roasting in the sun on the upper deck – along with most of the Embarked Force. The problem was finding a sheltered spot because the 'zephyrs', to quote one officer of the watch, were virtually howling gales caused by the speed of the ship. At about 5.15pm, I usually joined the throng of runners jogging the quarter-of-a mile around the promenade deck with the aim of running 3 miles. Mick Marshalsay developed a ploy of confusing the 'racing snakes' and 'whippets' sprinting past by slowing down at the end of each straight, allowing the sprinters to pass, then dart inside, run across to the other side, and continue running. The 'whippets' would hare around the bend, and overtake Mick, their flushed and sweating faces a picture of confusion and question, clearly asking themselves 'When did he pass me? I overtook him on the other side!' Sometimes, the runners were joined by the P&O officers and crew, and John Shirley of the *Sunday Times*, who I believe, was the only journalist on board. By this time the Serviceman's traditional suspicion of journalists was resurfacing, largely generated by some returning to UK on the first Hercules or who had taken Casevac ships to Montevideo and then flown home. Most of the stories revolved, and still do, around the Army and very few of the Royal Marines. Clearly the Army's public relations machinery was working well. The presence of Mr Shirley on board and an article he later wrote about the campaign and the Royal Marines helped to alleviate the intense disappointment felt by Royal Navy and Royal Marines that the Army were in the limelight. I later learnt that midway through the campaign, the Royal Navy Director of Public Relations was posted to Hong Kong and as a consequence the Royal Navy public relations faltered; which, in turn, seemed to have a detrimental effect on Commando Forces' public relations output. In contrast, the Army despatched their Director of Public Relations, Brigadier David Ramsbotham, to the Falklands on the first C-130 to Stanley. Major-General Thompson,

He (Brigadier Ramsbotham) ensured that the Army PR worked. The Royal Navy did not see fit to grip the situation. The result is that most people know all about the Army contribution to victory, which was considerable. But next to nothing about the

Royal Navy winning the biggest Air/Sea battle since the Second World War. And little about 3 Commando Brigade planning and executing an amphibious operation carried out at greater distance from home base (UK) to intermediate base (Ascension) to targets (South Georgia and Falklands) than any in modern history, including the Pacific campaign of the Second World War, except for the landings in Madagascar in 1942.

The total statistics added together from both sides between 22 April and 14 June tell the story:

103 aircraft lost or damaged (69 fixed wing, 34 helicopters).
24 ships sunk or damaged.
1 submarine damaged.
904 killed in action on land, sea and air.
2,432 wounded.

On South Georgia on 3 April, Lieutenant Mills and his Royal Marines damaged a corvette, shot down a Puma helicopter, killed three Argentinians and wounded seven at the cost of a Royal Marine wounded.

The shower after the evening run was preparation for the evening. Dinner, served at 7.30pm, consisted of soup, fish, a main course, a sweet and cheese and biscuits, usually accompanied by a French red or Liebfraumilch. Officers ate an hour later. This was followed by the evening entertainment in the Mess, which was often a film. The final seconds of a sequel to *Friday the 13th* of the tranquillity of a lake being shattered by a disgusting thing emerging from the depths drew the most laughs.

After about ten days, the liner slowed as it passed Ascension Island and took on mail and supplies, some flown by a RAF yellow-painted search-and-rescue helicopter, the first time such an aircraft had flown on board. The same cloud hung over Green Mountain and the anchorage was less full. I managed to write a quick letter to Penny that I was on the *Canberra* and on my way home.

The second-half of the voyage seemed to become more chaotic as we headed for the warmer weather of the northern hemisphere summer. The Embarked Force Mess Quiz team convincingly defeated a composite team consisting of two padres, two ladies from the *Canberra* and a RN Fleet Chief. The following night, the 40 Commando 'Sods Opera' on the temporary Flight Deck became more raucous as the night wore on with several rounds of *Zulu Warrior*, rugby songs complete with the actions and a diving competition from a board to the pool, a deck below. Several female crew members joined in and a ship's officer on his Rounds was hustled into the swimming pool. Three days later, the Combined Services Entertainment show, which had joined the ship at Ascension and performed for the Sergeants Mess, turned out to be a memorable evening with the main act being Roger 'Idiot', a talented clown with a wide variety of sketches. I had last seen him in Norway when he entertained 42 Commando. His act also featured his wife, who did little except sing 'Zoo-bee-doo-bee-doo'. For the finale, as the whole Mess sang *Land of Hope and Glory*, *Rule Britannia* and *Jerusalem*, Roger nearly wept with emotion. Who could blame him? Four days later the Mess had a cabaret evening. This turned out to be excellent, the highlights of which was Guy, one of the wine waiters, playing the piano and Sue, the shop girl, who courageously sang a few songs, if out of tune; indeed when she sang, there were few dry eyes. Other acts included a hilarious Morris Dancing routine and the 'Chelsea Pensioners in wheelchairs' parade, performed by several 'Mess members'.

As the ship neared England, when the range of drinks began to diminish and the Junior Ranks' Mess was rationed to one beer a day, the Sergeants Mess voted that all canned beer be passed to those in greater need. The reward for this sacrifice was John

Collins and Brandy Alexanders not by the cocktail glass but by the pint. I rather fear that the very tolerant bar staff in the Meridian bar, more used to genteel clients, were rather overwhelmed by the rapid consumption of alcohol.

The evening after a formal Mess Dinner Night, the ship's crew were entertained to a Horse Racing Evening with syndicates donating profits to the South Atlantic Fund. The 10th was 'Up Channel Night', so called because it is the last night at sea during which the Royal Navy traditionally consume any alcohol remaining on the night before the ship docked – except there was no drink. As the faded shores of southern England gradually crept over the evening horizon, excitement grew. I packed my kit for the final time with my souvenirs and gifts at the top of my bergen. A gaggle of journalists flown on board by helicopter was roundly booed.

The ship was then joined by several large cabin cruisers motoring parallel with the ship and a RAF Meteor that buzzed us twice at low level, the first time climbing straight into the evening sky, doing victory rolls above the ship and then diving down and streaking past, level with the upper deck, before blasting back to the shore, waggling its wings as it disappeared. On some cliffs, car headlights twinkled. The Band of Commando Forces 'Beat the Retreat' on the Flight Deck, during which, for the first time, the march *San Carlos*, composed by Major John Ware, was played as a tribute to the Task Force. The Band had played a significant role supporting RN Surgical Support teams ashore and afloat. An element of Medical Squadron had remained on *Canberra*. Other tasks included moving immense amounts of stores, rations and ammunition from the depths of the ship to the Flight Deck to be helicoptered ashore. They had also guarded the last of the prisoners of war when they were ferried from Port Stanley for repatriation via *Red Beach*. One of the bandsmen had taken six conscripts to a cabin and showed them how to use the en-suite shower. But he did not speak Spanish and so he turned on the water and pointed to one of the Argentinians to enter and left. He returned about 20 minutes later to find five conscripts looking very miserable and still dirty and the sixth in the shower fully clothed and shivering under a cold shower; he was under the impression that he was being punished some for some misdemeanour. The steward showed the Argentinians the intricacies of the shower and found some dry clothes for the soaking conscript. Some conscripts were so overwhelmed by the generosity of the *Canberra* that they did not want to go home.

Sunday 11 July dawned misty with the sun straining to split through the low and brownish swirls of early morning mist and the promise of an English summer day for our last day at sea and finale to our historic adventure. Reveille was early and the four of us breakfasted on steak washed down with several glasses of champagne. We claim the distinction of being the first to open a champagne bottle that day – as others did! The ship and Embarked Force's officers then conducted Rounds inspecting every nook and cranny. This was no pointless check. *Canberra* would soon be back on her commercial operations and the less cleaning and repairs to be done, the quicker she could revert to the job she does best. We piled our kit in the corridors. Our cabin was passed as fit. When a 'buzz' (rumour) circulated that the Royal Military Police were going to search for weapons and other dangerous souvenirs, the automatic pistol given to me by the Argentinian officer and which I intended to donate to the Intelligence Corps Museum, went over the side, along with a substantial number of other weapons. Afterwards Neil and I strolled around the promenade deck with, it seemed, the rest of the Embarked Force and one or two embarrassed but nevertheless bemused Royal Marines being interviewed by television crews and journalists flown on board.

As the ship glided through calm seas near the Isle of Wight, through the mist a tall sailing ship silently headed towards England, her topsails shrouded by the sun-pierced brown mists. On the other side, another sailing ship glided through the twinkling sea. I later learnt that they were gathering for the Tall Ships Race. The sun drove away the swirling grey mists exposing blue sky and a flotilla of pleasure launches converging on *Canberra*. Overhead circled helicopters, some carrying television crews. The Embarked Force units lining the decks assembled at mutually agreed places and watched them with mild interest. The Brigade HQ and Signals Squadron gathered port side aft on the promenade deck. As the ship slowly crossed the Solent, we watched with disbelief as the flotilla of launches grew into a fleet. Some launches were very near the ship. On one, a red haired girl in her twenties was sitting in the stern of a launch wallowing in the wake of the ship and every time that the boat crept underneath our position, there was a chorus of wolf whistles. A dozen canoeists joined the throng, their fragile craft being tossed on the crazy waves, a generous round of sincere applause rippling around the stern. Some boats came close and beer cans were dropped on board, some expertly caught. On another cruiser, two women changed into bikinis, which was applauded. And then the inevitable happened. A smart launch pulled alongside and then two women looked at each other, climbed onto the roof of the cabin and whipped off their tops, clearly mother and daughter. When photographers rushed over to see what was happening, they reached the rails with some difficulty to find the bare chests had been covered. As three 'Jack the Lads' dropped their shorts and offered their naked backsides, a barrage of beer cans hurtled onto the deck of their little boat. BBC and Southern Television launches kept pace with the liner and sometimes sped forward, their bows pushing aside the churned up waters, causing some small boats to rock dangerously in their wake. A blue P&O ferry crowded with people hove-to and hooted madly as her elegant but slightly battered elder sister glided by. Someone on board *Canberra* had hoisted a banner that read 'P&O cruises where Cunard refuses' referring to the *Queen Elisabeth II* cross-decking 5 Infantry Brigade at South Georgia. What must the foreigners on board the ferry have thought?

Canberra was eventually forced to slow down, such was the mass of launches, yachts, dinghies and boats. I suspect most of the Embarked Force were overwhelmed by the welcome home and sometimes we were very silent. It was a reminder of our families, parents and girlfriends in Plymouth and homes across the country. Near the entrance to Southampton Water, the armada grew, 'gin palaces' vying with humble yachts to escort *Canberra* past the shoreline crowded with people waving placards or handkerchiefs and cars hooting and blinking V for victory. We entered through the picturesque and ancient entrance and the choppy waters, usually so calm on a sunny summer's day, whipped against the historic quays where the nation's sailors had once waited for gigs and whalers. Now modern Royal Navy warships were dressed overall. *Canberra* slowed down and a helicopter carrying Charles, Prince of Wales, who had joined the ship earlier, clattered off the Flight Deck. He had joined some of the Embarked Force for coffee, which included some from the Intelligence Section. The armada was now surrounded by the escort of little boats and when a police boat attempted to organise order out of the chaos, it was booed and backed off with good grace.

To our astonishment, the quays were jammed with people, many holding placards and all of whom were frantically waving, children and babies held aloft. Our families! As a military band ashore struck up *A Life on the Ocean Wave*, the deck crew hurled ropes and springs ashore, snaking and curling onto the quay. The liner imperceptibly edged closer to England. No one moved and there was complete silence and then at 11.30 precisely, as *Canberra* gently nudged the large wooden floats of Quay 105 of Southampton Docks and was secured, home after nearly four months at sea, there was a great burst of cheering. She was safely back in the UK, if a little battered, on a glorious summer's day. Captain Scott-Masson, the Master, had said he would dock at 11am, but even when P&O make broken promises, who could but forgive him on this extraordinary day?

The generosity of *Canberra* was extraordinary and also a platform that allowed the Embarked Force to wind down and relax after the rigours of the war. Nothing was too much trouble. Raw emotions played havoc with excitement. This astonishing day had become truly extraordinary. This was no time to be aloof. The band played *Land of Hope and Glory* and we beat in time bruising our hands on the stained hull, utterly happy to be home. Two gangways were lifted into position and a small welcoming party came on board. Assumed to be Immigration and HM Customs, they were also booed.

Shortly afterwards, orders were received for the Embarked Force to go ashore and Brigadier Thompson followed by his commanding officers and senior Staff officers filed down the gangway to cheers and applause, as were several wounded on stretchers who were lifted into military ambulances. How were the families of the killed feeling on this extraordinary day?

A 45 Commando company, who had walked from San Carlos to Port Stanley, landed and would be flown to Arbroath, their base. The remainder of the Commando had been shipped home on RFA *Stromness* and had arrived to a tumultuous welcome the day before. In the meantime, my brother Nigel had found me and hurried away to find Penny and my mother and we held shouted conversations as they stood on the quay and I was on the bow, perched precariously across a handrail. Imogen was at home, which was wise. They had been there since about 8am and had watched *Canberra* brush aside the morning mist and as she was escorted to her berth. 42 Commando disembarked, then 40 Commando, the gunners of 29 Commando Regiment RA, 59 Independent Commando Squadron RE, Medical Squadron of the Commando Logistic Regiment, 3 Commando Brigade Air Squadron and finally at about 1.30pm, Brigade HQ and HQ Signals Squadron. We went down the gangway and tottered onto firm ground, our heavy equipment now light and unnoticed, and then Penny burst out from the crowd and we hugged each other.

We filed into a Customs Shed decked out with flags, bunting and balloons and after placing my seaman's kitbag on a pile, rejoined the Brigade HQ and Signals Squadron watched by a detachment of smart Royal Military Police. We were then released, 'nothing to declare' and joined our families. Nigel, bless him, gave me a can of warm beer, which I sank in one draught. Before going our separate ways, my mother and brother to Canterbury and Penny and I to Plymouth, we had a drink 'on the house' and a meal at the Star Hotel. It was good to be back in England, although somewhat humbling. There was an agreeable air of pride in the people, still suffering from the recession and in the midst of a rail strike. We had done what we were trained and paid to do, the word 'defeat' was never contemplated and 'Can do' was the watchword. No wonder a banner on *Canberra* had read 'Call off the rail strike or we will call an air strike' from those who needed to go home by train. On recognising the uniform, people would come and tell us what a good job had been done and how good it was to be British. The only response was 'Thank you'.

Mid-afternoon Penny and I left Southampton and drove to Salisbury and then joined the A303 heading to the South West. It was a peaceful *England, Their England* drive on a summer's afternoon passing village cricket matches and tourists wandering around Stonehenge. But as we neared Honiton, people were standing on the pavements, some holding banners inscribed 'Well done' and 'Glad you're back', while others waved, clapped and cheered. But why? It was only as we drove under bridges decorated with messages and packed with people that the full significance of the victory was emerging. Not since the Second World War had the British people had the opportunity to welcome its Armed Forces home after sending them away to fight a war. Ours had been 8,000 miles across oceans in winter on and around bleak but nationally important islands about the size of Wales that few had heard of until March, fighting against a nation with which we had once had good relations. Victory had been against all military logic. I assumed then, and still do, it was a welcome gleam of light in a country ravaged by recession, unemployment and political stagnation. Britain, once a major Imperial power, had been humiliated internationally but had surfaced as victor. One hoped that countries would think twice before stealing our territory again.

A mile short of Plymouth, home to 3 Commando Brigade, the crowds were larger and more vocal. I switched on my headlights, not to signify that I was a returning member of the Task Force but because it was raining. At the A303 exit to Plymouth, a traffic jam had piled up and a policeman apologised for the delay. Although the rain became a steady downpour, still the happy Britons waved and cheered. Some seeing a coach of Royal Marines or a car with returning troops, cried 'Look, there's one!' and surged over to the occupants.

The crowds had massed at the Valley Forge roundabout and there was nothing the police could do the keep the traffic on the move. Our car was stormed by pumping handshakes, hugs and kisses. Behind us, the coach carrying the Intelligence Section had been stopped and looking back, I saw that Scotty was walking down the road. He accepted a lift and we followed a Mercedes with Hannover number plates up the hill to his house. It was locked. His wife was in Southampton. They had missed each other. Penny and I had spent a year posted to Hannover.

And so back to 8 Tiverton Close, Widewell Estate, Southway, our married quarter, 118 days since I had left it at midnight on 4 April. The small military neighbourhood was normally neat but today it was decked in garlands, flags and welcoming messages. Our kitchen window had a Union Jack on the ledge. I crept upstairs into Imogen's room, peeped into her cot and wobbled as she smiled.

14

THE END AND REFLECTIONS

Even though the fighting was over, Argentina had not surrendered unconditionally. The Critical Intelligence Requirements of the LFFI as approved by No. 10 Downing Street and the Joint Intelligence Committee were classical 'Will the Argentine Forces attempt another attack on the Falkland Islands? If so, when, where and in what strength?' The Commander LFFI therefore kept the Royal Navy, Army and RAF on a war footing.

In July, Major Burrill handed his role as G2 to Major John Hughes-Wilson. Port Stanley was still recovering from its occupation. The Intelligence Section was Joint Service and consisted of six Intelligence Corps, two Royal Navy and two Royal Air Force, all on six-month tours and based in the New School. Hughes-Wilson became Head of Service Intelligence.

When Major Hughes-Wilson flew to Ascension Island in a RAF VC-10, the female cabin staff wore flying suits. The flight to Port Stanley was in a C-130 Hercules and included three in-flight refuelling legs in which the Hercules climbed to 24,000 feet and then dived to get maximum speed while connected to a Victor tanker 'braking' at 260 knots almost to a stall. Refuelling took place at 800 feet a minute in a descent to a minimum height of 5,000 feet. Hughes-Wilson was invited to the Flight Deck on one refuel and found it 'nerve wracking'. When the Hercules flights were later diverted to Senegal to refuel, Hughes-Wilson debriefed a crew that had experienced fuel injectors freezing at high level to the extent that three engines cut out. As the aircraft began to descend, the crew ditched the entire cargo until at about 2,000 feet, the captain managed to restart the engines in the warmer air. He concluded the aircraft had been refuelled with a mix of paraffin and water.

Argentinian attempts to encroach into the Falkland Islands Protection Zone by sea and air were monitored, as were the political and military fallouts from their defeat. Some events revealed different intelligence appreciations between the three Services. For the Royal Navy, intelligence was mainly 'strategic stuff' and anything coming towards a ship was 'action on' and a job for Operations and Weapons. For the RAF, intelligence was mainly what Strike Command in the UK said it was and therefore get aircraft onto the target. Force Intelligence focused on good communications with the Defence Intelligence Staff, No. 10 Downing Street and the SAS, which allowed the Intelligence Corps to collate events and build the intelligence picture. One issue was lack of appreciation for communications security by the merchant ships' captains.

Force Intelligence briefed that intelligence had been received that the Argentine Air Force planned to fly their Boeing 707 airborne intelligence collector into the 200-mile Falklands Island Exclusion Zone to nibble British electronic signals from the north-west sector of the Zone at the extreme intercept range of the RAF Harriers at Stanley. The Harriers had no air-to-air in-flight refuelling, which would limit their range and time on target. A detailed plan was put in place, which included the Navy agreeing to send a ship to act as a radar sentry. During a planning meeting, the Air Commander agreed to broadcast an international warning and if that failed, he indicated a karate chop. The Boeing 707 never turned up.

On 14 July, after Argentina surrendered unconditionally, the 593 Special Category prisoners were repatriated at Port Madryn where the officers received a warm welcome. They had been on the Sealink Ro/Ro ferry St *Edmund* since 30 June in considerably healthier conditions than at Ajax Bay. When Brigadier-General Menendez and several other senior prisoners were embarked on 2 July, resistance stiffened. Their departure allowed the Joint Service Interrogation Unit to close down and, with the last of those who had served with 3 Commando Brigade, it flew back to UK.

Major Hughes-Wilson widened Force Intelligence tasks to hunting for Argentine minefields maps for the Royal Engineers and documents relating to commercial intelligence. The Argentinians had burnt some maps. There was a suspicion that some maps had been retained as souvenirs or were in military museums. When Hughes-Wilson suggested that such maps be recovered by buying them in the clubs and pubs of Aldershot, he was met with raised eyebrows and a hard stare from a Royal Military Police officer. The result was that the Force Minefield Recording Team had to find the minefields the hard way.

The Section conducted technical intelligence assessments of Argentinian small arms. Counter-intelligence was minimal because Argentine sympathisers had been evacuated to Argentina before the surrender, nevertheless, every settlement was visited.

When its remit was expanded, Force Intelligence learned to detect mines and booby traps. Most of the operations took place in positions formerly occupied by the Argentinians and the hazards included corpses and battlefield litter, such as ammunition, boxes of explosive and abandoned weapons. On a search of Mount Harriet, the team were accompanied by an unflappable Royal Engineer bomb disposal lance-corporal. The position was surrounded by minefields and booby traps and yielded intelligence, such as state-of-the-art US night sights, and also a much-needed electricity generator. A corporal escaped certain death when he noticed that a pile of FAL rifles was connected by a trip wire to a grenade necklace. Major Hughes-Wilson was even luckier. Reaching into a hole in the rocks to retrieve a document, he triggered a microfilament wire attached to a cunningly wedged rifle grenade. He also dragged from a bunker a small metal object that looked like a green airbed pump. The Royal Engineer identified it as a Spanish anti-personnel mine and commented 'Gutsy stuff, boss.' A corporal tasked to locate unburied bodies often returned to the office with the rich scent of *eau de mort,* however, he had first pick of abandoned Argie ration packs, which often contained a small bottle of whisky or brandy.

Three large old-fashioned laundry baskets full of Government House letters were sent to the Ministry of Defence. Before sending them, Major Hughes-Wilson found several letters from UK-based chief executive officers, dated April, seeking from Brigadier-General Menendez exclusive commercial rights in Las Malvinas. When he returned to the UK in February 1983, he came across the letters in a Ministry of Defence cellar, all marked 'No Further Action' and was advised not to pursue his concerns as 'nothing must be seen to mar the great victory'.

As new units arrived, Force Intelligence formed a briefing team that gave presentations on the war and its legacy to new arrivals, reinforcements and the Harrier squadrons. The threat of mines was hammered home, although a proposal by Force Intelligence to drive sheep through suspicious areas was vetoed by publicity officials and startled sheep farmers. The team also flew to aircraft-carriers to brief Naval Task Force commanders and were winched by helicopters to submarines patrolling the South American coast.

As military normality began to develop, Force Intelligence lost its Argentinian Mercedes jeep reclaimed by the Brigade Ordnance Warrant officer, along with dark mutterings from the Royal Military Police about 'having no work ticket and unauthorised misuse of Ministry of Defence petrol'. Two members of the

Section had collected dozens of Argie steel helmets, which they repainted and sold to souvenir-hungry sailors on their only run ashore in Stanley. A corporal organised a weapon training day to assess captured Argentinian weapons and ammunition. They found that the .45 ammunition was unstable and the Halcón 9mm submachine gun was better than the Sterling.

When, at the height of the southern summer in early January, Prime Minister Thatcher paid her visit to the Falkland Islands, she impressed with her decisiveness and speed of comprehension of the problems and the requirements on the ground. Her visit also brought a sea change and the immediate post-war casual approach to life was replaced by a more ordered approach. When Major Hughes-Wilson handed over to his successor in February 1983, a visit to the 'Int Section House' was high on the list. When his successor asked to see the Section account and was advised one did not exist as the Section paid for food and drink in a shop, this was met with disbelief by the new arrival. The Army had arrived.

On his return to the UK, Major Hughes-Wilson was interviewed by a Metropolitan Police officer concerning an allegation that a dead Argentinian soldier found with his hands bound with signals cable had been shot in the back of the head. When Hughes-Wilson pointed out that the body was 20 yards behind the Argentinian company headquarters, the cable was Argentine and that it was unlikely the paras had the time to execute someone in battle, he suggested it could have been a summary execution by the Argentinians. Hughes-Wilson agreed to testify, if required. He heard nothing more about the matter.

Two years after the war, an Intelligence Corps major and I were summoned to the Ministry of Defence to provide answers for a Parliamentary question from a Labour MP alleging the misuse of interrogation. Frankly, we were not surprised because interrogation as a valuable asset had been undermined in 1970. Afterwards, we were taken into a store and as mentioned earlier on the table were the very postbags I had filled while searching Government House and still tied with tape that I had found. Other documents on the table included the log book of the Argentine submarine *Santa Fe*.

In conclusion, the Falklands War had proved that provided that information is handled with logic, common sense and sensitivity, it can be converted into intelligence, which – if handled properly and in time – is of value. The converting of information into intelligence is not an exact science. This is usually either because not enough is known about an enemy, as was the case throughout Operation *Corporate*, or because the enemy has taken counter-measures to hoodwink, confuse and mislead. It follows, therefore, that estimates of enemy deployments, strengths and weaknesses, orders of battles and intentions are an intelligence reality. Historically, it appeared there was very little intelligence on British interests in the South Atlantic, in particular those territories at risk from Argentinian aspirations. This was a serious deficiency that placed lives at risk. The Argentinians were well prepared, except their conclusion that Great Britain would not respond.

The weakest brigade, in terms of experienced intelligence provision, was pitched into battle impeded by peacetime rules protecting the distribution of operational intelligence on the 'need to know' principle. Our inability to disseminate intelligence to those who needed it most, the front line, resulted in distrust and in the tendency of some units to ignore good intelligence from credible sources. While the 'need to know' principle is a crucial principle, 'security must make sense'.

Interrogation of prisoners and translation and interpretation of documents was rarely practised on exercise, however they were important intelligence resources on Operation *Corporate*. There were several instances when 'amateur' interrogations risked the quality of intelligence by reducing wholly or partially the 'shock of capture'. Practical resistance to interrogation training in 1982 was confined to 'prone to capture' individuals, such as aircrew and

Special Forces, and yet the Falklands proved, yet again, that those regarded as 'not prone to capture' were more liable to be taken prisoner. While theoretical resistance training was regarded as adequate, the evidence gained during Operation *Corporate* is that some of those taken prisoner had little idea how to resist and consequently Argentinian interrogators were able to extract intelligence within the Geneva Conventions. The same weakness also applied to Argentinian prisoners.

In conclusion, Brigade Intelligence had risen to the intelligence challenge and its commitment was absolute. 3 Commando Brigade was fortunate that it had a Brigade Commander who recognised the principles and limitations of intelligence. In his Post Operation Report, Brigadier Thompson, as Commander, 3 Commando Brigade wrote:

> As the Brigade Commander, what impressed me most was the quality of the intelligence assessments that were produced from quite early on and right through the campaign, by the Intelligence staffs in my superior HQ, and in my own HQ. The *pièce de résistance* was the identification of positions occupied by the Argentine regiments before we landed, which proved amazingly accurate. I also felt that the way the Intelligence staffs in the theatre of operations coped with the interrogation of prisoners, a mammoth task, when one considers the numbers taken, and the short time available in which to process them, was a model of efficiency and humanity. The response by members of the Intelligence Corps was positive and professional.

INDEX